Words Upon the Word

QUALITATIVE STUDIES IN RELIGION

GENERAL EDITOR: Janet Jacobs

The Qualitative Studies in Religion series was founded to make a place for careful, sustained, engaged reflection on the link between the kinds of qualitative methods being used and the resulting shape, tone, and substance of our empirical work on religion. We seek to showcase a wide range of qualitative methodologies including ethnography; analysis of religious texts, discourses, rituals, and daily practices; in-depth interviews and life histories; and narrative analyses. We present empirical studies from diverse disciplines that address a particular problem or argument in the study of religion. We welcome a variety of approaches, including those drawing on multiple qualitative methods or combining qualitative and quantitative methods. We believe that excellent empirical studies can best further a critical discussion of the link between methods, epistemology, and social scientific theory, and thereby help to reconceptualize core problems and advance our understanding of religion and society.

Words Upon the Word

An Ethnography of Evangelical Group Bible Study

James S. Bielo

NEW YORK UNIVERSITY PRESS

New York and London

NEW YORK UNIVERSITY PRESS
New York and London
www.nyupress.org

Library of Congress Cataloging-in-Publication Data

Bielo, James S.
Words upon the word: an ethnography of evangelical
group bible study / James S. Bielo.
p. cm.—(Qualitative studies in religion)
Includes bibliographical references (p.   ) and index.
ISBN-13: 978-0-8147-9121-9 (cl : alk. paper)
ISBN-10: 0-8147-9121-2 (cl : alk. paper)
ISBN-13: 978-0-8147-9122-6 (pb : alk. paper)
ISBN-10: 0-8147-9122-0 (pb : alk. paper)
1. Evangelicalism—Michigan—Lansing Region. 2. Bible—Study and
teaching—Michigan—Lansing Region. 3. Small groups—Religious
aspects—Protestant churches. 4. Church group work—Protestant
churches. 5. Christian sociology—Protestant churches. I. Title.
BR1642.U5B54   2009
277.74'27083—dc22   2008047905

New York University Press books are printed on acid-free paper, and
their binding materials are chosen for strength and durability. We
strive to use environmentally responsible suppliers and materials to
the greatest extent possible in publishing our books.

Manufactured in the United States of America
c   10 9 8 7 6 5 4 3 2 1
p   10 9 8 7 6 5 4 3 2 1

For John S. Bielo, my father—I miss you
and
Judith S. Bielo, my mother—I love you

✳ ✳ ✳

Contents

* * *

Acknowledgments

This book is many years in the making, and there are so many to whom I feel indebted. First and foremost, I am pleased to thank the Bible study groups and congregations that agreed to participate in this research. They were kind, patient, intuitive, insightful, and forgiving, even when I failed to be. I owe a special thank you to Tony and Jan Luttrell. Not only did they offer warm friendship and wise council, but they also provided a home when I was in need.

The Department of Anthropology at Michigan State University was instrumental in helping me see this project to fruition. Support, encouragement, and productive criticism arrived from faculty, staff, and graduate students alike. At New York University Press, I have benefited greatly from having Jennifer Hammer as a supervising editor. She was enthusiastic from day one and provided sound advice. Two anonymous reviewers were also extremely helpful in their reading of the initial manuscript. Over the past few years my conference travels and blind emails have brought me into contact with wonderful scholars, many of who offered valuable feedback on this project. In particular, I would like to thank Brian Malley, Joel Robbins, Matthew Engelke, Tanya Luhrmann, Jon Bialecki, and Eric Hoenes. My students in undergraduate classes at Michigan State University and Grand Valley State University have been kind enough to listen intently and respond to my work, often in the early stages of analysis. This book is truly better for all this insight.

Throughout my academic career I have had the great fortune to be surrounded by kind and keen intellects. As an undergraduate at Radford University, Drs. Mary LaLone and Melinda Wagner provided as firm a foundation as I could have ever hoped. My dissertation committee at Michigan State University was truly a blessing. Dr. Amy Derogatis was an insightful and reliable reader and an unfailing resource in the field of American religion. Dr. Mindy Morgan was utterly consistent in her commitment and encouragement. Her trust and interest in my work has never failed to leave me inspired and reaffirmed. Dr. David Dwyer has been a source of wisdom, intellect, and humor since I met him in 2001. I can only hope to have his boyish enthusiasm when I find myself near the end of a career. Finally, I owe a tremendous debt to Dr. Fredric Roberts, my dissertation advisor. His influence on me—as an anthropologist, a scholar, and a person—is more profound than I could ever articulate.

Over the years, many, many friends and loved ones have shaped my experience in this life—and, in turn, this project. My family: Judy, Mary, John, Roger, RJ, Charlotte, Ed, Julie, and Clay; thank you so very much. Carri and Rowenn: in this life, I have loved you most. You have been most privy to my shortcomings, and your forgiveness leaves me astounded. Cristian, Jason, Bobby, Will, Aaron, Tim, Dillon, Duane, Christian, Michael, Jubin, Terry, Freddie, Kaley, Ryan, Rita, Andrea, Kate, Natalie, Cris, Emily: cheers to you all.

Ultimately, this project and my life only have been artifacts of the sovereign grace of God. Lord, Jesus Christ, Giver of New Life, have mercy on me, a sinner.

* * *

Introduction

Group Bible Study in American Evangelicalism

My alarm rings at 6:15 a.m. I am up, through the shower, dressed, and ready to go by 6:40. I kiss my girlfriend on the forehead, jealous she can sleep in at least until the sun rises. It is the first week of January, and, predictably for mid-Michigan, several inches of new snow has fallen overnight. The wintry air wakes me, along with an anxiety that the extra minutes of scraping windshields could make me late for the seven o'clock start. I begin the short drive east, cautious of my speed and traction. Luckily, there are few other cars on the road.

On my way to the restaurant I pass the "main drag" of downtown. To the left are coffee shops, bars, student bookstores, the newly built Barnes & Noble, the Gap, all manner of restaurants, more coffee shops, and more bars. To the right is the university campus, also still asleep. The quiet sidewalks are a sharp contrast to the typical, hectic feel of 40,000 students bustling and biking. It is just now seven, but I suspect the weather has slowed others' trips as well.

The Coral Gables restaurant sits less than a mile from the edge of campus. It is locally owned and has an interesting history. In the 1950s and 60s it was the first spot across municipal lines to serve alcohol, giving it a lively reputation. When the dry laws ended, "the Gables" slowly morphed into its present status—a "family restaurant" serving mainly middle-aged, older adults, and retirees. My first step into the warm building on this morning held no surprises: the owner—a white-haired gentleman who has operated the Gables since 1968—greeted me and directed me to the back meeting room; several elderly couples had just sat down for breakfast; the smell of fresh-cooked bacon melded with the sterile air; and a quiet stillness dominated the main room. This was not the place my colleagues and I met for coffee, went for weekend cocktails, or (quite frankly) sought out for any reason whatsoever.

I was right; the weather had delayed some of the other men too. Apparently, it had even deterred some from coming, though there were still thirteen who braved the snow and ice. When I arrived, most were ready to begin. There was an elevated eagerness this morning because the group was discussing the first chapter from the latest book they were reading together. The round tables in the private room were covered with copies of the book, along with the usual fare of Bibles, ink pens, scattered notepads, and the occasional yellow highlighter. I was excited too; this was my first tape-recording of this group and only the sixth Bible study I had attended since the official start of my fieldwork. The group's discussion that morning mirrored the few I had observed previously and the forty-seven more I would attend throughout the coming year: a striking mix of humor, seriousness, curiosity, intimacy, intellectualism, consensus, and amiable contention.

In the early days of my fieldwork with Evangelical Bible study groups I remember the reaction of my colleagues—graduate student and faculty alike. A slight few were curious about what I would eventually discover, others were baffled at the decision to undertake such a project in the first place, and still others were politely dismissive. If anything, they would suggest an ethnography of North American Evangelicalism should investigate the relationship between religion and politics, namely the political maneuvering of conservative Christians resulting in the two-term presidency of George W. Bush. Or, why not study the faith-based social activism of Evangelicals and their increasing involvement in national and global inequities? But these were not my concerns. I had chosen to observe, listen, record, and analyze what happens while conservative Evangelicals are (to quote one of my more skeptical colleagues) "just sitting around talking." I had chosen to attend to the conversations Evangelicals share among themselves, conversations that help orient their more visible forms of social mobilization.

In recent decades, scholars of American religion have had much to say about the Evangelical Christian movement. A great deal of attention has been paid to the varieties of Evangelical culture (Hunter 1983; Miller 1997; Muse 2005); the dynamics of congregational life (Warner 1988; Ammerman 1997; Becker 1999; Eiesland 2000; Watt 2002); paradenominational and educational institutions (Balmer 1989; Wagner 1990); rhetorical practices (Stromberg 1993; Bielo 2004, 2007b; Harding 2000); the embodiment of spiritual experience (Griffith 1997; Luhrmann 2004); social activism and mobilization (Elisha 2004, 2008); economic logics (Bialecki 2008); and strategies of Bible use and interpretation (Ammerman 1987; Bartkowski 1996; Bielo 2007a, 2008; Crapanzano 2000; Malley 2004). This body of research has been extremely productive and one could easily argue that, along with the global spread of Pentecostalism (Robbins 2004), the scholarly understanding of American Evangelicalism is the most intricate for Christian cultures worldwide. Among these historians, sociologists, and anthropologists, there has been an enduring interest in where and how religiosity happens for these Christians. Where is it that we see Evangelical culture "in action"? Despite a rich ethnographic record, a significant and surprising lacuna persists—an in-depth, comparative analysis of that most pervasive of social institutions in Evangelical life: group Bible study.

Evangelicals throughout the United States emphasize the need for Bible study in their individual and collective lives. As I demonstrate throughout this book, Bible study contends strongly for being the most consequential form of religious practice to the ever-evolving contours of American Evangelicalism. From a sheer numerical perspective, it is the most prolific type of small group in American society, with more than 30 million Protestants gathering every week for this distinct purpose. As a matter of substance, it provides individuals a unique opportunity to engage in open, reflexive, and critical dialogue. If we are serious about developing the anthropology of Christianity in the United States, we must attend to sites of cultural production and reflection. A claim to which I return throughout these chapters is that in the midst of "just talking," much happens—much that informs us about what it means to be an American Evangelical at the beginning of the 21st century. What are Evangelicals interested in? What are they concerned about? What are they conflicted about? And what are the narratives, vocabularies, and cultural models used to articulate them? In responding to these questions I am attempting to theorize a practice that is globally recognized as significant across Christian traditions. Yet, no one has thus far been able to provide a systematic account of what happens when Evangelicals gather to read, discuss, and debate.[1]

Bible study groups form in numerous ways. Congregation-wide efforts are launched to bolster participation in short-term church programs, and individuals act on an impetus to explore their faith with fellow believers. Most groups meet once a week, though some prefer only two or three monthly gatherings. They meet in homes, churches, coffee shops, restaurants, and other public and private venues. There are groups organized strictly for men, women, couples, couples with young children, college students, empty-nesters, retirees, business owners, dieters, church leaders, young professionals, and so on, almost indefinitely. The typical meeting begins with prayer, usually a brief request for God to "bless" the group members' time together. The majority of the meeting alternates between reading and an interactive discussion about the text of study. As we will see time and again through the case studies presented, Bible study conversations are distinctive in Evangelical life for their blend of self-deprecating and insightful humor, curious inquiry, intense intellectual banter, and intimate exchanges of information. Groups move with ease among topics as diverse as theological doctrines, hermeneutics, moral questions, politics, social mores, history, current events, congregational concerns, and personal experiences. Biblical texts are often the basis of discussion but are certainly not the only type of text that is read. Members are voracious readers, systematically working through Biblical texts, Biblical commentaries, devotional materials, best-selling Christian books, and print and online articles from Christian periodicals. (A select few groups also interspersed video or audiotape study series or lengthier films into their group schedules.) Discussions are followed by a closing prayer, which can be brief or extensive, sometimes lasting upwards of thirty minutes. Bible studies rarely last for less than an hour and often exceed two hours. Before and after the typical Bible study meeting, participants socialize with one another: laughing, trading stories, exchanging books, and generally enjoying each other's company. Within this generic structure a host of themes central to Evangelical culture are habitually performed and consciously reconsidered. These themes appear as textual practices, religious dispositions, and discursive formations.

In this book I present an ethnography of Evangelical Bible study life. In doing so I seek to address a series of questions: what are the defining characteristics of this practice? Why is Bible study so important in the lives of Evangelicals? What are the continuities and tensions among and between individual Bible study groups? Why is Bible study so crucial for understanding Evangelical culture? What are the broader discourses—Evangelical and American alike—that help shape Bible-study life? What role does Bible study play in making religiosity happen for Evangelicals? And how does the world of Bible study translate and become effectual for individuals as they go about the remainder of their religious and social lives? To get at these questions I rely on three frameworks for studying cultural life: (1) a focus on social institutions, emphasizing the role of face-to-face encounters; (2) a focus on the use of texts to mediate relationships, ideas, and motives for action, highlighting the role of collective reading; and (3) a focus on close analyses of spoken discourse as a means of studying institutions and the social life of texts. As I discuss these approaches, I point to their mutual compatibility and utility in an ethnography of Bible study life and, ultimately, for enhancing our understanding of American Evangelicalism.

Words Upon the Word is based on nineteen months of ethnographic fieldwork carried out between June 2004 and December 2005. I conducted this research in and around the Midwestern city of Lansing, Michigan. The project included six Protestant congregations: three United Methodist[2] and one each from the Lutheran Church-Missouri Synod, Restoration Movement, and Vineyard Fellowship. In total, I observed 324 Bible study meetings with 19 groups, and audio-recorded 167 of these meetings. The chapters that follow provide an up-close portrait of five groups and include audio-recordings and observations from 89 meetings. These case study groups, as well as the wider project sample, encompass a variety of ethnicities, gender compositions, ages, social classes, educational backgrounds, income levels, and political postures. I do not advance any specific arguments about the racialized, gendered, or otherwise demographically rooted qualities of Bible study life. Rather, I rely on the diversity of the project sample to strengthen my overall claim: Evangelical Bible study is organized by a series of practices, logics, and tensions that are deeply embedded in the broader cultural scene of American Evangelicalism.

Toward an Ethnography of Bible Study

In presenting this research to friends, students, and colleagues I am predictably confronted with one question: "How did you ever get interested in doing *that*?" My path toward an ethnography of Bible study life is strikingly academic. I did not grow up attending small groups, always wondering if others found them as rewarding or questionable as I did. My parents were not preachers or missionaries. I did not attend a Christian college or begin my career as a seminarian (only to later convert to anthropology). I was not intent on unmasking the negative impact of Evangelicalism in American life, nor did I start out as an unapologetic advocate for Evangelical Christianity. I was, in fact, in the office of my dissertation advisor. I was in my second year of a Ph.D. program in cultural anthropology (not yet overridden with cynicism but increasingly sleep deprived and over-caffeinated) working as a research assistant. I was helping to analyze a rather large corpus of data from a four-year ethnographic project that included eight mainline Protestant congregations and four Roman Catholic parishes (see Roberts 2005). During the fieldwork among mainline churches, the project researchers attended and took copious hand-written notes among several Bible study groups. Unsure of how to incorporate this particular data set into his other analyses, my advisor relied on the time-honored practice of turning to his graduate advisee. Having never attended a Bible study, I accepted the task with great curiosity. As I read through these notes, three thoughts slowly dawned on me. First, the content of these meetings was an amazing record of lay theology and spirituality "in action." Second, surely scholars had already taken advantage of this opportunity. Last, verbatim transcripts of these discussions would be far more advantageous than hand-written notes.

I return to the first and third of these thoughts in the next section. As to the second—what scholars, namely sociologists and anthropologists, have already said about Bible study—I was shocked. At the time, and still today, there are only three substantial works that focus principally on group Bible study among American Christians. Robert Wuthnow's companion volumes, *Sharing the Journey: Support Groups and America's New Quest for Community* (1994a) and *"I Come Away Stronger": How Small Groups Are Shaping American Religion* (1994b), were the first to analyze this phenomenon at length. *Sharing the Journey* is a quantitative account of the diversity of small groups in American life. Wuthnow argues that, beginning in the 1960s, Americans have steadily rearranged their search for community belonging, seeking small group opportunities in place of larger, more formal institutional structures. Among these, small group Bible study is the most prolific in American life, with more than 30 million men and women participating in these groups at least once a week (68).[3] This bears repeating: no other form of small group, religious or otherwise, is as widespread in American life as group Bible study. Despite recognizing the ubiquity of Bible study in American Christian life, Wuthnow fails to recognize what it accomplishes. Instead, in a surprising final analysis, he seems to de-emphasize its uniqueness:

> What counts is less the studying of specific lessons . . . but activities that
> people enjoy, that allow them to interact informally with a few other peo-
> ple, and that, in many ways, are not decidedly different from the activi-
> ties that other people who are not in such groups do in their leisure time.
> (148)

If nothing else, I hope this book convinces that Bible study is not best
theorized as just another "leisure" activity and that it *is* a "decidedly different" practice.

"I Come Away Stronger" is a collection of twelve ethnographic essays
depicting small groups in mainline and Evangelical Christian congregations, as well as Jewish synagogues and nonsectarian organizations. However, the essays are almost exclusively descriptive, identifying the varieties
of composition, purpose, and "feel" one finds in the small group movement. These narrative portraits are certainly valuable, but it is left to the
reader to decide what each group is telling us about Evangelical culture.
The chapters by Bender (1994: 225–50) and Olson (1994: 125–47) stand out
for attempting to move beyond documentation to create some sort of focused analytical argument. The collection as a whole, however, raises far
more questions than it answers about how Bible studies work, how social
discourses structure group interaction, what continuities and tensions define Bible study life, and generally why this cultural practice carries any
social significance whatsoever. Finally, *Women in the Presence: Constructing Community and Seeking Spirituality in Mainline Protestantism* (1995)
is an in-depth ethnography from the anthropologist, Jody Shapiro Davie.
Focusing on one women's Bible study in a New England Presbyterian congregation, Davie picks up where the Wuthnow collection falls short. Based
on extended fieldwork with the group and one-on-one interviews with
each member, Davie suggests that Bible study is a highly unique practice
in American religious life. Consider the following statement from the
opening pages of Davie's book in comparison to Wuthnow's conclusion:

> Attendance at a Sunday church service permits worshippers to gather to-
> gether for a common enactment of faith, but the service is a public per-
> formance: meaning-laden, surely, but fully corporate, consensual. It is not
> a time for dialogue, not a time for active personal negotiation of meaning
> except on the most inward level. . . . [It is in] small groups where per-
> sons who share a religion come together by choice in order to be actively

engaged in the enhancement and enactment of their spiritual lives on various levels, the potential exists for not only the creative articulation of individual faith, but also for a joint, or collaborative, search for and discussion of meaning and experience, and the affirmation of the life of the spirit. (1–2)

Davie goes on to analyze the communicative boundaries and type of spirituality cultivated by this women's group in their meetings. Despite an impressive analysis, we are left wondering about several crucial questions: how indicative are Davie's observations outside of mainline Presbyterianism? How indicative are her arguments for Bible study groups that arrange their meetings differently and perform different types of religious reading? Thus, while Davie's conclusion about the value of Bible study is far more accurate than Wuthnow's, she is handicapped by a lack of comparative analysis.

By picking out these three works I am not suggesting that Bible study has been completely ignored by other sociologists and anthropologists of American religion. Brief depictions and references to the importance of group Bible study appear in numerous widely cited works (e.g., Titon 1988; Ammerman 1997; Griffith 1997; Miller 1997; Becker 1999; Crapanzano 2000; Eiesland 2000; Ault 2004; Malley 2004). The collective shortcoming of this work, along with the valuable contributions from Wuthnow and Davie, is twofold. First, the only semblance of an explanatory framework has been to understand Bible study in functionalist terms. Congregationally, Bible study has been explained as functioning to foster participation in the local church, increase bonds of fellowship, help make important policy and program decisions, and socialize new members into the local culture of the church (e.g., Eiesland 2000). In short, Bible study is viewed as satisfying distinct needs and purposes within the local church community. Individually, Bible study has been described as functioning to provide emotional support and accountability, generically reinforce beliefs and values, and serve as a source of spiritual growth for participants (e.g., Becker 1999). My objection to these analyses is not that they are inaccurate but that they are vastly incomplete. I argue for an analytical framework that extends well beyond local and individual functions. Second, what is lacking throughout the existing literature on Bible study is a sustained focus on this practice for itself: an in-depth, comparative account that situates Bible study within a defined framework to understand the cultural significance of this phenomenon. In other words, Bible study must not only be regarded as a means toward other ends (e.g., as a barometer for church growth), but also as an event that accomplishes its own cultural work and is appreciated as such by its participants. To achieve this there must be an account of the themes that define Bible study life and how these connect to prevailing discourses and trends within the broader Evangelical movement.

The lack of systematic research on the practice of group Bible study is striking for a number of reasons, some of which I have already indicated. The sheer numerical presence, greater than 30 million people each week, provides ample reason to wonder why more attention has not been paid to Bible study. The importance of Bible study as a unique congregational and religious event, as described by Davie, is equally compelling. We should also question this scant attention on historical grounds. At its core, group Bible study is a practice that centers on the interaction between Christians and their sacred scriptures. Beginning at least with the 16th-century European Reformation, Protestants have been supremely concerned with their ability and duty to read and comprehend the Bible for themselves. Among others, Martin Luther, William Tyndale, and John Calvin all charged Christian believers to assume a personal responsibility in reading scripture and grasping theological truths (Frei 1974; Cummings 2002). In the context of the United States, this responsibility has been understood as best met through collective endeavors. The birth and rapid spread of the Sunday school movement in the 19th century testifies to the centrality of scriptural study and the voluntary, church-based, group focus of American Evangelicalism (Boylan 1988). Studying the Bible indexes a broader schema among Evangelical Protestants, a firm connection between literacy and spirituality. The authority invested in religious reading and a fundamental affinity for all manner of texts has been an organizing feature of conservative Christianity since the late 1800s (Brown 2004). Finally, the paucity of analytical, critical work on Bible study from scholars is astounding in light of the rather voluminous attention paid to it by pastors and church leaders. Widely popular church campaigns such as Rick Warren's *40 Days of Purpose*, Bill Hybels and Mark Mittelberg's *Becoming a Contagious Christian*, and scores of others are centered on the formation of weekly small groups. Monthly congregational newsletters devote entire sections to the types of Bible study opportunities offered by the church. Christian bookstores have special sections devoted solely to Bible study materials. A (very unsystematic) search on Amazon.com for "small-group Bible study" returned a not-so-modest 1,766 results. (Compare this to the same search for "Evangelical politics," which produced only 208 results!) It seems as though everywhere in the worlds of church leadership, church growth, and spiritual development, Evangelicals are talking about group Bible study.

Thus, there is little reason to wonder if there is a need for more substantial research on this religious practice. The question remains, however, what is the best way to go about this research? I argue that group Bible study is most fruitfully understood as a vital social institution, rooted in the processes of collective reading and intersubjective dialogue. Through the weekly exchanges that occur between texts and readers and among those readers about those texts, we see the continuities and tensions of American Evangelicalism "in action."

Institution, Reading, and Discourse

The arguments I raise in this book locate important lessons about the current shape of American Evangelical culture in the details of Bible study conversation. This approach rests on a series of assumptions about the nature of culture and what happens when a group of readers interact with a text together. As an anthropologist by training, part of my socialization into the discipline was first to embrace and then question "culture" as an organizing analytical concept. Indeed, more so than any other theoretical-methodological device, anthropologists have spilled their ink over the status of "culture" (e.g., Clifford and Marcus, eds. 1986; Marcus and Fischer 1986; Rosaldo 1989; Abu-Lughod 1991; Kuper 1999). My approach towards Evangelical "culture" emerges primarily from theories of social practice (e.g., Bourdieu 1977), which emphasize the integral and active role of social institutions.

Institution

Approaching "culture" as collections of overlapping, interreliant institutions is not simply a matter of identifying organizational structures. Rather, "institutions" in this sense refers to "any relatively durable set of social relations which endows individuals with power, status, and resources of various kinds" (Thompson 1991: 8). More explicitly, institutions are stable social forms—of all sizes and types—that contribute to the formation of dispositions: inclinations of action, thought, embodiment, interpretation, belief, interaction, and speech. Thus, when we speak of "culture" we are in reality grasping for the social processes by which such dispositions are formed, become habitualized, made attractive and worth seeking, or defined as oppressive and worth rejecting. To borrow from Brian Street, "culture is a verb," a "signifying process" in the "construction of meaning," not a "fixed inheritance of shared meanings" (1993: 23).

A key element in this conceptualization of social institutions is their capacity for production (see Berger and Luckmann 1966). Institutions are not simply social arenas where individuals congregate to passively receive and exchange information about their surrounding world. Rather, as sites of knowledge production, institutions provide social locations where we can actively engage the history of the ideas and epistemologies with which we live. The cultural scene of American Evangelicalism, for example, encompasses numerous bodies of knowledge, including theology, hermeneutics, science, nationalism, legality, and everyday ethics, just to list a few. An institutional approach to "culture" recognizes that much of individuals' interactions with these systems of knowing occur through various types of social settings and relations. And if we want to see how individuals and collectivities are experiencing forms of knowledge we must look closely at the sites where this actually happens.

This framework for studying "culture," however, is not strictly mentalist and ideological. It is ultimately concerned with how the life of an institution relates to the life of individual and collective action that ensues from participation in that institution. Cultural life cannot solely be about thought, belief, value, and the like, but must also attend to action, strategy, change, coercion, and resistance. Thus, in the analysis of institutions we find the breeding ground for intention, creativity, motivation, and ambition. And while the analyses I present in this book focus on the life of one Evangelical institution, it is clear in each chapter that what happens in Bible study is destined not to stay in Bible study but most certainly informs the logic and decision making of participants as they leave the group setting to be mothers, fathers, spouses, bosses, workers, and citizens.

Of course, not every social institution in every cultural setting functions equally as a site of knowledge production and disposition formation. Theories of practice have been most interested in observing those scenes where the dynamic and conflicted nature of social life is made apparent—either as public performance or backstage reflection. Among American Evangelicals, group Bible study is just such an institution. This returns me to Jody Davie's key observation about the nature of group Bible study, namely, its uniqueness in the context of the American Christian experience. It is a site where individuals are able to critically and reflexively articulate the categories of meaning and action that are central to their spiritual and social life. This happens primarily in and through the act of collective reading.

Reading

Group Bible study is an event defined by the interaction between a collection of readers and a text. While this does distinguish Evangelical Bible study, it is certainly not unique. Cross-culturally, numerous events have been observed that are built around this same phenomenon. Orthodox Jews gather to read and study the Talmud (Boyarin 1989); Muslims from varying regions find a host of performative and interpretive uses for the Quran (e.g., Baker 1993; Bowen 1993; Lambek 1990); literary clubs seem to form around most any available genre (Long 2003; Radway 1984; Reed 2004); and thousands of university students huddle around assigned texts every week in undergraduate and graduate seminars. Without question, texts are crucial to a variety of social institutions. In all of these, texts are not read only to be discarded. They are not forgotten. Sacred or academic, ancient or recently published, texts become embedded in the lives of readers and serve as guides to action. The use of texts is not static or stagnant, and the relationship between reader and text in the group context is never uniform. Indeed, collective reading is as likely to produce tension as it is continuity, depending on the text under study, the composition of readers, and their recognized purpose of being together. These dynamics require an understanding of the social qualities of textual consumption.

The empirical study of reading has been taken up most intentionally by those within "the ethnography of reading" (Boyarin, ed. 1993). This field of inquiry seeks to understand the cultural logics that organize reading—as a structured form of social action, an emergent performance event, and a defined category of practice. Ethnographers of reading have shown interest in all manners of literacy, from the most mundane reading events to those at the center of ritual and communal life. This body of research has posed a series of fundamental questions about the culturally constructed nature of reading: what constitutes an act of reading? Who reads alone and who reads together? What does reading accomplish? Who has the access and legitimacy to read? What is deemed worth reading? Who deems it so? Whose readings are authoritative? And what sociohistorical processes—local and global—structure acts of reading? The fundamental strength of this scholarship is its recognition that the act of reading is about so much more than just consuming information. It is, in fact, a forum for (and form of) social interaction, moral discourse, and epistemological formation.

Words Upon the Word, alongside other works in the ethnography of reading, is a product of the "turn toward the reader" within literacy criticism and cultural hermeneutics in the 1970s. Reader-response theory, as it came to be known, objected to the assertion that texts contain finalized meanings via defined authorial intentions or specific properties of genre. For its proponents this model implied a rather passive reader whose job was simply to excavate the buried meaning from a text. Instead, reader-response theorists sought to demonstrate how meaning is invested in a text by its interlocutors, thereby restoring a more active role to the reader. In turn, the idea of an active reader is a social problem, not only because the baggage brought to the reading of texts is culturally derived, but also because the consumption of texts (even when performed alone) is always done within particular settings of society and history. Stanley Fish (1980) captures this in his model of the "interpretive community" whereby readers read the way they do because of their participation in defined communities of practice. Such communities operate on common procedures for engaging texts, sharing hermeneutic assumptions, interpretive strategies and performative styles. It is from this collective reading context that meaning ensues, not from the individual reader and not from the text itself. As a result, we see reading and interpretation as fundamentally cultural acts, and we open a space to view the multiplicity of social meanings that arise from the reader-text interaction.

Studies of "scripturalism" have continued in this tradition of thinking about readers, their texts, and the social contexts of reading (see Malley 2004 for a critical review of this field). Scholars of comparative religion, most famously Wilfred Cantwell Smith (1993), have called attention to the fact that "scriptures" rely on communities of practice to recognize them as such. For a text to be "sacred" or "scriptural" it must be endowed and continue to be endowed with the appropriate significance by a defined group of interlocutors (see Levering, ed. 1989). There are many questions to be asked about the "social life of scriptures" (Bowen 1992: 495; Bielo, ed. Forthcoming)—what communities of readers do with their sacred texts across settings and involving different social actors. As textual artifacts, scriptures can experience change due to their social circulation. In the case of American Evangelicals and the Bible, one need look no further than paraphrases, children's Bibles, Biblezines, and graphic novel Bibles to see evidence of this. Moreover, scriptures are implicated in all manner of normative rhetoric, quoted irrespective of occasion, and invested with divergent meanings for divergent reasons. In short, the social life of scriptures is a busy one, hectic even. The work I present here on group Bible study provides an up-close vision of where Evangelical readers take their scriptures (as well as texts that comment on scriptures) in their own anthropological imaginations.

A collective strength of the reader-response tradition is that it stresses the formative impact of texts on the lives of readers. The social life of scriptures includes the propositional beliefs they encourage, the emotions and motivations they cultivate, and the practices they shape. This relationship between text and world foregrounds the need to better understand what happens between readers and texts. After all, these processes and products are quite meaningful outside a closed circle of religionists huddled around their scripture because they eventually enter the surrounding social world through those religionists. In the chapters that follow I analyze various products of collective reading, such as Bible interpretation, spiritual intimacy, and personal witnessing. These scenes should therefore be understood as both a form of mutual knowledge production and potent incitements to action.

Discourse

A framework that emphasizes institutions and collective reading does well to identify where to begin observation and what to look for. It falls short, however, on the question of how to look. The methodological complement I employ is that of "discourse analysis." Following the tradition of symbolic interactionism (Mead 1934), I understand intersubjective institutions to be constituted by their semiotic, linguistic, and interactional features. The knowledge and orientations toward action that are produced within social institutions rely on processes of signification (e.g., the exchange of talk) and the rules and strategies that organize this behavior. Thus, to study an institution necessarily entails the study of its discourse.

By "discourse" I mean language-in-use, that dialogical stream of communicative activity that helps to define group identity and purpose. At least since the 1960s (Hymes 1964) anthropologists have studied speaking not simply as a vehicle through which culture gets transmitted. Rather, it is in the details of linguistic practice that the study of culture can take place. Questions of meaning and social structure can be understood through the combined analysis of speech content, strategies of talk, discourse organization, and accompanying interactional features (Sherzer 1987). The discourse-culture link has been recognized as particularly salient within "religious language," where ideas about the nature of language and the identities of speakers, patterns of linguistic form, and contexts of performance are all integral to religious formation (Keane 2004). In fact, the analytical connection between language and religion appears quite natural, given their shared interest in questions of meaning making, identity performance, and establishing common bonds of sociality.

The close coupling of religion and language has been highlighted in the study of American Evangelicalism. Two of the most widely cited works among anthropologists and sociologists, monographs by Susan Harding (2000) and Vincent Crapanzano (2000), are both linguistically oriented investigations. Harding, in particular, sees language as central to born-again Christianity. She argues that "speaking is believing," suggesting that religious conversion is marked by adopting forms of discourse and, by extension, modes of thinking and being in the world (33–60). Harding's now influential claim is evident also in the work of Peter Stromberg (1993), whose analysis of Evangelical conversion narratives emphasized that such performances are not simple retellings but effectual rituals where emotions and experiences are reframed in born-again terms. Perhaps the ultimate lesson of this research tradition is the inseparability of language and religion in Evangelical culture and that the former is among the most useful ways of understanding the latter (cf. Csordas 1997, Meigs 1995, Muse 2005, Shoaps 2002, Witten 1993).

Of course, American Evangelicals are not the only Christians to pay close attention to words, discursive forms, and attitudes toward language. Indeed, the history of Christianity could be sketched in linguistic terms. Augustine is widely recognized as setting the theoretical agenda for both signification and reading in the West (Ando 2001; Stock 1996). Aquinas was invested in both Aristotelian semiotics and the doctrine of analogy (Ayres 2006). Erasmus struggled to balance the limitations of language with his desire for vernacular translations (Boyle 1977). The European Reformation recast Protestant language ideologies. Namely, the spoken and written word were ascribed an unprecedented trust as a communicative vehicle for accurately conveying exterior realities and internal states (Cummings 2002; Keane 2007). The struggles—from the 17th century through the 21st—over Biblical literalism, systematic theology, common sense philosophy, Enlightenment philosophy, German neo-orthodoxy, "fundamentalism," "liberalism," and "postmodernism" are all anchored in questions about what language can and cannot do (Macquarrie 1967; Ward 1995; Jeffrey 1996). We might go so far as to suggest that Christians are as much *homo linguisticus* as they are *homo religiosus*. Alongside theologians, historians, and literary critics, anthropologists of Christianity have honed in on the historical, cross-cultural intersection of Christian culture, linguistic ideology, and discursive practice (e.g., Robbins 2001; Engelke 2007; Keane 2007). In many ways *Words Upon the Word* emerges from this tradition as I analyze how conservative Evangelicals, through their dialogue and collective reading, articulate their versions of Christian language, identity, and culture.

What I have presented above are the guiding analytical assumptions and principles for this study of American Evangelicalism. The framework I am advocating focuses on the life of social institutions, the practices of collective reading and interpretation, and the discourse that gives life to these processes. Ultimately, this book is about what happens when American Evangelicals gather to read and discuss various texts and the very real impact that this form of social action has on the remainder of their lives. I focus on group Bible study because of its dialogic, reflexive, and dynamic characteristics as an event where this type of action occurs.

Plan of the Book

In the chapters that follow I argue that there are definable themes in Bible study life. The five themes I address in this book are both the most prevalent and most significant for understanding group study. They are, however, not the only themes one might observe. For example, I do not directly address the role of local congregational life in shaping the content and organization of group study. By leaving certain themes out, I am, necessarily, drawing an inevitably partial portrait of Bible study. It is my hope that readers will sympathize with this dilemma as they are introduced to the themes on which I do focus. For each theme, I argue explicitly for its priority within group life, and its (often very serious) consequences for understanding the status of Evangelicalism.

In the course of highlighting these themes, I stay attentive to two crucial realities of Bible study life. First, group study is dialectically implicated in broader discourses of American Evangelicalism (e.g., prosperity theology, gender ideologies) and American society (e.g., democratic ethos, religious pluralism). By dialectical I mean simply that these discourses help to structure processes of reading and dialogue, while also being placed under self-conscious scrutiny through group interaction. Second, while my primary focus remains on the continuities among and between Bible study groups, I make clear in each chapter where tensions are likely to and do arise. Through their disagreements and contradictions (potential, seeming, and real), these groups come face-to-face with the heterogeneity that defines American Evangelicalism. And as a result, they reveal that their faith and their group life need not be threatened by these elements of diversity and conflict.

I begin in chapter 1 by addressing several questions of ethnographic reflexivity. I examine the methodological decisions made in designing and carrying out this research. In the latter half of the chapter I turn to the question of how I participated and related with the project groups, outlining the ways in which my presence undoubtedly impacted the ethnographic scene I was there to document. Ultimately, the goal of this chapter is to intentionally reflect on the myriad of decisions I needed to make throughout the project and how those decisions impacted the shape of the research.

In chapter 2 I examine the organizing theme of group life: Bible reading and interpretation. While reading directly from biblical texts is not always a part of group meetings, scripture remains at the center of why these groups meet and how their conversations are structured. My analysis focuses on a Lutheran men's Bible study and their thirteen-week study of the Old Testament book of Proverbs. I argue that the practice of group Bible reading is best understood through an analytical scheme that pairs distinct ideologies articulated about the Bible as a text ("textual ideology") and distinct hermeneutic activities that groups perform with Biblical texts ("textual practice").

Chapter 3 takes up the question of how participants understand the event of Bible study and what they expect from this event. Employing the sociolinguistic concept of "interactive frames," I argue that Evangelical Bible study is defined by the sustained attempt to cultivate increased intimacy among participants. I focus this analysis on fourteen meetings of a mixed-gender home group from a Restoration Movement congregation. I emphasize how this frame of intimacy helps organize group meeting structure, norms of interaction, and modes of Bible interpretation.

Chapter 4 analyzes the ways in which the personal interests of participants work to structure religious reading. Like other forms of collective belonging, Bible study groups often coalesce because they share certain interests and passions. In the case of Bible study, the shared interests of participants provide a "subtext" for reading (Long 1993: 194). The case study for this chapter is a mixed-gender home group from a United Methodist congregation. This analysis is based on the group's sixteen-week study of the best-selling Evangelical text *The Jesus I Never Knew* by Philip Yancey (1995). I illustrate how this group's shared interest in the general category of "history" constitutes their subtext for reading, organizing their discussion of the book itself, its biblical references, the moral-political issues it raises, and the group's prevailing mode of hermeneutic activity.

Chapter 5 explores how Bible study participants use group meetings as an opportunity to practice "witnessing." The sociological and anthropological research on American Evangelicals has identified "witnessing" as a distinct speech genre in which "believers" attempt to convert "nonbelievers" to Christianity. I argue that a prevailing theme in Bible study life is a form of performance rehearsal, wherein participants reenact past witnessing encounters and imagine potential opportunities. Ultimately, the aim is to define what constitutes effective and ineffective witnessing. My analysis is based on over thirty hours of discussion from a United Methodist men's group and their reading of the New Testament book of Acts.

The final analytical chapter considers how religious identity is constructed and negotiated in group Bible study. The issues addressed in chapters 2 through 5 all speak to the tensions and emphases of Evangelical identity. In chapter 6 I focus my analysis on one Lutheran women's Bible study group and their ongoing struggle to identify the nature of their religious identity. Based on observations and recordings from eighteen group meetings, I argue that this ongoing articulation of identity is grounded in conceptualizations of what distinguishes a defined Lutheran Self from a variety of "misguided" Christian others.

In the last chapter, I return to the necessity of developing an ethnography of Bible study life. In particular, I highlight the theoretical and methodological lessons available in this type of research. In the spirit of encouraging open-ended scholarship, I end by pointing to three areas of Bible study ethnography that deserve more attention and might provide a useful starting point for others. Throughout the course of this book, readers will encounter a variety of Bible study groups from different Protestant traditions that have cultivated different group dynamics. The arguments I pursue are always presented in the context of verbatim group interactions. As I move between qualitative analysis and primary empirical data, I am confident that readers will be struck by the creativity and acumen of these groups and the individual participants. I have suggested in this introduction that a key aspect of social institutions is their ability to encourage reflexive dialogue and that Bible study stands out in this regard. I believe this assertion is borne out time and again in the chapters that follow as these individuals reveal themselves as critically engaged social actors. In short, I believe that the analyses in this book repeatedly demonstrate the importance of what happens when Evangelicals are "just sitting around talking."

Doing Bible Study Ethnography

On two occasions—for two months in 2006, and a four-month stint in 2007—I lived with a host couple from a United Methodist Bible study. My final meeting with a Lutheran women's group in December 2005 took the form of a "good-bye" party the group insisted on throwing for me. A Vineyard group, whose Wednesday night meeting happened to fall on my birthday, replaced their weekly study with a celebratory dinner. I spent a hot July afternoon helping one Bible study facilitator jackhammer his decaying asphalt driveway. A difficult end to a three-year relationship was eased by the friendship of a woman from a Restoration Bible study. My Memorial Day in 2005 was spent grilling, talking, and playing kickball (at least attempting to play) with a Sunday night group. Still today, I meet regularly with several Bible study facilitators to wax theological and drink coffee.

These events and relationships index an important reality of this research: while observing nearly 500 hours of Bible study was an intense ethnographic experience, it was also an emotional and spiritual one. On the other end of my fieldwork, before I attended 324 meetings and formed these relationships, I spent over six months designing the project sample. Before proceeding to the more empirical and theoretically oriented chapters of this book, I reflect here on several crucial questions regarding the methodology and experience of this ethnography.

On "Being Reflexive"

It is gospel among social scientists that ethnography is a means of knowledge production—one that always struggles to manage a series of formative institutional and relational contexts (Clifford 1986). How we know what we know as ethnographers occurs against the backdrop of tough sampling choices, practical necessities, cultural biases, histories of power and meaning, personal biography, political turmoil, and real relationships with real people. The goal of reflexive ethnography is to attend to the ways in which one's particular fieldwork encounter and the interpretations that arise from it are shaped by these various contexts. At its worst, "being reflexive" amounts to little more than unnecessary autobiography (navel gazing, as it were), illuminating little that helps better understand the analytical questions being posed. At its best, "being reflexive" scrutinizes how research is conducted and the experience of doing fieldwork, all in pursuit of helping readers better understand the claims being made.

Ethnography is no longer the strict purview of anthropologists. It is practiced (and practiced well) by those in sociology, communications, media studies, and host of other disciplines. But of all the fields that "do ethnography," anthropology holds it closest as a methodological badge of self-identity. Since the beginnings of cultural anthropology in the United States (Boas 1920) and Britain (Malinowski 1922), cultural anthropologists have first and foremost been fieldworkers. We are more interested in abduction than induction or deduction, committed to the ongoing generation of new theorizing based on ongoing empirical observation (Agar 1996: 35–41). As the discipline has matured, though, the classic statements on ethnography (and the model of doing ethnography that informs them) have been opened to critique. In particular, the idealized (but never actualized) process of the lone ethnographer leaving home to live in the field as part of a wholly different culture has been shown to rest on a series of fundamentally false dichotomies. Distinct separations between subject/object, insider/outsider, native/nonnative, colonizer/colonized and self/other have all been questioned or rejected by anthropological theory and philosophy (e.g., Clifford and Marcus, eds. 1986; Marcus and Fischer 1986; Narayan 1993). In my case, while I may appear to be a "native" (or, "insider") in certain subject positions (for example, I am a Christian; I was born in the United States), there are as many others where I do not (for example, I am not a conservative Evangelical; I am not a card-carrying Republican). In 2008, almost a century after Boas and Malinowski "established" cultural anthropology, reflexive ethnography is not simply a niche interest among postmodern anthropologists. Rather, it is an integral sensibility for all who recognize the reality of situated theorizing and data collection.

Anthropologists, alongside other social scientists, have identified numerous reasons why ethnography must attend to questions of reflexivity. At least three are particularly relevant to the research I conducted among Evangelical Bible study groups: (1) being reflexive is not tantamount to an absence of methodological rigor (e.g., Wolcott 1995). The reflexive turn among anthropologists has been particularly keen to the reality that ethnography does not function the same as a natural science—that is, the experimental testing of discrete variables in a controlled environment. However, this is not to say that ethnographic fieldwork cannot or should not be concerned with the systematic use of well-defined data collection techniques. Any presentation of methodology should include the decision-making logics that guided the formation of the research agenda. While we are not in the business of deriving scientific laws, we are still able to make comparable claims based on empirical evidence. (2) Ethnography is not a matter of providing mirrorlike reflections of cultural scenes. Rather, ethnography always takes the form of a cultural representation (e.g., Clifford 1986). The observations and arguments depicted in a piece of ethnographic writing are always partial in several senses. They are a particular selection of empirical evidence, born from a particular research design, translated by a particular individual, understood through a particular set of analytical frameworks, and presented via a particular style of writing. And (3), an ethnographer's observations are not always of naturally occurring events, but often performances enacted for the benefit of the ethnographer (e.g., Crapanzano 1980). Ethnographers frequently constitute, or are thought to provide access to, an audience that would not otherwise be part of a cultural scene. Laura Graham (1995), for example, was surprised to learn that a primary reason the Xavante Indians of Brazil allowed her to videotape rituals was because they deeply desired the global audience they presumed her camera lens represented. Ethnographic subjects find many reasons for this, from individual benefit to community good, mockery of the ethnographer or, in the case of evangelizing Christians, the endangered eternal soul of an imagined listener.

In this chapter I situate my ethnography of Evangelical Bible study life and honestly address how I designed the research, what my experience of "being there" was like, and how I collected the project data. I have organized this discussion around four questions: How did I choose the project churches? How did I choose the project groups? How did I observe myself during Bible study? And how did I collect and organize the project data? Throughout this book readers will encounter a variety of Bible study dynamics and the commentary they provide on the nature of American Evangelicalism. My goal here is to ground those analyses within a set of ethnographic experiences that shaped their outcome. My arguments emerge from the social scientific study of religion and language. But still, I applied these ideas to a body of data that materialized through my identities as an ethnographer (an individual of a certain sex, age, religious background, and social status) and the conditions of doing ethnography in a certain place. In short, the portrait of group Bible study I present is my own portrait, and this chapter details the boundaries of that frame.

How did I choose the project churches?

As I mentioned in the introduction, this project consisted of nineteen months of ethnographic fieldwork, encompassing 324 Bible study meetings, nineteen groups, and six Protestant congregations. I began with a series of goals regarding what the project sample should include and thus what it would enable analytically. From the outset, a primary aim was to build a comparative ethnography of Bible study life. I wanted these points of comparison to illustrate several issues: the heterogeneity across Evangelical denominations; representation of different socioeconomic classes; and congregations with varying senses of mission and identity. Given my concerns with scripture reading and interpretation and Bible study as a dialogical space for lay theology, it was significant to include churches claiming different Evangelical histories. I prioritized socioeconomic class because of my experience analyzing data for the "People in the Pews" project, a comparative ethnography of eight mainline Protestant churches and four Roman Catholic parishes conducted by my dissertation advisor from 1994 to 1998 (Roberts 2005). The central question of this project was how local congregational styles of worship, fellowship, and organization equate with "success" in local religious economies. Among the more surprising findings was that the typical variables emphasized by scholars of American religion (for example, age, gender, race/ethnicity) were less important in shaping congregational life than members' education, occupation, and income. Finally, because I was interested in congregational Bible study and because of the tight coupling between congregational culture and religious activity, I sought to include churches emphasizing different types of mission work. The final sample of churches, then, was meant to reflect these interests. In addition, a deciding factor for any church I consulted about the project was the expansiveness of their Bible study program. I knew that only congregations offering multiple Bible study opportunities throughout the week and Bible studies of varying types would be suitable for comparative research.[1]

My first field note entry documenting the sampling process is from May 27, 2004. I began by delimiting the geographic area where I would collect information on Protestant congregations,[2] which included seven municipalities in the Lansing, Michigan area. This included a population of roughly 200,000 people and an area of thirty square miles. Using up-to-date telephone and Internet listings, I determined that this area included nearly 300 churches. I used three means for evaluating all 300 churches to gauge their available Bible study opportunities: (1) I talked to regional denominational representatives about the project, asking them which Lansing area churches would be best suited for study. (2) I examined congregational websites. This was an extremely productive method because churches consistently (and accurately) list the current (and often, previous) Bible study classes they offer. (3) For the remaining churches for which no data was found, I telephoned the church office and inquired about their Bible study program. This initial survey produced forty-eight churches matching the criteria described above.

Beginning on August 10, 2004, I visited these forty-eight churches. I met the senior pastor and/or the small group director and explained the project. These visits ended in one of three scenarios: (1) the pastor declined on behalf of the church, usually because the congregation was struggling with some type of controversy; (2) I learned that the small group opportunities were not as abundant as I had recorded during my initial survey, removing the church from consideration; or (3) the pastor or small group director expressed interest in their church participating. In these cases, I left a packet of materials describing the project to be presented to the church board or other decision making body. By late September 2004, ten of the forty-eight churches had granted me permission to do fieldwork. From October through mid-December I talked with other staff members at the church, attended worship services, and met with Bible study facilitators. Based on these discussions and observations I chose the six churches that best met the initial goals of having ample Bible study opportunities and representing different Evangelical traditions, socioeconomic compositions, and local mission emphases.

The experience of exploring congregational websites, visiting churches, and meeting with leaders provided an introduction to the culture of Bible study life. It was at this point when I first realized the wide circulation of particular nonscriptural texts and favored Christian authors among Evangelicals of different denominational and theological stripes. In some cases, as I would realize later when reviewing my field notes, building the project sample offered clues as to what analytical themes would ultimately prove important. The following example from my first visit to the Missouri-Synod Lutheran church provided one of the more memorable encounters. It was late summer, and I arrived at the church in the early afternoon to find a large parking lot occupied by only one car—an Audi convertible. The car's owner was a man in his late fifties, working diligently at the front desk. His name was Al, a man who appears frequently in the analysis in chapter 2 of "Reading the Bible." Al informed me that the pastor was on vacation but would return the following week. After I described the project and left a letter for the pastor, Al suggested that Dave—the facilitator of the LCMS Men featured in chapter 2—was "an academic," "loves to read," and was "always looking for ways to improve the church." He went on to describe a men's Bible study—the LCMS Men—that met on Thursday mornings at a local restaurant and would be "great for this sort of thing." During our conversation, Al asked what type of church I grew up in (Southern Baptist). As I was leaving, Al assured me that the congregation would be interested. He described them as "theologically conservative," and promised to "rid me of the heretical teachings [I] grew up with in the Baptist church." We laughed and I left. I soon realized that this brand of identity discourse—constructing a Lutheran self through non-Lutheran, Christian others—would be a major theme in my analysis of the LCMS groups.

How did I choose the project groups?

During the tenure of my fieldwork, the project churches respectively had nineteen, nine, eleven, twenty-two, twenty-seven, and six groups meeting each week. Given this abundance of research opportunities, I had to decide which groups to approach about being in the project and then which to include. Through the scant literature on Bible study, my reading of field notes from "People in the Pews," and a predissertation project I conducted in 2003, I knew that my forthcoming Bible study experience would be anything but uniform. Individual Bible study groups can have unique (even idiosyncratic) histories, interactional dynamics, demographic compositions, and preferred texts of study. Amid this diversity, I wanted to build a sample of groups that followed two criteria: First, I sought out groups that had a steady membership. I wanted to avoid a situation in which numerous groups ceased meeting partway through the fieldwork. Second, I wanted a variety of group types, including groups with wide age ranges; male, female, and mixed-gender groups; recently formed and long-established groups; and groups practicing different study formats and texts. This last point is of particular importance given my theoretical interest in religious reading. During November and December 2004 I requested participation from groups with these aims in mind.

The process of soliciting consent involved several stages. First, I arranged a time with the facilitator when I could visit the group, present the project, and, if they allowed, stay for the remainder of the meeting. During these presentations I spoke for only a few minutes, explaining my methodology and main research questions. In most of these situations groups listened intently but had few (if any) questions. A small minority of groups preferred that I leave after this presentation, while most invited me to stay for the study session. Groups then voted (formally and informally) to decide if they wanted to be included in the project. Most agreed only if there was unanimous consent, though a few accepted the will of the majority. This approach led to one of three responses.

Several groups, primarily women's Bible studies, did not want to participate. Comparably, these groups were few, but in three cases there was a decisive decline of my request. At one of the United Methodist churches, Janet Simmons—a mother of three in her late thirties—volunteers as the small group director. Among the six project churches, Janet was certainly the most organized in this capacity. In our first meeting she gave me a spreadsheet detailing the existing groups: when and how often they met, what type of group it was, and who the facilitator was. As Janet progressed through the list of fifteen groups, she marked them as "appropriate" or "not appropriate" from which to solicit participation. Nine groups were placed in the latter category and all were either women only, couples with young children, or newly formed groups. Janet felt my presence would be awkward[3] in the first two and disruptive for developing cohesion in the third. A second case was a "young mom's" Bible study at the Missouri-Synod Lutheran church. I presented the project to this group at one of their Friday morning meetings and later that afternoon I received word via email from the facilitator that there was too much concern among the women that my presence would disturb their current level of intimacy. A third case comes from the Restoration Movement church. Mary (who appears in chapter 3) organized and facilitated several women's Bible studies as part of First Place, a national program that combines Bible study, scripture memorization, prayer, and an exercise/diet regimen (cf. Griffith 2004). Per her request, I provided Mary with a letter to read to the groups instead of me presenting the project. None, however, were comfortable with the possibility of being observed or tape-recorded by a man.

In addition to these denials, there were two cases in which my ethnographic presence was allowed conditionally. The first was a women's group in a United Methodist congregation. They were openly willing to let me attend and take hand-written notes during their meetings but were uniformly against the idea of being tape-recorded. Thus, my conversational data from their meetings is far less precise than the other groups. The second group is the Prayer Circle, which appears in chapter 3. After discussing the project, they reached the unanimous agreement that I could attend, take notes, and tape-record, but only if I participated as a "regular" member. I agreed, unsure at first of how to balance the dual roles of participant and observer. However, as I describe in chapter 3, the meeting structure and conversational order employed by the Prayer Circle was such that my participation did not guide or change the nature of their interactions.

The third outcome, which occurred most often, was a collective decision by the group to allow me to attend and observe in any way I preferred. A total of twenty-nine groups offered their unconditional participation in the project, although I was only able to include seventeen due to scheduling conflicts (plus the two groups described above comprise the total sample of nineteen). In those seventeen groups, though the decision was advertised to me as "collective" and "unanimous," there was still a lingering concern of coercion. Did certain individuals feel compelled, perhaps against their preference, to allow my attendance, observation, and recording? This is an important ethical question and a difficult one to evaluate.

Since designing the project in early 2004—and still today, four years later—I have returned to four measures when responding to this question: First, did individuals—immediately or at any time during the fieldwork—express to me any discomfort about being observed or recorded? There were several individuals—primarily women involved in mixed-gender groups—who, near the end of my fieldwork, informed me that they were hesitant about my involvement at first. In each of these cases, they assured me that their worries subsided after observing my observational style during the initial period of fieldwork. Second, did facilitators inform me, based on their knowledge and experience, that individuals were uncomfortable? None of the facilitators expressed this type of sentiment to me at any time during or after my fieldwork tenure. Third, did individuals cease their attendance with the group? Unfortunately, this did occur on one occasion. In one of the United Methodist men's Bible studies a retired pastor who regularly attended and frequently contributed to discussions stopped coming after the fifth meeting. I was informed several months later that my presence, and specifically the use of a tape-recorder, was responsible for his decision. There was no attempt by the group as a whole, or this individual, to discuss his discomfort with me. And fourth, were there identifiable changes in individuals' discussion participation during the fieldwork that would signify a change in their opinion about my presence? This was certainly the most difficult measure to gauge but perhaps the most revealing. In the various transcript analyses I performed, I also documented how individual contributions to group discussions changed over the course of fieldwork, in both amount and in type. Surprisingly, there was very little difference between the first and last recordings. Individuals who were talkative at first continued to be talkative, and those who were more observant remained so. Moreover, the type of participation—for example, the level of intimacy involved in contributions—remained stable. Taken together, these four measures suggest to me that I had very little (though, in isolated cases an undeniable) impact on these groups' Bible study performance.

After twelve months of tape-recording, I had collected data from nineteen Bible study groups. My length of participation varied greatly, from one to forty-eight meetings with a mean of seventeen meetings per group. I observed and recorded eleven mixed-gender groups, four men's Bible studies and four women's Bible studies. The equal number of men's and women's groups is misleading, however, considering the number of meetings I attended for each: 120 men's compared to sixty-two women's. Eight groups studied directly from Biblical texts, while the remainder organized their study sessions around nonscriptural texts of various genres (such as scriptural exegesis, inspirational nonfiction, print and online periodical articles).

How did I observe myself during Bible study?

My reflexive account thus far has primarily been methodological in tone. I have outlined the logics that guided my conceptualization of the project, its design, and my entrée into particular group settings. Yet, reflexive ethnography is also about the autobiographical and relational element of fieldwork. What was it like "being there?" Who did you come to appreciate, love, and find abhorrent? What did you learn about your own preoccupations and deep-seated biases? What impact(s) did your presence have on the setting you were documenting? And when reflexive ethnography is at its best, how do these questions enhance your analysis and arguments? In my case, how must my interpretive readings of group Bible study take into account my positionality as a researcher? To begin, I address the central issue of being an ethnographer of Christianity: my spiritual identity and the community's reaction to this. Very simply, how do I respond when my informants ask, "Are you a Christian?"

Most anyone who has done ethnography in Christian communities will attest to the significance of this question. It is often the first question we are asked when attempting to gain research permission, when we are making our entrance into the field, and as we encounter new individuals in the field. Even when it is not the first question, it never seems to linger too far from anyone's consciousness until it is finally voiced.

Why is this question so crucial? In many (if not most) varieties of Christianity worldwide, the status of one's spiritual/religious identity (one's "relationship with God," as my consultants might phrase it) is the matter of utmost importance to consider in this life. It takes precedence over any other identity we might claim (as a husband or father, for instance) because it is tied up in questions of salvation, right living, moral obligation, and community belonging. For the ethnographer of Christianity there is a certain understanding that much of the fieldwork agenda is influenced by his or her answer to this question. At stake are issues of access (to spaces, to information, to people), social relations with local adherents (sister/brother in Christ, target of conversion, antagonistic opponent, lost soul, seeker), and subject position (advocate, critic, teacher, conversation partner). Establishing one's posture toward Christianity (and, as I argue below, the local variety of Christianity one encounters) is often the first, and often the most crucial, element of doing ethnography in Christian communities.

How have anthropologists responded to this question? Frankly, the most common approach is silence, an avoidance of how this matter of identity impacted the research. It is a sort of don't ask-don't tell policy— one that is always conspicuous in its absence. For those that do address the issue, the dominant narrative is hardly surprising. It is somewhat of a truism, at least in the United States, that religious faith can be hard to come by in the academy—a fact appearing in exaggerated form among anthropologists. Dean Arnold (2006) points to a survey conducted by the

Carnegie Foundation to lend some empirical evidence to this stereotype. In responding to the question "What is your religion?" anthropologists refused to claim any affiliation at a rate of 65 percent, ten points above the next discipline (philosophy) and more than twice the mean for all others. If this survey is representative in the least, it would seem that anthropologists are rather nonreligious folk.

Among ethnographers of Christianity there seems to be little exception to this general rule. The voice of reflexivity among this crowd has been sparse, hesitant, and quiet, at best. However, the dominant narrative (if only existing implicitly) has been a stance of assumed distance: "As an anthropologist I am most definitely *not* a Christian, and while this may not prohibit ethnography, it does raise the problem of forever being the subject of conversion attempts." There is little room for faith in this equation and little desire for it. Some ethnographers who fall in this ilk are interested in the structural environs of economics and politics that relate to religious life, while others are committed to elucidating the inner world of the believer and translating it to those who have never glimpsed it. In either case, there is a want to keep plenty of personal distance from the life of faith. This dominant narrative, this posture of assumed distance, dominates two of the most widely cited works in the emerging anthropology of Christianity, both of which provide ethnographic portraits of conservative Christianity in America: Vincent Crapanzano's *Serving the Word: Literalism in America from the Pulpit to the Bench* (2000) and Susan Harding's *The Book of Jerry Falwell: Fundamentalist Language and Politics* (2000). If an ethnography of Christianity in the United States has indeed arrived, these are its most visible statements.

Look at any bibliography in the anthropology of Christianity—be it grounded in American ethnography or elsewhere in the world—and one or both of these works is bound to be there. In many ways they are hardly similar. Crapanzano's fieldwork was recent and conducted for the sole purpose of this particular monograph; Harding's dates to the early 1980s and has resulted in several major publications prior to the book. Crapanzano's account is comparative, drawing a parallel between conservative Christianity and conservative law practitioners; Harding's is ferociously single-minded, focusing on a suite of institutions connected to or influenced by Jerry Falwell's fundamentalist empire. Crapanzano's ethnography is critically minded, claiming at every turn the problematic and contradictory nature of a literalist approach to language and interpretation; Harding's is much more sensitive, trying to explain a world that can seem both utterly

strange and utterly familiar at once. Yet, they are not altogether different books. Both concern themselves with a particular stream of American
Christians: rigid, white fundamentalists. Both are theoretically grounded
in issues of language, text, and hermeneutics. And most integral to my
concern here, both authors adhere strictly to a position of assumed distance. Crapanzano's negative posture toward conservative Christianity is
not even thinly veiled as he terms the movement "potentially dangerous"
(xviii) and defined by "intolerance" (xx) in the opening pages. Both authors attempt to temper their analysis with an awareness that their interactions and observations in the field need to be understood as a discourse
of witnessing *to them*—as opposed to something akin to naturally occurring data. Harding, in particular, capitalized on this in her now infamous
depiction of Reverend Milton Cantrell and his finely tuned, structured,
rehearsed performance of witnessing rhetoric (33–60; cf. Harding 1987).

I dwell on Crapanzano and Harding because of the considerable currency their work carries in the discipline and because they are indicative
of this dominant reflexive narrative among anthropologists of Christianity. Their tone—and their envisioning of positionality—is the tone and the
vision of many. Though many follow Crapanzano and Harding's visions, a
counter-narrative has appeared among ethnographers who openly claim
a Christian identity. In my view, the best articulation of this comes from
Brian Howell (2007). In a recent article, Howell argues that the positionality of being a Christian in doing ethnography among Christians should
be viewed as a viable and useful standpoint. This subject position is "characterized by moral/ethical commitments" (372) and is therefore much like
"the feminist studying women, the leftist studying labor unions or the
Muslim studying mosques" (385). The real power of Howell's claim is not
simply that Christian anthropologists can or should claim their religious
identity, it is that in doing so they can productively explore theoretical
and methodical issues that are comparative in nature and applicable outside the study of Christianity and outside the study of religion.

This counter-narrative—the notion that the anthropologist, including those doing ethnographies of Christianity, need not eschew religious
faith—is much closer to my own subject position. The argument I want
to develop in the remainder of this section is that the answer to "Are
you a Christian?" is not simply a yes/no affair—an ethnographic cruci-
ble with one's fieldwork hanging in the balance. This speaks to the larger
theoretical issue of cultural diversity within local, regional, national, and
global Christian economies. I will argue that this question is effectively

not always the same question, an artifact of the difference among and between Christian traditions. Apologists such as Brian Howell have suspected this argument but, in my reading, have not developed it fully. For example, Howell is right to quote Fenella Cannell (2006) when he suggests, "in identifying the selfhood of commitment between me and my Christian interlocutors, I became aware of the situatedness of our cerebral and emotional subjectivity. . . . This echoes the insights of many recent anthropologists of Christianity who demonstrate that 'it is not impossible to speak meaningfully about Christianity, but it *is* important to be as specific as possible about what kind of Christianity one means'" (Howell: 381, italics in original). We would do well to heed this mandate of specificity in all matters, including those that are reflexive in character.

Six Iterations of "Are You a Christian?"

1. Three of the project churches were affiliated with the United Methodist Church (UMC). Still, this question was not the same in even these three places. Of all the major and minor denominations in the United States, United Methodists are well known to be among the most diverse in their memberships (Kirby, Richey, and Rowe 1998). The UMC is part of the National Council of Churches, which nominally makes it a "mainline" church, which for many means "moderate" or "liberal," denomination. However, UMC congregations across the United States are theologically, politically, and ethnically diverse. Indeed, the UMC counts all manner of Christians as part of their fold, from charismatics to conservative Evangelical Wesleyans, moderate and Progressive Evangelicals, and liberal/ecumenically minded Protestants. This national diversity was reflected in the first project church: Downtown UMC (DUMC).[4]

This church has been a fixture in its city's downtown for 155 years. In the mid-1970s DUMC was considered among the city's largest and most affluent churches. In the mid-2000s, the weekly attendance hovered around 150, and the membership is now comprised of individuals and families from every socioeconomic stratum. Theologically, the congregation is defined by division and contestation. Their theological clashes have taken place on numerous fronts, from homosexuality to gendered references to God to the Iraq War. Leaders and laity recognize these divisions as a source of some ambivalence, generating anxiety over divisive tensions alongside a pride in diversity and mirroring of their denomination. As an ethnographer, the result is a local culture where difference is expected and, if not accepted, allowed to linger. Thus, my positive response to "Are you a Christian?" was always the end of discussion. This was fully sufficient among religionists who are used to embracing different and divergent interpretations of the Christian faith. The meaning of the question, in short, is one of minimal identification.

2. The second UMC congregation—Suburban UMC (SUMC)[5]—presented a different scene. Like many UMC churches nationwide, this congregation has sought second affiliations with conservative Evangelical parachurch organizations. This is often done for purposes of church growth. It is no secret within the sociology of American religion that mainline denominations declined in memberships throughout the 20th century, giving way to the growth of Evangelical and Pentecostal traditions (Finke and Starke 1992). The response of many local congregations has been to adopt models of program development that promise growth, most all of which are born from more conservative milieus. Perhaps the most widely adopted model comes from Willow Creek Community Church, a nondenominational suburban megachurch south of Chicago. Willow Creek is the paradigmatic "seeker" church: catering to Baby Boomers who want their religious life to mirror their corporate and entertainment life. Seeker megachurches are distinct for providing pop-infused praise and worship music, self-help–infused sermons, childcare, tutoring, and most any other service the suburban family needs. The Willow Creek Association is a sponsored parachurch organization that organizes seminars, publishes books, and sells church programs.

SUMC is a Willow Creek Association church and consistently attempts to implement the methods and programs produced by the organization. As a local culture, the result (and a common one at that) is a family-focused environment with a strong emphasis on everyday evangelism (though one imbued with middle-class politeness). What does "Are you a Christian?" mean in this setting? It is not the same as the minimal identification of DUMC. Rather, this question seemed to assume several implications: are you married? Do you have a family? Where are your sites of evangelism? Who can you bring to church with you next time you come? My answer of "Yes, I am," was thus never the end of discussion. It instead moved on to these other questions, with the assumption that while I was there to do research, I could still aid their mission of church growth. I am not married, I do not have children, and I hold to a different theology of evangelism. This required me to navigate with care conversations where my "Christian-ness," defined by living a family-centered life and evangelizing at work and with friends, was under view.

3. Divisive heterogeneity and megachurch mimesis are not the only options taken up by UMC churches. The third project church—Inner-City UMC (IUMC)[6]—offers yet a third vision for developing a local culture. When Pastor Bill accepted the call at IUMC in 2002, he took over a congregation that was ready to permanently close its doors. The fallout from a controversial pastor and several interim pastors had left a significantly lowered membership disillusioned. Bill brought with him aspirations but not megachurch aspirations. He wanted to cultivate a more intimate community of faith. This was welcomed by a church body that felt disconnected from their Christianity. One of the most influential resources on Bill's approach to worship and congregational life comes from the "Emerging Church." This is a rather recent movement among American Evangelicals that denounces the corporate feel of the megachurch in favor of a more "authentic" religious experience. It is an extremely interesting and complex movement that refuses easy summation. But a central theme is an affinity for "mysticism," meaning that an unfailing certainty in matters of faith is not required. Doubt and mystery are productive, beneficial places to dwell, not dangers to guard against (see chapter 5; Bielo forthcoming).

The "Emerging" character of IUMC casts "Are you a Christian?" into a still different web of meanings. To simply answer "Yes" is met with some skepticism, taken as a tacit denial of the complexities that define the life of faith. "Are you a Christian?" at IUMC is not meant to elicit an exposition of the kind of Christian you imagine yourself to be but is an invitation to share the doubts, questions, challenges, and confusions you struggle with. Similar to DUMC, diversity and difference is expected, but unlike their downtown neighbor, the response at IUMC is not silence. The assumption is that articulating theological differences and doubts is an edifying experience, one that draws a community closer together and defines their life of faith as an ongoing dialogue.

4. The fourth church is affiliated with the Lutheran Church-Missouri Synod (LCMS).[7] The LCMS denomination is unique in the landscape of American Evangelicalism. Its distinctiveness is partly theological and liturgical but is also derived from the importance placed on denominational identity. For most Evangelical traditions, the dominant trend has been to downplay the significance of denominational affiliation—what some have

called the "post-denominational era" in American Christianity (Wuthnow 1988). In contrast, LCMS churches place great emphasis on their uniqueness among other varieties of Christianity, Protestantism, Evangelicalism, and Lutheranism. There is a distinct sense of correctness in LCMS circles, convinced—to the extent humans always fall short of God's ideals—that among all streams they come closest to getting doctrine and church life "right."

And indeed, this was the case at this local LCMS congregation. There was an abundance of talk in Bible studies, sermons, and hallway conversations about what it does and does not mean to be a Missouri Synod Lutheran (see chapter 6). Against this backdrop, "Are you a Christian?" was still the first question posed to the incoming ethnographer. But it was always followed closely by "Are you Lutheran, then?" I am not. And to be perfectly honest, growing up in coastal Virginia, I did not know that Lutherans existed until a university education informed me of the fact. For the entirety of my fieldwork, while I did not face conversion attempts like Harding and Crapanzano, I did face attempts to explain the superiority of Lutheran doctrine.

5. The post-denominational thesis that is so inconsistent with Missouri Synod Lutherans was represented with great clarity in the fifth project church.[8] The Restoration Movement is a conservative Evangelical denomination that began in the late 19th century. In the United States there are over 6,000 Restoration churches with more than 4 million members and an affiliated network of Bible colleges (Jones et al. 2002). Restoration Movement churches (RMC), like the one in which I conducted fieldwork, espouse a rather strict Evangelical theology including requirements of baptism by immersion and affirmation of an "infallible," "inerrant" Bible. RMC was, in fact, the closest approximation in my sample to the brand of Christian fundamentalism featured by the ethnography of Crapanzano and Harding.

Given the theological and cultural identity of this denomination and the close adherence of this local RMC church to those frames, the meaning of "Are you a Christian?" was quite clear. What I was really being asked was "Are you born-again?" This is a much trickier question. It is dialogically loaded with political and otherwise cultural baggage in America, as Harding has so aptly demonstrated. In this case, my typical answer of "Yes, I am," also became tricky. Have I ever experienced a dramatic, personal, story-worthy encounter with the Holy Spirit? No. Do I self-identify as a "born-again Christian?" No. Can I look back on my spiritual relationship with God and identify a transformation in how I understood that relationship? Yes. Did askers of this question care to hear about these distinctions? No. This is a ritual of inquiry, a way of asking about shared identity and signifying community belonging. It is supposed to, and normally does, happen at the speed of the sound of an everyday greeting. Would answering "Yes" exploit the assumed background knowledge implicit in this ritual? Would it have been dishonest? And would I be risking getting "found out" later on as actually not sharing certain theological assumptions? Yes. So, what did I do? I answered, "Yes," and I risked dishonesty. This never came back to haunt me, but it did create several surprised reactions when lengthier conversations of faith occurred with individuals I befriended.

6. The final church in the project sample was affiliated with the Vineyard Fellowship (VFC).[9] Vineyard churches trace their roots to the "Jesus Movement" of the 1960s, eventually establishing a distinct denominational identity in the early 1980s (Bialecki 2008; Miller 1997). The Vineyard is a self-consciously charismatic denomination, meaning its followers accept (expect?) the gifts of the Holy Spirit to be just as operative in today's world as they were in the world of the New Testament apostles. Oddly enough, the VFC and LCMS churches were most alike because in both settings there was a high emphasis placed on denominational identity. Much like the Lutheran case, being a part of the Vineyard was very important to these religionists.

What happened, then, to "Are you a Christian?" at the VFC? This question encoded a separate theological commitment: "Are you charismatic?" Because this is a distinguishing feature of the denomination, and because of the stress placed on denominational identity, this was an important implication. Unlike the case of "being born-again," this question was much easier to handle. I do not classify myself as a charismatic Christian, and I have never experienced any gifts of the Holy Spirit. Thus, much like the LCMS situation, this created a fieldwork-long dynamic of hearing biblical and historical justifications for the acceptance of charismatic gifts.

What is one to make of all this? I am arguing that "being reflexive" in the ethnography of Christianity entails more than thinking about "Are you a Christian?" Namely, it entails attention to the different forms, meanings, and consequences invested in this question across different Christian contexts. The question and the ethnographer's response both take shape against the backdrop of distinct Protestant histories of tradition, theology, and identity. To assume otherwise is folly, and to ignore this reality is bad policy for the anthropologist of Christianity.

Moreover, this analysis highlights a key theoretical concern in the anthropology of Christianity: accounting for the cultural diversity that defines global Christendom. The social fact is that there are many ways to be Christian in the world. To echo Cannell again, "it *is* important to be as specific as possible about what kind of Christianity one means" (2006: 7). And while the ways of dividing up the Christian economy are definitely theological, they are also always already cultural because individual and collective lives of faith are already caught up in contexts of history, power, meaning, and action. While I am perfectly willing to argue that certain doctrines are true and others are not, I am equally willing to argue that all doctrines arise and are enacted through all things cultural. In the United States, the boundaries of the Christian economy are defined by denominational traditions, parachurch organizations, new church movements, and ideological discourses that cut across institutional lines. Elsewhere, there are concerns of colonialist histories, nation-states, educational and economic formations, and a host of other forces impinging on what it means to be Christian and how many ways are available for doing so. With regards to ethnographic reflexivity, this requires the anthropologist to keep aware of what these boundaries are, the cultural meanings that surround them, and their own relationship to the divided Christian economy with which they are confronted.

The End of Being Reflexive?

The social meanings invested in "Are you a Christian?" are but one argument I want to advance. As a second objective, I suggest that the job of "being reflexive" in the anthropology of Christianity (and, I would extend this to the anthropology of religion more broadly) is not finished once this all-important question of religious/spiritual identity is answered. No doubt, struggles around that question are likely to index defining moments in one's fieldwork. I do not dispute this in the least. What I am suggesting is that this is not the only question that matters. Other questions—always emerging from the ideological and material realities of the surrounding social context—can be equally formative for the research encounter. I consider two such examples below.

"Are you young in your faith?"

Unlike "Are you a Christian?" this question was not necessarily one I encountered immediately. In many cases, I had been actively conducting fieldwork for weeks, sometimes months, before the temporal length of my Christian identity was inquired about. But conversations of faith, including those with ethnographers, eventually come around to how long you have been "saved." In all six of my fieldwork settings, no matter what emphasis was placed on having a born-again experience, one's life is calculated according to how long one has "known Christ." A fifty-year-old woman who converted to Christianity at forty-seven is, in many respects, a three-year-old. The underlying motive that gives this question meaning is to understand how long I have been a professing Christian, and thus, how "mature" I am in my faith. Much like responding to "Are you a Christian?" this question makes clear that one's spiritual status is not a yes/no affair. At work here is a dominant trope among Evangelical Protestants: a life-cycle metaphor that produces "baby" and "mature" Christians (Muse 2005). Just as we grow physiologically and emotionally—becoming wiser, more knowledgeable, more discerning—we "grow in the Lord."

Counting one's years "in Christ" provides both a known role structure as well as a set of expectations and responsibilities that accompany the social positions in that structure. The Evangelical life-cycle metaphor helps organize congregational life and establishes conceptual frames for interacting with other believers. Baby Christians are not expected to facilitate Bible study groups, be go-to lay theologians for other church members, lead prayers, and the like. Mature Christians, on the other hand, are looked to for all these tasks and more. Just like any other new arrival in their midst, my informants constantly used this trope to situate my presence in their community. And because of my status as a relatively young Christian, the relationships I formed with individuals were always structured by this subject position. Many of the individuals I encountered—particularly pastors, lay leaders, and group facilitators—were mature Christians. As they did with other younger Christians, they assumed a posture of being a spiritual mentor to me. It is their duty within "the body of Christ," as older Christians, to make themselves available to me in this way: with or without my solicitation. Thus, my interpretive readings of group Bible study have had to remain attentive to the very real possibility that, even though I was mostly silent for nearly 400 hours of Bible study, I often constituted an audience for a form of mentoring discourse. While I did not elicit witnessing attempts I did help to produce words of exegesis, instruction, and advice during Bible study.

"Are you an academic?"

Questions regarding religious identity are, of course, not the only ones that matter. The question "Are you an academic?" proved to be a crucial one in my ethnography of American Evangelicalism. It is certainly a loaded question. The relationship between Evangelicals and "the academy" (that is, the public and secular private university system) is one defined by tension. On the one hand, there is a dominant discourse among conservative Evangelicals that the academy is a territory where Christians must tread lightly. It is the breeding ground of "liberalism," "humanism," "secularism," and a variety of other unsightly "isms" that are antagonistic to Christians and to Christianity. The university is where human evolution, existential philosophies, and non-Western epistemologies are used to sweep the legs out from under Christian theology. It is where "tolerance" and "diversity" are "liberal"-speak for the evaporation of moral absolutes. This particular narrative plot includes the overly cerebral, smart-ass professor who intellectually abuses unsuspecting Christian students, forcing them to doubt their faith. Despite my own self-identification as a Christian, my status as a career academic necessarily casts me as part of the problem.

Yet, on the other hand, conservative Evangelicals are not anti-intellectual, nor do they renounce post-secondary education. They are voracious readers who conceptualize their Christian heritage as one of brilliant thinkers and writers. They point to St. Augustine of Hippo, Martin Luther, John Calvin, John Wesley, G. K. Chesterton, and C. S. Lewis as learned men, exemplars of intelligent Christianity, and individuals who are genealogically important to the literary and intellectual culture of contemporary America. They are well aware that the field of hermeneutics (though many do not call it by name) exists because of scriptural study. And they point to the Christian origins of many universities, including several Ivy League institutions. Many of the individuals I encountered during my fieldwork had earned baccalaureate and advanced degrees from secular universities. Many of these same individuals send their children to public universities and emphasize the necessity of higher education. It is well worth noting here that the site of my fieldwork (Lansing, Michigan) is home to a major research university (Michigan State University) where I was completing a dissertation and teaching classes. East Lansing is a true university town in that everything tends to revolve around what is happening on campus. Many of the Bible study participants were MSU alums, many others had children enrolled at MSU, and most all of them were avid supporters of the university.

In short, conservative Evangelicals have a conflicted relationship with "the academy." It is both friend and foe and is all the while acting as a "spiritual battleground," a place where the public status of Christianity is at stake. I was reminded of this social fact time and again during my fieldwork. On occasions that were too numerous to count, I was asked how openly Christian students are treated at Michigan State, if I had any colleagues who were not anti-Christian atheists or "secular humanists," if I was a "liberal," if I let my personal politics enter the classroom, if I taught evolution, and so on. How I handled these questions constituted defining moments in my relationships with individuals, my status as a trusted confidant, the willingness of individuals to be interviewed, allow me to tape-record Bible study meetings, recommend me to other groups, and trade books and resources with me, and, of course, which books and resources they chose to share. I often wondered if controversial political topics (for example, the Iraq War) were avoided because groups wanted to stay away from these discussions generally or if they were wary of my reaction as someone who would be writing about them. Here, then, is a moment when my status as an "insider," or "native anthropologist," became ambiguous. While I was most certainly "among them," and most thought me to be "with them," I was not always "one of them" (cf. Narayan 1993).

Alongside "Are you a Christian?" the questions "Are you young in your faith?" and "Are you an academic?" were therefore vital reflexive inquiries. In using these examples, I am drawing attention to the reality that the truly reflexive ethnographer in a Christian community must imagine what other questions are necessary to ask given the social, religious, political, and economic backdrop of one's fieldwork scene. Ultimately, I am speaking about multipositionality in ethnographic fieldwork. Researchers inhabit numerous identities that are likely to shift as we move across social settings and interpersonal relations. This raises a series of necessary questions. What subjectivities do we bring with us to the field? Which ones do we step into? Which are we thrust into? And how do these subject positions impact the process of empirical observation? In regards to this last question, one final issue needs to be addressed. In presenting my research to colleagues, questions inevitably arise about my level of participation in group meetings. To what extent did I contribute to group discussion? Did I function as a "participant observer" in the usual sense of the term?

The default position I assumed when beginning my tenure with each group was to be a silent observer. I explicitly stated that I was perfectly willing to respond if addressed directly but would otherwise remain a nonparticipant during discussions. In certain cases, like with the LCMS Men, I was completely silent for forty-eight meetings. In other group situations, however, I consciously departed from this default position. The determining factor for my decision making was group size. In the case of the LCMS Men this was particularly unproblematic. In a group with as many as twenty-five people in attendance, I was certainly not the only one who would pass from meeting to meeting without contributing. In smaller groups meeting in more intimate settings, my presence would have been far more disruptive were I not to speak at all. One of the Restoration Movement groups provides an exemplary case. The group met in the home of a married couple on Monday evenings from seven to nine at night. In addition to the hosts, there were four individuals who made at least one appearance. Most evenings, though, there were only four participants besides me. We sat around a living room table facing one another, each with our Bibles open for reading and reference. In a situation such as this, sitting silently, taking notes, and running a tape-recorder would have been an obvious deterrence to this group's free-flowing dynamic. My adjusted position in this group was as a full participant observer, contributing periodically to discussion often without request from other members. My goal, each time I spoke, was to join the conversation in a way that did not direct it somewhere that it was not already going. I refrained from introducing new information. I did not challenge others' contributions or ask them to elaborate. And I did not pose questions about the text. I cannot claim to have been completely successful in this regard, but this guiding intention allowed me to view this group's discourse as I did the other project groups—as occurring as naturally as possible given my presence.

The question of my potential impact on group life is particularly salient in regards to gender. I count myself very fortunate to have been granted the opportunity to observe and, in several cases, tape-record all-female Bible study groups. Yet, my presence as the sole male among these groups of women raises serious questions about how they may have altered conversations and relationships in response to my being there. Certainly, I caused more than a few gender-specific jokes. And certainly I was responsible for more than a few hesitations before individual women spoke. I can never be fully aware of how I may have changed (if only temporarily) the lives of these women's groups. I can say, though, that the standards and criteria I described above were applied with no change in the cases of these groups, and I am therefore as confident about my observations among these groups as I am of those from the all-male and mixed-gender groups. Ultimately, I am overly pleased to be able to include these women's voices alongside the others in this research, even if those voices might sound a little different than they "normally" do.

How did I collect and organize the project data?

Unlike many ethnographic accounts, which propose to represent whole communities, *Words Upon the Word* is a comparative account that focuses on a particular social institution. Moreover, I am less concerned in this book with the life of Bible study groups as such. Rather, I am concerned with the details of their interactions, the continuities and tensions evident in their talk, and the presence of larger social discourses in and among those details. In turn, the central methodology of this research aimed to represent Bible study interactions.

The analyses in chapters 2 through 6 derive from eighty-nine group meetings, all of which were tape-recorded, transcribed, and supplemented with field notes. Discourse analysts rely on audio recording to capture language-in-use and recreate speech events because it has several fundamental advantages over the use of hand-written notes (Johnstone 2000). It allows for verbatim records, providing a more accurate and reliable corpus of data. It allows the ethnographer to return to the original recording and, in a sense, relive the event. It frees the ethnographer to focus on other contextual features in his or her field notes. In group situations in which full participation is expected as a speaker or reader, tape-recording prevents valuable data from being lost. And once the recorder becomes an accepted presence, it gradually becomes less distracting to participants than an ethnographer who is constantly scribbling.

The path from tape-recording to transcription is neither brief nor direct, presenting still more choices of selectivity and representation. Transcription is always a process laden with the ethnographer's theoretical, methodological, and analytical interests (Ochs 1979). Producing transcripts of Bible study meetings required me to make numerous decisions about what to include and what not to include. All of the transcripts are verbatim, meaning that they represent (as precisely as possible) the referential content of each meeting's conversation. In order to capture the interactive qualities of group discussions, I marked features such as interruption, overlaps, laughs, lengthy silences, and nondiscursive agreement (such as collective affirmation via "Mhmm"). I indicated various paralinguistic features, the verbal cues that accompany talk such as emphatic stress, prosodic changes, and mimicry. And last, given my interest in Bible use, I marked the recontextualization of scriptural texts into speech (which are marked by italics in the examples I present). Conversely, other types of transcript conventions were not necessary given my analytical aims (for example, phonological pronunciation, crutch phrases).

For each meeting, I also took hand-written field notes that focused on a variety of nonverbal cues and behaviors that accompany talk. This included interactive strategies employed by speakers and listeners such as facial and bodily gestures, indications of agreement or disagreement, and indications of confusion. I also recorded other behaviors occurring during the meeting that were not captured on the audio-recording, including participants in side conversations, someone searching through a Bible or other text, and individual's temporary absences from the room. While these field notes were far from exhaustive, they did aid in the transcript analysis on numerous occasions by providing information about the interaction that would have otherwise been lost.

In addition to these methodological decisions, a few words are in order about my selection of groups and examples. While no two groups were identical, I employ the case-study approach precisely because the arguments I make are representative for the entire sample. For example, in chapter 2 I discuss the hermeneutic assumptions and procedures of Bible reading. The findings I present for the LCMS Men typify how the other project groups engaged with the Christian scriptures. In certain cases— such as the Prayer Circle's intense focus on spiritual intimacy in chapter 3—the case study is exaggerated but still representative of what characterized the remaining project groups. This same logic is in place with my use of discourse examples to illustrate various claims about Bible study life and American Evangelicalism. In no case do I show the reader the only instance from a group's study in support of a particular claim. Rather, I have sought to show the more articulate and clear examples produced by these groups that are associated with each argument I make.

In this chapter I have considered a series of questions about the nature of my fieldwork among Evangelical Bible study groups. In addressing these four questions, my aim has not been to argue for the near-perfection of my chosen methodology or of my approach toward acting as a participant observer. Neither has my goal been to present these strategies as a means of achieving the status of an objectively neutral, positivistic ethnography. Rather, I have attempted to demonstrate how issues of reflexivity—methodological and personal—can enhance the analysis of cultural scenes. The next chapter provides the first of these analyses: the theme of Bible reading and interpretation.

Reading the Bible

Every Thursday morning at seven a.m. a group of fifteen to twenty-five men gather at a local restaurant to eat breakfast, socialize, pray, and study the Bible. They are part of a growing congregation affiliated with the Lutheran Church-Missouri Synod (LCMS). Unlike most Protestant traditions in America's subculture of conservative Evangelicalism, the LCMS denomination has been declining in membership for decades (Jones et al. 2002). In spite of this national trend, the local congregation of the LCMS Men has steadily increased over the past three years. The registered membership now exceeds 700, and the weekly worship attendance tops 350. This growth has paralleled a proliferation of small groups within the church, a program consisting of twenty-two weekly gatherings during my fieldwork. Founded in 1994, the LCMS Men were one of the first Bible study groups in the church to be established.

The original facilitator, Eric, is a lifelong LCMS member and still attends every week. For nearly eight years Eric organized the group's meetings, maintaining a weekly attendance of between eight and ten participants. In 2003, after Dave accepted the call as head pastor, he took over the role of facilitator. The group has grown ever since, and the weekly attendance during 2005 averaged nineteen men, attracting as many as twenty-seven on one Thursday in November. They were, by far, the largest group I observed.

Dave's skill as a facilitator is one reason for the group's success. He performs the role to near perfection. Hardly an imposing figure, he stands five-foot-five with a bookish demeanor. He is affable, extremely well liked by the congregation, has an inviting manner and wry sense of humor. The men raise their hands to speak, and Dave notifies them when the floor is theirs. He keeps primarily to open-ended questions. He tacks a brief comment onto the end of their contributions, creating a space for others to pick up the conversational thread. He has a way of softening dogmatic comments and sharpening the more benign ones. He avoids long, preachy exhortations and manages to raise potentially controversial and divisive issues without being controversial or divisive.

During an interview, Dave told me, "I eat breakfast with the leadership of this church every Thursday." Most of the building committee, the youth minister, the church administrator, several ministry directors, and most of the church elders are regular participants. Many are lifelong LCMS members, though several converted from other denominations in their adult years. All of the men are white, and aside from the youth minister, who is twenty-five, the group is composed of middle-aged and older adults. They are a highly educated crowd, with lawyers, state education consultants, engineers, entrepreneurs, politicians, professors, physicians, and policemen in their midst.

They meet in a large room in the back of the restaurant. It contains over a dozen circular tables, and the men habitually fill the three or four closest to the front of the room. Each table sits five to seven people, and with a few exceptions, most gravitate toward the same seat each week. Dave facilitates from the front of the room: standing, staying mobile, and clearly signifying his leadership role.

From June through September 2005 the LCMS Men studied the Old Testament book of Proverbs. They did not use any formal study-guide text, but their meetings did follow a consistent format. For each meeting they read two to three chapters on their own time during the week and then gathered for the hour-long group discussion. Dave began each meeting with a brief summary of the reading, followed by a statement addressing any overarching themes (such as "wisdom" or "temptation") and connections to other Biblical texts. He then opened the discussion to everyone, asking what verses "stuck out" for them. Roughly halfway through the meeting, Dave identified the verses he thought most compelling or confusing if they had not been raised already. If time still remained, he returned to asking the group what verses they highlighted or had questions about. He was always prompt to begin the brief closing prayer at or near the eight o'clock hour.

The LCMS Men's discussions were frank, detailed, lively, and laced with humor. Their reliably dynamic exchanges are very much an attractive feature to potential members and an important factor in the group's continued growth. The LCMS Men provide an illuminating case study for the logics and practices of reading scripture as performed in group study.

Evangelical Bible Reading

Definitions of Evangelicalism and the definitive characteristics of American Evangelical culture often begin with the issue of Bible belief. Scholars have taken a cue from Evangelicals' self-identification as "Bible-believers," and their placement of "God's Word" at the center of everyday and ritual life, in prioritizing how scripture figures in the Evangelical imagination (e.g., Hatch and Noll, eds. 1982; Ammerman 1987; Bartkowski 1996; Crapanzano 2000; Harding 2000; Wimbush, ed. 2000; Malley 2004; Muse 2005). Attention to scripture, not surprisingly, is arguably the most pervasive element of what happens among groups of Bible readers. Yet, despite a rich ethnographic record, there are notably few attempts to propose a defined framework for understanding how Evangelicals interact with the Bible (see Malley 2004 for an important exception). From this work, there are three general conclusions that can be culled about the social life of the Bible among American Evangelicals:

1. Despite the claims of adherents, literalism does not constitute a hermeneutic method. That is, it is not a self-conscious or tacit means of actually reading and interpreting biblical texts. In his extensive account of Evangelical biblicism, Brian Malley (2004: 92–103) argues that literalism functions primarily as a signifier of theological and religious identity. To identify as a literalist is to claim affiliation with certain Christian traditions (conservative, born-again, Evangelical, fundamentalist) and separate oneself from others (moderate, liberal, mainline, progressive). This phenomenon is traceable through the post-Reformation era (Keane 2007: 63; Ward 1995: 21), the rise of neo-Orthodoxy and its opponents (Ward 1995), and the fundamentalist-modernist debates of the early 1900s (Harding 2000). Appeals to being a "biblical literalist" may be an increasingly important means of identity expression given the ambiguity and unwanted baggage of many institutional affiliations (denominational, parachurch, or otherwise). Literalism is also informative as an expression of distinctly Western and Protestant language ideologies. Vincent Crapanzano (2000), Simon Coleman (2006), and Webb Keane (2007) have each argued convincingly that claims of literalism embed fundamental assumptions about the nature and function of language. In particular, literalism prioritizes referential over performative meaning functions (that is, preference is given to language's ability to make propositional statements about reality instead of the use of

language to create a state of affairs). With this close coupling of language and reality in place, literalism stresses the ability of words to accurately convey inner states of intention, sincerity, and moral character. Thus, while literalism is not a direct channel to hermeneutic practice, it does convey important lessons regarding other aspects of Evangelical culture.

2. The most widespread form of interpretive activity that American Evangelicals perform is an ongoing attempt to apply biblical texts to their everyday lives. A number of authors have provided a vocabulary to capture the goings-on of this practice. Jeff Titon (1988), based on his ethnographic fieldwork among Appalachian Baptists, frames this as an outgrowth of an explanatory imagination that is analogical in nature. Harding (2000) suggests that this is merely the most recent iteration of the longstanding practice of typological interpretation, in which the Bible is read as consisting of types and antitypes that are continually in the process of fulfillment. Malley (2004), with cognitive interests in mind, contends that Bible reading functions much like other forms of communication in that it is motivated by a search for relevance. These explanations, respectively, view this phenomenon as part of a broader cultural reasoning process, a historically established interpretive tradition, and a base cognitive necessity. Yet, they all recognize this process of finding application as the most familiar way that American Evangelicals read the Bible.

3. Evangelicals assert an extremely close relationship between text and action (Watt 2002). In other words, their logics for decision making—from everyday ethics to political voting, financial giving, and volunteering—are figured in biblical terms (Elisha 2008). Malley (2004: 143–44) is careful to point out that Evangelicals' use of scripture to guide action is not completely uniform and typically takes shape in ad hoc and selective ways. Still, much of what Evangelicals do is presented and justified with explicit reference to scripture. As I suggested in the introduction, the social life of the Bible is not simply a matter of reading and exegesis, but translates to various forms of action in the world. This tight link between text and action in the Evangelical imagination is among the more compelling reasons for a more detailed understanding of what happens in institutions such as group Bible studies, where adherents engage in substantive interaction with scripture. These three observations, though extremely helpful, still beg for a more fundamental insight into how the myriad of reading and interpretive practices Evangelicals perform with scripture are part of the same cultural

logic. We should ask, in short, what organizes how Evangelicals treat the Bible? I argue in this chapter that Evangelical Bible reading is structured by a relationship between well-defined presuppositions and distinct textual practices. These assumptions pertain to the nature of the Bible as a text, and they encourage certain hermeneutic activities while discouraging others.

I frame this analysis as a matter of "textual ideology" that denotes the expectations that guide how individuals and groups read specific texts. Textual ideologies operate similarly to "genres" in that both are centrally concerned with dialogically producing expectations (Bahktin 1986) and structuring social practice (Hanks 1987). Textual ideologies are thus a formative mechanism in social life. They exist prior to any given act of reading, and they orchestrate how readers evaluate different (and divergent) interpretations, what they read, when they read, where they read, and who has the access and legitimacy to read. As readers, we are the bearers of multiple textual ideologies, some as simple as a single presupposition and others as complex as an interconnected system of propositions. We assume different orientations toward cookbooks, comic strips, pornography, encyclopedias, textbooks, novels, personal letters, self-help books, and sacred texts—ad infinitum. Our expectations are realigned anew not only as we traverse genres, but also as we move among different texts within the same category.

Of course, textual ideologies (particularly those as intricate as surrounding scriptures) are not birthed from nowhere and cultivated by no one. Textual ideologies are always formed and negotiated among defined communities of practice:

> aggregate[s] of people who come together around mutual engagement in some common endeavor. Ways of doing things, ways of talking, beliefs, values, power relations—in short, practices—emerge in the course of their joint activity around that endeavor . . . defined simultaneously by its membership and by the practice in which that membership engages. (Eckert and McConnell-Ginet 1992: 95)[1]

In the case of group Bible study, that common endeavor appears in many forms, from congregational involvement to denominational affiliation and spiritual fellowship (among others). More than any of these, though, Bible study is bound together by the practice of collective reading. As a social institution, and in regard to the cultivation of textual ideologies, reading performs important cultural work. It is a place to inherit conceptions from a shared social and theological history and is a moment to take ownership of those conceptions in ways that make sense for readers' own social scenes. In the analysis that follows, I examine the composition of the textual ideology surrounding the Bible for American Evangelicals and the forms of textual practice that result. Throughout their reading of Proverbs, the LCMS Men adhere to three distinct principles regarding the authority, relevance, and textuality of scripture, all of which boast a substantial historical precedent within Western Christianity.

Textual Ideology, Textual Practice

Biblical Authority

In their second meeting for the Proverbs study, the LCMS Men read chapters three and four. At the end of this discussion Dave provided the group with some instruction for the remaining twenty-seven chapters:

> As we read through this let's keep in mind that all this stuff [is] true. I think we should tell ourselves that every once in a while when we pick up the Bible. Now, I might not be able to figure out the whole Truth. I might not be able to figure out how to apply all of that Truth in all of the ways in all of my life. But we should at least approach this from the standpoint: "This is right. And this is more right than anything I would have in mind if I'm thinking differently." This is the wisdom of the ages that comes to us from on High, as opposed to the newspaper [where we] say, "Well, maybe that's right, maybe it's not."

Dave's closing statement exemplifies the primary observation scholars have made about the nature of Evangelical Bible belief. Numerous authors have recognized the social fact that Evangelicals regard scripture as "God's Word," "the Word," "the Truth," "inerrant," "unswerving," and a host of other descriptions that indicate the unique authoritative quality that is attributed to the Bible (e.g., Ammerman 1987; Crapanzano 2000; Harding 2000; Malley 2004; Luhrmann 2004). Dave's hedging ("I might not be able to figure out the whole Truth") poses no trouble for his commitment to Biblical authority because it indexes an Evangelical conviction that there is a fundamental separation between the mind of the Creator and the minds of His creations. As I illustrate below via a moment of tension within the group, this assertion of separation can act as a dividing line between conservative Evangelicals and their Pentecostal counterparts.

The ideological principle of absolute authority is one that Evangelicals assign only to scripture. Two qualities distinguish Biblical authority from other alternatives: First, the Bible is absolute because of its source of authorship. It is not simply a human product but is God's revelation to humanity. The Bible's authors penned the original manuscripts under God's direct guidance. In this way, it is the only text that, in its entirety, bears the coauthorship and supervision of the divine. Thus, it is unparalleled in power, influence, and wisdom. Second, as a direct consequence of its divine authorship, the Bible prevails over any other type of instruction in all matters, ranging from the practical to the moral to the spiritual. The notion that something—a text, an event, an experience—can trump the Bible as a source of guidance is unthinkable in the Evangelical imagination. Biblical answers, as Dave's description indicates, are final answers. Ultimately, this is manifest in the oft-heard phrase among Evangelicals that "all truth is God's Truth." Anything accepted as true based on human wisdom can ultimately be confirmed by the Bible. And if not, its veracity should be doubted. The central assumption is that whatever we discover through human agency has already been stated, in some measure, in the Bible. As a result, various epistemologies (natural science or physical and emotional health, for example) are fully justified only when they are verified by the Bible, demonstrating the alignment of these discovered truths with the Truth as it has been recorded and revealed in scripture.

The conviction that the Bible is the authoritative Word of God crystallized in the Patristic Age (Bright 2006) and took center stage during the 16th-century European Reformation. Christians from Augustine to Luther, however, might find modern commitments to inspiration and authorship somewhat confusing. As the historical theologian Michael Horton notes, "Despite their appeal at times to mechanical analogies of inspiration, [Reformist] theologians did not think that scripture fell from heaven, revealed all at once as dictated to a prophet" (2006: 86). Stricter concerns with right interpretation and authorial intention began with Calvin's exegetical method, and continued through the rise of historical criticism in 18th-century Germany and England (Frei 1974; Zachman 2006). Assumptions of plenary inspiration were being championed in the 17th century by theologians such as John Owen, migrated to the "New" World with English Puritans, and took root in academic discussions of systematic theology among Charles Hodge and others (Noll 1992; Turner 2003; Ward 1995).

Early 20th-century debates among Pentecostals, fundamentalists, and neo-Evangelicals kept the nature of biblical authority in clear view (Malley 2004). And still today, it is used to draw theological, denominational, and soteriological lines within Evangelical culture (Bielo forthcoming).

Not surprisingly, this historically rich principle is evidenced by numerous ways that conservative Evangelicals interact with scripture. Perhaps the two most common examples are a strict refusal to overtly challenge the Bible and a never-ending impulse to recontextualize scripture (irrespective of the social context), thereby transferring authority to one's own words. Here, I focus on a less frequent but equally revealing form of textual practice: the hesitancy to interpret biblical texts as promises.

Throughout their study of Proverbs the LCMS men devoted at least one discussion in every meeting to whether or not a particular text should be read as a "promise from God": a timeless certainty unbound by circumstance, agency, or any other mitigating factor. Consider the following example from the group's seventh meeting in which they discussed Proverbs 20, 21, and 22. Scott, a man in his early fifties and a midlife convert to the LCMS Church, questioned Proverbs 22:6: *Train a child in the way he should go, and when he is old he will not turn from it:*[2]

> Scott: I guess my question is, how much of that [verse] can you hang on to?
>
> Dave: Is that a promise? Is that a general observation? Is it an unswerving truth? What do you think?
>
> Scott: I don't think it's a promise. But sometimes as parents you'd like to hang on to that. You think, "Yeah, maybe some day she'll come back to church."
>
> Dave: Right. Take it this way. This is a passage that heaps a tremendous amount of guilt on parents because the kid goes the way you didn't want the kid to go. And all you can think of is, "Maybe I didn't train the kid right."
>
> Eric: It's also a comfort to parents. When our daughter was with a cult for a while, we came back to this verse a lot.
>
> Dave: Does this suggest something that we should be focusing on as parents? Does this suggest something that we should be focusing on as a congregational community trying to support parents?
>
> Gene: I've had some who would interpret that as saying train up a child in the way *he* should go, and not the way *you* want them to go. And that there is an emphasis there that, maybe what you want for this kid is not the way he should go. And so, you need to look carefully at that.

Dave: Would this be speaking against the father whose dream it always was for his child to be an investment banker? But clearly, the child has the markings of a street artist. And "Fathers be wise."

Dan: I guess the real question comes in is, is it a lesson as to wisdom or is it speaking of our faith? And that's, I think, the real issue we need to look at. Are we looking at train up a child in terms of their faith, and that even though they depart from it for a while, God will cause something to happen in their lives that will bring them back? And I think that's really what happens. God will place something in their lives that they can't handle at some point in their lives, even if it's on their deathbed.

With his question, "Is that a promise?" Dave throws the group into an interpretive dilemma. If they argue in favor of this reading they risk the presentation of contrary evidence. What about the many cases, including among group members, in which "faithful" parents end up with "heretical" children? At stake here is not simply a conflict of opinion but the very nature of biblical authority. As "God's Word," the Bible does not lie and does not break promises. To risk dealing with contradictions, then, is to risk challenges to the authority of scripture, making this interpretive procedure a comparatively dangerous one in their hermeneutic repertoire. In response to this dilemma the group opposes the promissory interpretation. Scott, Gene, and Dan each present alternative readings that work to uphold the Bible's absolute authority. In short, though this proverb is not a promise from God, it does contain a fundamental moral and spiritual lesson that demands attention. Note also that none of the members directly address Dave's question regarding the status of the text as a promise, maintaining a safe distance from the dilemma while still actively participating in the discussion.

This is a particularly revealing issue of Bible reading for Evangelicals because it serves as a point of contrast with other conservative Christianities, namely Pentecostalism. A favored Evangelical method for articulating identity is to establish defined cultural others who highlight their own theological and moral correctness. The participation of Peter in the LCMS Men brings this dynamic into view.

Peter was one of the youngest men in the group at forty-one, a successful architect, and the son of a lifelong LCMS member who also attends the group regularly. He is also the only participant who is not a member of the LCMS denomination. Instead, he belongs to a nondenominational,

Pentecostal church in the city. This places Peter at theological odds with the rest of the group in several areas, namely his understanding of the relationship between contemporary believers and the work of the Holy Spirit. The Pentecostal theological self, unlike its Lutheran counterpart, emphasizes God's direct access to the individual believer and vice versa (Bialecki 2008; Csordas 1997). One outgrowth of Peter's denominational/theological dissonance from the group is his inclination toward reading the Bible as promise. Pentecostal theology, with its emphasis on an unmediated connection between humans and the divine, is much more receptive to interpreting biblical texts as promises from God. In turn, Peter was the only participant to consistently argue in favor of this interpretive style. His reading of Proverbs 3:7–10 during the group's second meeting illustrates this tendency:

> As your nondenom brother, I feel obligated that we don't skip over seven through ten, which reads like this: *Do not be wise in your own eyes; fear the Lord and shun evil. This will bring you health to your body and nourishment to your bones. Honor the Lord with your wealth, with the firstfruits of all your crops; then your barns will be filled to overflowing, and your vats will brim over with new wine.* And you know, *the Word became flesh and dwelt among us.* Jesus became flesh as the Word, and the Word we believe in has right there healing and prosperity. So, the nondenoms that you guys are always beating up for healing and prosperity, it's in there like Prego. I mean, it's in there.

Here, Peter raises the interpretive dilemma of promise, as well as the possibility that the group is at odds with the correct reading of scripture. His choice of text is particularly powerful because it indexes the discourse of prosperity theology, a hallmark of American and global Pentecostalism and a frequent target of critique from outsiders (Bielo 2007b). After a few conflicting reactions are voiced, this discussion ends quietly, with no resolution and no one's commitment to biblical authority under any real threat.

Peter's attempt to keep the genre of promise at center stage continues in the next two meetings. Through the course of these interactions a growing disquiet with Peter's persistence was evident among the other members. The following exchange took place at the end of the group's fourth meeting:

Peter: Proverbs 11 and 12. There are a lot of references in here to the right-eous man, or the righteous. And *the claims of the righteous are just. The righteous man is rescued from trouble. The house of the righteous stands firm. The righteous man cares for the needs of his animal.* And I know I was brought up on, *there is no one righteous; no, not one. All have sinned and fallen short of the glory of God.* But if you go over to Romans 4:13, there's another side to this. And it reads like this: *It was not through law that Abraham and his offspring received the promise that he would be heir of the world, but through the righteousness that comes by faith. For if those who live by law are heirs, faith has no value and the promise is worthless, because law brings wrath. And where there's no law there's no transgression. Therefore, the promise comes by faith.* And then, if you go down to verse 22: *This is why "It was credited to him as righteousness." The words, "It was credited to him" were written not for him alone, but also for us, to whom God will credit righteousness—for us who believe in him who raised Jesus our Lord from the dead.* So, those verses in Romans back up the notion that all of these promises made to the righteous man are made for all of us by faith. Just like we receive our salvation by faith we receive our right-eousness by faith. It's not by anything we do, it's just by faith. And if we don't believe that we're righteous by faith, then you might as well just tear these three chapters right out of the Bible.

Al: I got a question for Peter about that. Where are you going with this? So, this gets back to the idea that this is a book of promises.

Peter: Yeah, by faith.

Al: Yeah. I understand. But I still struggle with what that means when I see faithful people take it in the neck. How do you square that?

Peter: Well, I don't have all the answers. All I'm saying is that this is a book of promises from beginning to end. And life is more than just saved by grace. We have life, and a better life, by claiming all the promises in this book as ours. Our pastor has a saying. He says, "If you don't believe in that healing stuff, don't worry. It's not coming to your door."

[[Laughs]]

Peter: I'm not trying to cause division. I'm just saying there's a lot in here that we need to get into.

Al's objection (namely, his concerns about experience contradicting scripture) captures the group's reluctance to read the Bible as promise "from beginning to end." This puts Peter on the defensive. He explicitly challenges their adherence to biblical authority ("you might as well just tear these three chapters right out of the Bible") and takes a direct jab at LCMS tradition ("life is more than just saved by grace"). This was the last meeting Peter attended with the LCMS Men. His initial and continued absence occurred in silence, receiving no public discussion between July and when I ended fieldwork in December.

It was clear that Peter's exit issued directly from his theological/denominational distance from the other men, crystallized here by the interpretive dilemma of reading scripture as promise. Thus, while Peter and the group equally presumed the Bible to be the only source of absolute authority, Peter's Pentecostal inclinations put him at odds with the group's hesitancy to risk challenging that authority. The example of Peter and promises suggests that biblical authority—while a rather obvious and also self-conscious ideology—ultimately produces some tricky interpretive territory that Evangelicals must navigate.

Biblical Relevance

The LCMS Men's final meeting in the study of Proverbs was a review. They wanted to spend one meeting rethinking the recurring issues and questions that were raised during the previous twelve discussions. One of the closing comments in this meeting came from Art—a husband and father in his late fifties, retired state policeman, and lifelong LCMS member—who reflected on the relationship between the Bible and contemporary life:

Art: The Bible was written in the real world. Not today, but it's not some fantasy planet or something, like, that was given to us from another solar system. I mean, everything happens in the real world. You read the Bible, the problems people experienced back then and the solutions, like in Proverbs and stuff, we have the same things today. It's a different setting, but we all have that. All those things, mankind is still basically the same. The interpersonal relationships we have with others remain just a different venue.

Dave: Be interesting to know what we could do to change our mindset of this as a religious book and think of it as a practical book. There's a thing in our minds or a thing in our culture, maybe it's a thing always, that things religious, the word "irrelevant" is right by it. And that this is not about irrelevance, it's about real world and coordinating all this stuff we learn about science or all this stuff we learn about math and integrating it into our . . .

[[interrupted]]

Art: Right. I think it's a guide on how we should conduct our life.

Evangelicals understand the Bible's message to be eternal, just as true tomorrow as it is today, as it always has been. Part of this conception is that scripture reveals the spiritual and moral nature of humanity. People are born into this world as sinful beings, separated from the righteousness of God. This human nature has remained unchanged through time and is therefore always available in the pages of scripture. In turn, there is a certainty that the Bible has the unique capacity to be always relevant and appropriate and do so in ways that keep pace with the uncertainty of life. Evangelicals expect the experience of reading the Bible and the consequences of doing so never to be the same as the previous reading. Readers are assured of receiving something new to consider or apply. Because scripture is "alive" it can never be old, antiquated, or exhausted. No matter one's age, maturity in faith, or biblical expertise he or she can always count on (re)discovery. Not only is the Bible new with each reading, it is also precise in its application. Readers expect biblical texts to be relevant to their own, particular circumstances. The application is not vague, but specific; not general, but amazingly exact in how it aligns with readers' lives. There is no contradiction here for believers because the same process is at work: the Holy Spirit reveals what is needed when it is needed from the absolute Truth that is the Word of God. The ideology of relevance is intimately linked with the first principle of authority, because only the "Word of God" possesses this inherent assurance to forever be directly, personally applicable. As a result, each time transitivity is established, the authority that produces relevance is testified to (see chapter 3).

It is tempting to attribute this fixation on relevance to the character of contemporary American spirituality, with its focus on individuality and personalized religiosity (Luhrmann 2004). This would be misguided. Much like the ideology of authority, the assurance of scripture's relevance began in the Patristic Age, continued through the Medieval Period, and was advocated by different streams of Reformers (Horton 2006). The type of idiosyncratic application so characteristic of American Evangelical readers was equally visible with Martin Luther, for example, when trying to make sense of his wife's difficult childbirth (Mattox 2006: 95). Wesley Kort (1996) has described how the eternal relevance of the Bible figured centrally in Calvin's theory of reading, as it "moves from saving knowledge outward not only to the whole of Scripture but to the relation of Scripture to the whole of life" (30). The Wesleyan tradition continued in this vein, emphasizing the confirmation of the Bible in personal experience (Metts 1995). This transformative quality of Bible reading for the individual has been integrated into virtually all trajectories of American Protestantism.

The primary form of textual practice that results from this presupposition is the interpretive style of finding application. As discussed above, scholars have continually demonstrated that this is the predominant form of hermeneutic activity engaged by Evangelicals. However, to simply identify the ongoing search for relevance as a process is incomplete for characterizing Evangelical Bible reading. A more thorough account must understand how readers align themselves in specific types of relationship with biblical texts.

When reading the Bible, Evangelicals place themselves in some form of ideological relationship with their sacred text. In other words, they establish how they relate to what is being portrayed. This takes shape around a series of questions: am I doing what I understand the Bible to be saying? Is my life in conflict with scripture? Am I working toward the example set forth by biblical characters? Is scripture challenging my life of faith and daily habits? Is it affirming them? These questions are never answered solely from the perspective of an individual's idiosyncratic preoccupations. Rather, they are thoroughly social questions—always situated within broader cultural concerns. Such concerns are many and varied, but in the case of Evangelical men, the Bible's relevance is frequently subject to ideologies of gender. Consider the following interaction, which took place in the LCMS group's third meeting after reading Proverbs 5:8–9: *Keep to a path far from her, do not go near the door of her house, lest you give your best strength to others and your years to one who is cruel*:

> Dave: One of the things I wanted to ask this morning is, and I think we're getting able to do this, do you have practices, barriers in your life that serve to keep you pure and chaste?
>
> Art: Don't put yourself in a situation where you may be tempted, where you would be creating an opportunity to go down the wrong path. Avoid them.

Scott: Following up on what Art said, don't go to bars. Not that long ago I had a neighbor who had a little problem where he would start going to a singles bar on the west side of town after work. And it became regular. And it was just a matter of time, like half a year later, he went off with another woman.

Nate: Instead of focusing on not doing those things, focusing on loving your wife better. Aside from following Christ, our greatest commitment as men is our wives.

Dave: Yeah, a little later in this chapter it speaks about delighting yourself in your own wife. I want to say a few things about that in just a second. What else do you do to keep yourself away from the wrong path?

George: You have to stay away from self-reliance. If you leave it only to yourself, then you'll fail. Keeping these broad relationships with other people, if it just gets to one-on-one you're in trouble.

Gene: I think for a lot of men a time that you're most vulnerable is traveling. You're away from home. You stay in a motel. I think that's where you have to be aware ahead of time. What are you going to avoid?

Dave: Part of staying pure is making certain decisions in advance. I haven't traveled like some of you have, but I got so that when I travel I just wouldn't even turn on the TV set, because I didn't want to find myself watching stuff I shouldn't be watching.

Peter: I don't want to come off as sounding too self-righteous. You know, I struggle with this too. I work with professionals, executive women. I have these temptations like everybody else. But you have to look at the way Jesus faced temptation. I pray this prayer," God, why did you make women so gorgeous? What were you thinking?" You know, and why did he make us this way? But three verses come to mind. The first one is, *let no man say when he is tempted he is tempted by God.* Temptation comes from the Devil. And the second one is, *resist the Devil and he'll flee.* And you gotta remember when Jesus was tempted in the wilderness by the Devil he only spoke the Word. He didn't say, "Devil, you're bothering me. You're gettin' on my nerves [[spoken in wimpy, agitated tone]]." He said, *it is written.* The third verse I've got is 1 Corinthians 10:13, which is a really great one for all us to memorize as guys. And it reads like this in the NIV [New International Version]: *No temptation has seized you except what is common to man. And God is faithful; he will not let you be tempted beyond what you can bear. But when you are tempted, he will also provide a way out so that you can stand up under it.* You know, it's a struggle everyday, but there's the Word that we have to battle these temptations.

Dave: I think we have to watch building what seem like harmless intimacies with women that aren't our wives. It doesn't start necessarily with full-blown physical adultery. But when we start taking another woman into our confidence and building up intimacies that begins us down a path that we need to be careful of. I think also, in this realm, Philippians 4:7 or 4:8: *whatever's good, whatever's noble, whatever's pure. If there's anything honorable, think on these things.* We can share good things, and we ought to be speaking positively about the good and Godly things that are going on and not have intimacy with others. I knew a couple. They were close friends. We were out with them one night and they were joking with each other but in a cutting, negative way, all night long. And it wasn't too many weeks after that that they said, "Pastor, we need to talk." Nate kind of was pointing to this too. Let us look at 5:19: *A loving doe, a graceful deer—may her breasts satisfy you always, may you ever be captivated by her love. Why be captivated, my son, by an adulteress? Why embrace the bosom of another man's wife?* In my premarital counseling I always tell people that they are going to become, if they're not already, experts on what's wrong with each other. As time goes on they'll be able to write books about what's wrong about each other. I tell them to just lay off that stuff. You're marrying someone that's not perfect. And you've got, there are enough people in our lives reminding us we're not perfect. I always believe marriage is to be that spot in our life where we are there to encourage the other.

Discussions of sexual morality were less common among this group than other gender-infused topics (for example, religious responsibilities), but they clearly elicit how the group views the ideal subject positions of "male" and "female." The LCMS Men read the Proverbs text regarding adultery and immediately begin reflecting on their own habits and practices. While the men are forthcoming in the exchange (perhaps surprisingly so), their contributions remain abstract and hypothetical. Scott "had a neighbor" and Dave references "a couple" that were "close friends," but the men avoid structuring the discussion as one of personal confession. Alongside this removed quality to their reading, there is also a striking inclination to see scripture as having specific lessons for men. Nate, Peter, and Dave all suggest that certain biblical texts carry direct meanings for male readers. Through this gendered hermeneutics the group constructs an image of the ideal husband, committed to his wife and resistant to temptation. In examples such as this, Bible reading becomes a means of gender articulation, and, given the religious value of scripture, one imagines it is a distinctly important way of saying what it means to "be a man" in the world.

This method of grounding the relevance of the Bible is at the center of discourses of masculinity within American Evangelicalism more broadly (Bartkowski 2001). Evangelicals have no shortage of certainties about how males and females are "wired," how they are different, why they love and infuriate each other, and what roles they should play within the "Body of Christ." Parachurch organizations such as the Promise Keepers (Bartkowski 2004) and GodMen[3] articulate a vision of masculinity that is, innately by God's design, built for leadership, strength, and decisiveness but easily tempted and forever in need of spiritual guidance. The ideal Evangelical man is a breadwinner for his family, a caring husband, a devoted father, a model in his church community, and keenly aware of his reliance on divine help for avoiding sexual and selfish temptations. The group's reaction to Proverbs 5:8–9 illustrates the general process of biblical relevance unfolding in ways that establish a relationship between readers and their text. This relationship is typically informed by wider discourses that crisscross through the world of Evangelical institutions. Here, a particular version of masculinity popular among Evangelicals shapes the application made by the LCMS Men. It provides a vocabulary and a narrative for their search to find biblical relevance.

Biblical Textuality

In their discussion of Proverbs 29, Dave asks the men to read and "mull over" verse 25: *Fear of man will prove to be a snare, but whoever trusts in the Lord is kept safe.* After a lengthy exchange (to which we will return in a moment) Dave offers a closing statement:

> This is one of those words, like I suppose all the words, where we have to take the whole council of God. And this is not saying, "I'm trusting in God to take care of me; I think I'll go golfing all day." There are verses in here about *being a sluggard*, about *being a sloth.* So, this is another example of where we have to let scripture interpret scripture, take the whole council of God. A friend of mine says, "God feeds the birds of the air, but he doesn't put the worms in the nests." So, we want to take, well, this says *trust in the Lord.* But there are other places that say, *well, you better get up and go to work.*

Evangelicals do not understand the Bible as a group of disparate texts or as a single book lacking a unifying theme. Rather, it is understood as a collection of texts that tells a cohesive story about the nature of God and humanity, the purpose of history, and the unfolding of time. It is the story of fallenness and trials, faith in spite of hardship, the difference between human and divine wisdom, and ultimately, redemption through Jesus. Biblical texts are read within the context of this unifying narrative, providing an interpretive frame to situate any verse, chapter, or story. This assumption of unified textuality places certain traits, such as contradiction, in opposition to the Bible's inherent qualities. Scripture is characterized by continuity of form and theme with no room for contrary meanings or purposes. Much like the ideology of relevance, beliefs about the textuality of scripture emerge from the authority of scripture. The uniform authorship of the Bible—despite its variety of known and anonymous human authors—underwrites this assumed continuity. Because God is always ultimately the author, it is no mystery to find such coherence from Genesis to Revelation.

The ideology of unified textuality shares the same historical depth as commitments to the Bible's authority and relevance. Patristic and Medieval theologies of scripture assumed "that scripture speaks as a whole. Any seeming inconsistencies between the different books may be due to our lack of understanding, or they may even be intended to stimulate our minds to greater effort. But scripture agrees with itself" (Ayres 2006: 16). This principle was also necessary for Luther's "perspicuity of scripture" (Mattox 2006: 104) and his Christological hermeneutics because it requires the presence of a single, continuing narrative. It is an ideology of language and text that has informed the King James translation tradition (McGrath 2002). And it has persisted as a dividing line among American Protestants. Peter Thuesen (1999) describes how this single issue of narrative coherence posed constant difficulties for the ecumenical translation committee of the Revised Standard Version in the 1940s and 50s.

Even more so than the previous two principles, the presupposition of unified textuality engenders a wide array of inventive strategies for Bible reading. I will consider two of these strategies below: establishing intertextual linkages and resolving seeming tensions. Throughout their study of Proverbs, the LCMS Men made a practice of connecting texts from other sources in scripture to the verses in Proverbs. Consider the following example, which ensued following Dave's request that the men "mull over" Proverbs 29:25:

Dave: Do you know of another Bible passage or another Bible-something that reminds you of that or that would support this?

Don: Fear of the Lord is the beginning of knowledge.

Dave: Okay.

Gene: Rely not on your own understanding, but trust in the Lord.

Dave: Okay. Can you think of a biblical event that would be an example of someone *not* being afraid of man but who was trusting in the Lord and is kept safe? Can you think of a Bible picture of that?

Don: David and Goliath.

Dave: David and Goliath. Can you think of another one?

Art: Daniel in the lion's den.

Dave: Daniel in the lion's den. Go ahead.

Nate: Paul in prison.

Dave: Paul in prison.

Dan: Meshak, Shadrak.

Dave: Yeah, Chris.

Chris: Joshua standing before the people of Israel and he told them they had to choose that day whom they were gonna serve. And he said, as for me and my house, we're gonna serve the Lord.

Dave: We're gonna serve the Lord. Yeah.

Joe: Jonah.

Dave: Okay. Al.

Al: Gideon.

Dave: Perry.

Perry: Peter walking on the water.

Dave: Peter walking on the water.

Per Dave's request, they demonstrate no trouble finding comparable Bible stories. It is hard to appreciate from this printed transcript the quick, unflinching manner in which the men rattled off these connections. They provide ten examples, drawn from both Testaments, of where the message communicated by this proverb can be located elsewhere in scripture. In doing so, they assert a continuity of meaning that stretches throughout the Bible, continually supporting itself and redeclaring its consistent nature. This practice of establishing intertextual linkages is especially interesting because it was often done as an end in itself. Groups did not assemble these (sometimes lengthy) textual chains in pursuit of a particular study question; they did so for the sake of the chain itself, a concrete demonstration of the Bible's unified textuality.

In a related fashion, groups presented and resolved seeming contradictions among biblical texts. In many cases, individuals juxtaposed two separates texts, pushing their fellow participants to explain the apparent conflict between their meanings. This often began with someone playing the role of devil's advocate, pointing out a potential incongruence and, by extension, the possibility that one text is right, the other is wrong, and the Bible as a whole is inconsistent. Much like the earlier problem of broken promises, any hint of disparity within scripture necessarily raises doubts about its authority. In response, the poser of the conflict or someone else was quick to dispel the ostensible tension by appealing to further biblical references. Again, the LCMS Men provide a rather articulate, and in this case rather humorous, example in their reading of Proverbs 6:

> Dave: I love, beginning with verse six. I like the word sluggard. *Go to the ant, you sluggard: consider its ways and be wise. It has no commander, no overseer or ruler, yet it stores its provisions in summer and gathers its food at harvest. How long will you lie there, you SLUGGARD? When will you get up from your sleep? A little sleep, a little slumber, a little folding of the hands to rest—and poverty will come on you like a bandit and scarcity like an armed man.* Does that strike you in anyway?
>
> Art: Give up your remote control.
>
> [[Laughs]]
>
> Art: Couch potato is what I thought.
>
> Bill: I don't know. There's some verse that says *we're not supposed to take any thoughts for tomorrow.*
>
> Dave: And aren't there verses that tell us *we're supposed to rest.*
>
> Bill: Yeah.
>
> Dave: What's the difference between resting and being a sluggard?
>
> Bill: How many days a week you do it.
>
> [[Laughs]]
>
> Eric: Also, that means that we should work and be ambitious. But then, I always like Psalm 127, verse two here. It says, *it's vain for you to rise up early, sit up late, eat the bread of sorrows—for so he gives us the beloved while they sleep.* We're gonna have what we're supposed to have, but then of course, we can't just rest there because we're supposed to be ambitious. The two kind of balance each other.
>
> Dave: Yeah. A lot of Christian living, a lot of biblical living, is living in tension. We're saved by grace through faith, but God wants us to live a certain

way. We're not to be lazy, but we're not to be anxious. And we are to take the Sabbath rest. And so, lots of Christian living is living in tension between poles.

Bill and Dave present the group with biblical texts that pose a potential contradiction regarding the scriptural view of laziness. Eric responds, looking to the Psalms for a solution to the seeming problem. Dave supports Eric with his summation that "biblical living" is about "living between poles." Here, again, the unified textuality of the Bible is upheld by the group. The consistency of scripture leaves no space for discrepancies, a fact the LCMS Men reaffirm through their discussion of *sluggards.*

In both cases—establishing intertextual linkages and resolving seeming contradictions—the group's interpretive conduct is guided by the ideological principle of biblical continuity. God, through His Word, can be counted on to never lie, misdirect, or distort His purposes with conflicting messages. The hermeneutic activity of these men takes place against the backdrop of this assumed coherence. They read with an unfailing confidence, knowing from the outset that everything will come together.

Postscript: Continuity and Tension in Evangelical Bible Reading

It would seem from my analysis that Evangelical Bible reading is largely an uncontested affair. I have emphasized the continuity among these readers as they consider, grapple with, and ultimately affirm interpretations of Bible texts. Indeed, for the LCMS Men and the other project groups, this is most often the case. Even when group members disagree or when multiple and sometimes conflicting interpretations are left to linger, the status of scripture and the adherence to principles of authority, relevance, and textuality remain unthreatened. To end this account here, though, would be incomplete. There are also occasions, though they are far less numerous, when the collective reading of scripture is fraught with tension. In particular, there are occasions when biblical interpretations conflict with other ideological discourses in which groups are highly invested. Consider a final example from the LCMS Men, one in which their reading is defined by complication rather than stability. What happens, for example, when the cultural identity of Bible readers conflicts with what appears to be a clear biblical mandate?

In their eleventh meeting, Dave had just read Proverbs 29:2–3—*When a country is rebellious, it has many rulers, but a man of understanding and knowledge maintains order*:

Dave: Is there any statement of democracy in this passage? Can you read it backwards? If a country has many rulers, it is rebellious?

Al: I just don't get a sense, biblically, much of democracy at all, throughout the entire Bible. It almost seems to be that it recognizes that the best possible government is a benevolent dictator and that democracy is really gonna screw you up. Get all those people running around think they know what they're doing. I don't necessarily agree with that, but that's the sense I get biblically.

Dan: I was just gonna say, this implies less leadership, one person in control. In other words, the more people that are in control, the more factions you get. And this is implying one person. I mean, even in our form of government we only have one person in control.

Chris: I don't think this implies one person. I think this implies God in control.

Al: Well, the Bible says that democracy . . .

[[overlapping]]

Chris: Democracy being exactly the opposite of that, where *Every man* . . .

[[overlapping]]

Dave: *Is a law unto himself.*

Chris: *Is a law unto himself.* And I think this is implying the opposite of democracy, of not being human dictatorship, but the rule of God through His law.

Al: And in fact, we know that the only reason Israel had a king in the first place is because they begged for it. And God finally said, "I'm tired of listening to you. I'll give you one."

Joe: "And you won't like it."

Dan: I've got a question/comment for Chris. Are you saying when a country's rebellious, in other words, it doesn't follow God, it has many rulers, in other words, other gods? Is that what you're saying?

Chris: I don't think that's what this is saying. No, that's not what I was implying. Human rulers, and democracy, are really the ultimate form of every man is just a little human ruler. You look at this country as an example. God and His law are anathema in this country. And what do we have? We have more rulers than you can shake a stick at, in the formal sense, and then also in the theoretical sense of democracy.

Dave: Now, take this a step away from where we are. How do you apply that to governance in the Church? We might not be able to do much about governance in the United States of America. But we do have some influence over governance in the congregation.

[[Jokes about voters' meetings at church]]

Al: I think you could heat the city for a week with the steam that's coming off people when they walk out of most [voters' meetings].

Dave: Why do we do that to ourselves?

Chris: Because we are obsessed with this notion of democracy, and that's the way we view the church. We turn authority on its head and vest it in each individual, every man doing what is right in his own eyes and then we come together and argue about it.

Gene: Well, I think it's a measure of our own selfishness. We all want what we want. And when someone doesn't agree with what we want we get angry and we get upset. And if we don't get our way, we get even more upset. And I think that's the pull and the tug that goes on, not a willingness to give up and say: "It's not a matter of what I want, it's what's maybe best for the church and what everybody thinks is right." And a lot of us can't accept that.

The group's discussion of democracy places them in a difficult position. On the one hand, they are strict adherents to the Bible's absolute authority. On the other hand, they cling to a particular model of governance as democratically minded Americans (Hatch 1989). The reading advocated by Al, Chris, and Gene confronts the group with an interpretive dilemma. This dilemma is heightened by the fact that all three men are highly regarded exegetes in the group and in the larger context of the congregation. What recourse is left to them? Do they affirm the authority of the Bible on this matter of governance? If so, what does this mean for their patriotism and faith in democracy (read: Americanness)? If they deny this statement on democracy, what does this mean for the nature of the Bible as absolutely authoritative (read: Evangelicalness)? Unlike other matters where they were quite willing to pronounce the Bible's unswerving authority in spite of their own practice—regarding personal sins of greed or lust, for example—the question of democracy poses a distinctly different challenge. This is an ideological discourse in which they have large stakes, as it is tied up in identities of political affiliation and egalitarian individualism.

Ultimately, both are unshaken. No one rejected the authority of scripture, and no one renounced their citizenry responsibilities of participating in the electorate. Dave's question about church governance attempts to shift attention away from the veracity of the text to its application. This is a strategy frequently invoked by facilitators when facing a tense interpretive situation and one that is frequently successful. In this case, though, it is not. The discussion comes quickly back to democracy as an obsession and its conflicts with scripture. The lesson of this exchange is twofold. First, it makes clear that the ideology of authority is not always something to which Evangelicals simply or blindly give assent. Often, they must struggle with how that authority squares with their other ideological commitments. And second, it makes clear that Bible reading is always potentially a practice defined by tension as well as continuity.

Textual Ideology and Evangelical Culture

What happens when conservative Evangelicals go about reading the Bible? In this chapter I have addressed this question from the perspective of collective reading and interpretation as it occurs in group Bible study. These readers construct an imaginative yet restricted hermeneutic relationship with scripture. The structure of their reading is found in the link between the presuppositions held about scripture (textual ideology) and the various interpretive procedures used to take it up (textual practice). The LCMS Men have very clear notions about the Bible's authority, relevance, and textuality, and they rely on them to organize their reading from week to week. As a site of collective reading, Bible study allows contemporary Evangelicals to participate in a long history of grappling with the Word of God. This analysis makes clear how this space is one of both inheritance and ownership, where defined practices of reading scripture are both affirmed and made new. I have also made clear that local dialogues regarding textual ideology are not simply rehearsals but rituals of identity and pedagogy. These rituals bespeak both continuity and tension, and they occur alongside broader discourses of Evangelical and American subjectivity.

The framework of "textual ideology-textual practice" that I have proposed is particularly relevant to the comparative study of Bible reading cross-culturally (cf. Bielo, ed. Forthcoming). After all, the argument that textual ideologies take shape within defined communities of practice (themselves embedded in distinct sociohistorical formations) demands the possibility that very different ideas can be cultivated among other collections of readers. This is true among non-Evangelical streams of American

Protestantism (see Davie 1995), and for Christians elsewhere. John Pulis (1999) describes how Jamaican Rastafarians, while similar to orthodox Christianity in certain ways, uphold a unique set of ideas about the nature of biblical texts. In particular, there is a marked flexibility of interpretive limits among these Christians ensuing from the conviction that the scriptural canon is incomplete. Filtered through the lens of a racialized and colonialist history, Rastafarians are quite certain that the Bible as it appears in the present has been robbed of texts detailing African history. This absence of texts that belong allows exegetes to supplement the printed text of scripture with their own oral traditions.

Similarly, Matthew Engelke (2007) reports on Zimbabwean Apostolics who dismiss the written word entirely in favor of oral performances. A semiotic ideology that stresses the immaterial over the material and a national past that equates literacy with colonial oppression has produced devout Christians who not only reject reading the Bible but also suggest using its pages for toilet paper! Eva Keller (2005) represents a divergent literacy situation among Seventh-Day Adventists on the island of Madagascar. Unlike Pulis's Rastafarians and Engelke's Apostolics, Keller's Adventists fetishize the written word, spending as many hours as they can spare immersed in individual and group study. Their interest is not so much about excavating the "right" meaning of scripture but is to delight in the very process of discussion and intellectual pursuit. The act of Bible reading is thus an attraction for newcomers and the primary reason why adherents continue to practice their faith long after conversion.

These three cases suggest that any empirical analysis of Bible reading must attend to the presuppositions held by scripture's interlocutors and their various impacts on what people do with their sacred text. Returning to the example of American Evangelicals, the ideological principles of authority, relevance, and textuality exert the most influence on the practice of Bible reading. As I stated earlier in this chapter, the most pervasive form of reading is that of application, highlighting the importance of the principle of relevance. The interest in relevance is heightened because Evangelicals seem to carry it with them beyond scripture. Amy Frykholm (2004) and Lynn Neal (2006) have both observed this type of interpretive transference in Evangelicals' fiction reading, respectively interviewing readers of Christian apocalyptic and romance books. In both cases, the frame of relevance guided how readers consumed these texts.

In writing this I am reminded of an anecdote from my own fieldwork, again involving the LCMS Men. Several months after their study of Proverbs, the group chose to read G. K. Chesterton's *Orthodoxy* (1908). Collectively, the men applauded Chesterton's seminal work but thought many sections were challenging to the point of utter confusion. One morning I was sitting next to Art. He quipped to me while the group was discussing a particularly difficult passage, "I just skipped down until I found something that applied to me, then I started scribbling in the margins." Thus, the principle of relevance appears distinct from the Bible-specific ideologies of authority and textuality because it seems to have achieved a level of transitivity to other types of religious reading. Vincent Crapanzano (2000: 19) goes so far as to suggest that the model of relevance has even colonized Evangelicals' reading of everyday experiences, as they are always searching to pinpoint the lessons of every little action and event.

Earlier in this chapter we considered how others have made sense of this push toward relevance—namely through appeals to cognitive demands or reinventing received methods of interpretation. I then made clear that there is great historical depth to this practice (and the presupposition that buttresses it). Alongside Evangelicals' historical inclination toward establishing biblical relevance, we should also remember how attaching the details of one's own life and circumstances to the words of scripture works in tandem with the discourse of personalized spirituality that circulates among American Evangelicals. The next chapter focuses on this issue and its role in organizing Bible study life.

* 3 *

Cultivating Intimacy

Darren and Beverly are a married couple in their early fifties. They own a modest, three-bedroom home nestled in an affluent neighborhood. Beverly is a dental assistant at a local practice, and Darren is a formally trained engineer. Since 1995, though, he has been the executive director of an international ministry organization he founded after leaving a part-time position in university campus ministry. Every other Thursday night they host a Bible study in their living room. The group is one of twenty-seven groups offered by a local Restoration Movement church (RMC). Unlike the LCMS Men's group that places great value on its Lutheran tradition, Darren and Beverly's Prayer Circle, like their home church, is more typically Evangelical. They shy away from identifying the Restoration Movement as a "denomination" or themselves primarily as RMC members. Instead, they use various doctrinal signifiers to self-identify: "born-again," "New Testament Christian," "no creed but Jesus," "where the Bible speaks we speak, where the Bible is silent we are silent," and "we are not the only Christians, but Christians only."

In the spring of 2003, the congregation participated in Forty Days of Purpose, a church-wide campaign designed and distributed by pastor and author Rick Warren. Warren pastors a 20,000-plus member megachurch in southern California and his most widely read book, *The Purpose Driven Life* (2003), has sold tens of millions of copies in the United States alone. Like thousands of churches throughout the United States, RMC implemented the six-week program with hopes of generating new excitement in the congregation, increasing member involvement, and attracting new members. Forty Days is incorporated into most every facet of congregational life during its six-week tenure. One of its central projects is to organize as many home Bible study groups as possible. Each week, the groups meet to read and discuss material produced by the program, often in coordination with the previous or upcoming Sunday's sermon, which is also designed by the campaign. Most of the home groups at RMC began during Forty Days.

The Prayer Circle bonded quickly during these six weeks and immediately decided to continue meeting after the program ended. Of the original eleven members, nine regularly attended during my fieldwork.[1] Because of the close attachments they formed, midway through my fieldwork they decided to cap the group at its current size in order to safeguard this intimacy. Aside from Darren and Beverly, there are two married couples and three single women. Matt and Mary are in their late forties with two adult children. Matt is an elder at the church, and Mary leads several women's Bible study groups. Tom and Jenny are in their early thirties. Tom is an accomplished musician and plays for the church's praise band during Sunday morning worship. Jenny works as a full-time photographer. Julie, Mandy, and Tanya all recently turned thirty. Mandy is an elementary school teacher, and Tanya is an athletic trainer at Michigan State University. Julie is a lawyer for the state and is extremely active in the church. She teaches a youth Sunday school class and leads several youth worship events each year, and she helped organize the first-ever twenty-four-hour prayer vigil at the church. All of the younger participants were friends prior to the group's formation, spending time together socially outside of church activities. Julie and Darren are particularly close. She considers him her primary Christian mentor and regularly attends the ministry trips offered by his organization.

Darren is very much an authoritative voice in the group. His position as an ordained minister, coupled with his status as a spiritual mentor to Julie and others, creates a group dynamic that reveres his contributions. While everyone was quick to tease and trade quips with Darren, they listened closely when he spoke, relied on him when tough questions arose, and rarely challenged his conclusions. However, Darren did not lecture or act as an overbearing voice in the group. Aside from Beverly and Mandy's quiet personalities, conversations were remarkably balanced among the remaining members. Julie and Matt, in particular, were prone to speak at length. The brand of lively, analytical, and humorous interaction exhibited by the LCMS Men was replaced in the Prayer Circle with a more confessional, emotional atmosphere. Through their reading and discussion, the group exemplifies a defining theme of American Evangelicalism: the conceptualization of Christian spirituality as an intimate experience.

Intimacy in American Evangelicalism

In his recent ethnography of a Zimbabwean Pentecostal sect, Matthew Engelke (2007) describes a defining tension of the Christian faith. Christians everywhere face a "problem of presence," whereby believers must imagine how to construct a relationship with an Almighty God who is simultaneously, and paradoxically, both present and absent (12). While this God is said to be always there, He cannot be directly seen, touched, or heard. This dichotomy of presence-absence aligns with several other familiar oppositions embedded in the Western Christian tradition: objective-subjective, material-immaterial, mediate-immediate, knowledge-faith, natural-supernatural, and here-hereafter, to name a few. Through all of these dichotomies runs a confidence that God has the ability to transcend separated realms and believers can avail themselves of the chance to experience this. How do Christians respond to this dilemma of making a metaphysical God available, visible, and communicable in the physical world? The answer to this question—how Christians resolve the problem of presence—is a thoroughly cultural process. How God is experienced within Christian communities is formed alongside fundamental assumptions about the nature of the world, people, language, space, and materiality. The question I take up here is: how do conservative Evangelicals in America resolve the problem of presence, and why is group Bible study a significant site for doing so?

Tanya Luhrmann (2004) provides an apt description of how Evangelicals imagine the nature of God and spirituality. The defining characteristic at work is intimacy. This God is not distant, mediated by arcane rituals or rote formulas. He is always approachable, forgiving, loving, and desires the best for each person. One should seek to relate, talk, and listen to God everyday and in a frankly everyday manner. God should be involved in every decision, no matter its gravity: there are no "big" and "small" worries for God. He is depicted as a "best friend," "perfect love," and "heavenly Father." God cares about your prayer life and your mission work, but He also cares about your date tonight and the ongoing problem you have with your boss. As Luhrmann neatly suggests, "This God is not without majesty. But He has become a pal" (518). In turn, establishing and nurturing a personalized, one-on-one relationship with God is the defining goal of Evangelical spirituality. Having a "relationship with Jesus Christ" is not solely a matter of eternal salvation, it is also the key to enjoying the best life possible in this world. Luhrmann focuses on the experiential outcomes of this approach to Christianity—those that manifest themselves cognitively and bodily. States of trance, altered consciousness, and intense spiritual awareness characterize various forms of Evangelical religious practice and are articulated through a specialized language and felt through an expressive emotionality.

Evangelicals seek to imitate the close, intimate bond they desire with God in their expectations for relating with each other and with those outside their community of faith. The hallmark of a successful Christian community is one that is open, always willing to share personal thoughts and feelings. One's Christian family is ideally a safe haven, a place to reveal the utmost private triumphs, concerns, and problems without fear of ridicule or exile. This contrasts sharply with what Jodie Davie (1995: 25–27) calls a "don't ask, don't tell" spirituality characteristic of mainline American Protestants in which openness is often muted for the sake of maintaining an air of cohesion and belonging. A widely circulated utterance among Evangelicals, and one I heard often from Prayer Circle members, is that "Christianity is about relationships, not religion." This statement indexes a separation posited between Evangelicalism and other Christian traditions that have, in some way or another, "gotten it wrong." The basic sentiment is that strictly institutionalized forms of religious practice should always be secondary to personalized faith, which is best realized when developed alongside fellow believers interested in the same intimate spirituality. As such, the relationship being sought with God—as close, individual, unmediated—provides a model for the type of relationship desired with other people. In turn, brief moments and sustained periods of deep intimacy become unambiguous, iconic signs of faith, righteousness, and a healthy spiritual life.

Ethnographers of American Evangelicalism have tried to identify the locales and processes by which cultural dispositions, such as intimacy, are cultivated. As Luhrmann suggests, such sites of learning range from congregational worship to immersion in Evangelical literature, personal Bible reading, and devotional prayer. When Evangelicals look for concrete ways to cultivate their spiritual intimacy—and thereby respond to the Christian problem of presence—they look with great interest and expectation to group Bible study. The group setting is the ideal space because of its reputation in Evangelical life as a site of active, open, and reflexive dialogue. But how this happens—how Evangelicals use Bible study and the process of collective reading to achieve their desired intimacy—is open for analysis. To understand this process it is necessary to understand the nature of this event, which we will do through the concept of "interactive frames" (Tannen 1993).

Appropriate, acceptable, and attractive participation in any social encounter requires an understanding of what the event is all about. Scholars interested in intersubjective communication have built a rich tradition around analyzing what distinguishes events and how we are able to transition seamlessly between them on a daily basis (e.g., Bateson 1972; Goffman 1974). Following Deborah Tannen (1993), the frames we apply to our interactions constitute "structures of expectation" (15) we build on previous experiences in similar encounters. We pattern our behavior based on how we expect the event will unfold, what we expect from others, and what we expect others are expecting from us. Such interactive frames provide an orientation for how to act, how to arrive at proper interpretations, and how to understand relationships. What, then, is the dominant frame that Evangelicals use for group Bible study?

It is easy to imagine a variety of guiding expectations these Christians might bring to their weekly meetings. The goal of Bible study could be to improve Bible literacy, be exposed to new theological or spiritual ideas, arrange church business, mobilize resources for mission and outreach, increase fellowship with friends, evangelize new people, publicly express doubts about faith and seek affirmation, or raise doctrinal questions that are troubling or puzzling. While these are all part of the Bible study experience, the guiding expectation of meeting together is to cultivate intimacy and thereby grow in personal faith. As I outlined above, this directly aligns with a central theme of Evangelical culture: imagining a spirituality consumed with intimate relationships. This argument is representative of the larger project sample but takes on an exaggerated form with the Prayer Circle. It is striking how inclined they are to this aim, how deeply it is ingrained, and how closely they adhere to this logic. They use three ways, in particular, to cultivate this frame of intimacy: the meeting structure, Bible reading, and prayer.

"THIS is Christianity"

Meeting Structure

Ethnographers of language have repeatedly shown that the organization, format, and method of an event contain important lessons about what cultural work it accomplishes (e.g., Frake 1964). When I first began attending the Prayer Circle in January 2005, Darren was solely responsible for planning the meetings. During the two-week period between each meeting, Darren listened closely to "what God had been speaking to [him] about." Based on God's prompting, Darren chose a study topic intended to "further everyone's relationship with God." In addition to his own thoughts, Darren selected biblical texts that exemplified the lesson. These were usually texts that Darren "felt led to," often arriving in his consciousness in the wee hours of the morning when he was unable to sleep. Examples of topics included "My Body: God's Temple," "Stop Grumbling among Yourselves," "Jesus' First Miracle," "King Saul and his Sin," and "'Interruptions' or 'Bumps' in the Road of Life." This last lesson was based on Acts 16:16–30, the account of Paul and Silas being arrested in Rome, beaten, imprisoned, and eventually praising God in jail. Darren poses five questions on the study handout, asking the group to identify "unpleasant people issues," "sickness and suffering issues," "family issues," "financial issues," and "spiritual issues." For each, he asks what "characteristics to learn" can be gleaned from the story in Acts. This combination of scripture reading and personal application typified the first few meetings I observed.

The group would spend anywhere from twenty-five to thirty-five minutes discussing Darren's lesson. They then transitioned to a period of prayer that lasted just as long as the study proper. Each participant spent several minutes informing the group of their "prayer requests" and "praise reports" from the preceding and upcoming weeks. Darren provided everyone a sheet divided into equal blocks of space reserved to write down each person's requests and reports. These sheets filled up after two or three meetings, at which point Darren furnished new ones. Following the last person's requests and reports, Darren systematically prayed for each individual in turn. He rarely skipped any of the specific points that had just been given. The others bowed their heads and prayed silently, sporadically echoing affirmations of "Yes, Lord" and "Thank you, God."

The group had followed this meeting structure since the end of Forty Days of Purpose in mid-2003. If Darren was absent for some reason, someone else would lead in his stead mimicking this format. As far as I know all of the members were pleased with this approach. The attendance was consistently high and no one expressed any overt objection or boredom about the method. However, at the end of my third recording, Darren proposed a new format he was excited to implement:

Okay, I had this thought. I've been reading this book called *Cultivating a Life for God* [Cole 1999], and the author talks about getting together in triads and holding one another accountable and encouraging one another. It involves prayer, confession, reading the Bible, and outreach. Then, what they do is they come together. They don't have a leader. Each one shares what God's been teaching them through what they've been reading. And I thought, "We ought to try that some time." So, here was the thought: read [the New Testament book of] James. It's got five chapters. I think you can read it in about twenty minutes. And what if we attempted, between now and two weeks from tonight, to read James everyday. And let's say the minimum is that we do it ten times. And that's not sitting down and reading James ten times in one day. It's reading James ten days or more. Now, my guess is if we spend that much time in James, God's gonna teach us something.

Everyone present—Beverly, Julie, Jenny, and Tanya—received the idea with great enthusiasm. Their appreciation for the proposed method is directly traceable to its resonance with the idea of an intimate spirituality. "Accountability," "encouragement," and "sharing" are all key signifiers in the Evangelical lexicon of building relationships. Replacing "a leader" with God as the primary teacher ostensibly places everyone on equal footing, engendering an environment where relationships are more egalitarian. And connecting Bible reading and learning from God places the individual believer in direct communion with the Almighty. The group resumed meeting two weeks later, with all nine members except Tanya present. They had their Bibles in hand and their teachings ready to share. Darren went first and they moved around the circle clockwise. Julie, for example, commented on a verse that "convicted" her:

[James 3:9] says *we give blessings to the Lord and then we curse from the same mouth.* It really convicted me on my interactions with other people that I show grace and compassion and that I not be judgmental. And one example was this snowstorm we got within the last two weeks. And my sister and I live in a duplex. I have this shovel that I bought two years ago. I don't care if she uses it. But oftentimes when it snows she uses it and then she leaves it way on the other side of her house. I've asked her time and time again, "Will you please put the shovel back?" So, that morning when I woke up and there was all this snow and I was running late for work, the shovel wasn't there. So, I had to go get it from her side of the house. So, I shoveled my drive and I put my shovel in the house and left for work. Well, she called me at work and said, "Do you have the shovel?" I said, "Yes. It's in my house." She was very upset and hung up. I was really convicted. I realized I didn't handle that in the best way.

Julie's narrative speaks directly to the Evangelical concern with relationships, using an encounter with her sister as an iconic representation for what she is striving to achieve in all her "interactions with other people." This sequence of reading, sharing, and moving on to the next participant continued until all eight had spoken. Everyone read at least one verse but more often read multiple verses. Their contributions always consisted of an example from their life—sometimes generic but usually specific—to demonstrate the veracity and relevance of the text. On some occasions the truth was one they were living out, illustrating how the text confirmed them. At other times, as with Julie, the truth was one they were failing to live out, illustrating how the text convicted them. Further discussion about what someone shared rarely ensued. Instead, participants listened intently and allowed one another to speak uninterrupted. Cultivating intimacy emphasizes the detailed "sharing" of participants' personal struggles and victories. The aim of meeting together is to grow spiritually through increased fellowship, signified here by exchanging how their patterns of thought and behavior aligned and broke with biblical ideals. The group moved back and forth among applications as diverse as sibling troubles, occupational hazards, parent-child relations, the woes of being single, and marital issues. These applications traversed theological principles of trust, obedience, prayer, love, forgiveness, and punishment. Yet, attention to such principles was a tacit affair, and the explicit focus remained on the concrete examples identified in the lives of group members.

After everyone shared, Darren and others reflected on this new meeting structure:

Darren: James is so convicting. I mean, James is so much different than most of the other books of the New Testament, especially Paul's letters or even Jude. This is just such practical stuff. I didn't expect it to happen, but can you imagine someone reading this regularly and then coming to a group to discuss it and say, "I didn't find anything applicable in there?"

Jenny: Mhmm. . . .

Darren: It just talks to us where we are. And wow, I've read James. I've memorized James. But I've never read it all the way through several days in a row. Wow. That's good stuff.

Julie: Mhmm.

Darren: But I think it goes beyond James. I mean, this is what Julie and I had talked about with this book *Cultivating a Life for God*. They meet in triads, once a week, and their assignment from one week to the next is to read thirty chapters of scripture. I often read that many chapters, but not the same thing over and over again. I just found it was really encouraging.

Jenny: Mhmm.

Julie: I just want to say I liked it a lot because I've been trying to read through on a regular basis, trying to work my way through the Bible. But the thing I liked about this, because I actually felt like it was more of a study, that I became so familiar with material, that not only did something new pop out to me all the time, but it was also because I became so much more familiar with it. I was able to teach it in a way.

Mary: Use parts of it, yeah. . . .

Jenny: When I read, I'm a horrible reader. So, like, I can read the whole chapter and couldn't tell you what it's about. I didn't read this everyday, but I did read it a lot. And I finally got through the whole thing where I could say, "Oh yeah, I remember that! I remember that!" So, that was really good.

The group's positive evaluation of the method is clear. They emphasize its uniqueness compared to other ways that they have read scripture. And they attribute to the method a hypersensitivity toward making biblical relevance apparent.

The Prayer Circle's revised format exemplifies how the frame of intimacy is constructed. The Bible study experience provides an opportunity to reveal what remains hidden in the rest of these believers' everyday interactions. For this reason it serves as a unique event in their lives, one they distinguish from all other social encounters. They anticipate each meeting for the chance to unburden themselves: sometimes excitedly for what they learned, sometimes anxiously for what they feel compelled to divulge. Bible study, in turn, becomes a space defined by an increasing knowledge of one another's preoccupations, worries, joys, and questions. And the process of collective reading becomes the avenue through which this knowledge is constructed. "Sharing" is a particularly powerful signifier in the Evangelical lexicon. It carries the specific denotations of trust, vulnerability, openness, and ultimately, intimacy. The lack of dialogue following individuals' contributions is equally striking. By not responding to what is "shared," group participants respond to their guiding expectation. They are there for support, not advice; to listen and pray, not listen and correct or critique. This conversational ideology also accounts for the near total lack of disagreements and tense interpretive situations that inevitably arise in other groups. Occasionally, individuals were asked to elaborate on what they intended, but never was someone's application disputed or their treatment of scripture criticized. Darren's method, and the group's eager reaction, defines the event of Bible study as one that is about the continued cultivation of close, intimate interpersonal relations. This, in turn, feeds the lifelong effort to become closer to God.

Given Darren's level of authority in the group, it might be assumed that he chose the texts for the remaining nine meetings. Not so. It was common procedure for everyone to agree on the first text suggested, reinforcing the sense of egalitarianism introduced by removing the presence of "a leader." The choice of choosing the study text, in fact, fell to Darren only twice more. On several occasions, though, suggestions were quietly ignored or questioned because they were not suspected to serve well for this new method. Revelation, Isaiah, and several Old Testament prophets were all considered "not as easy to apply." Consider this alongside Darren's closing statements following their reading of 2 Timothy:

> This is different than what we've read before in Colossians, Ephesians, and Philippians. Those were written to groups of people. This was written to a person. And wow, you can just see the relationship. I mean, in 1 and 2 Corinthians Paul talks about the relationship with the church in Corinth and how much he loved them. But here, it's more intimate, not so general. We just gotta love this. You know, we thought James was so applicable. But 1 and 2 Timothy and Titus are too because they're so personal and personable.

Evangelicals are full of ideas about the Bible. Not only do they have specific notions about scripture as a whole, they have well-formed thoughts regarding individual books. This reminds us of Brian Malley's distinction between principle and practice in Bible belief (2004: 143–44; see chapter 2). In reference to biblical authority, he describes a difference between what Evangelicals say about scripture and what they actually do with scripture. The same can be argued here regarding biblical relevance. The ideology of a full commitment to the entire Bible's ongoing relevance, from Genesis to Revelation, exists alongside a clear preference for certain texts over others when it comes to finding application.

Bible Reading

The format of the Prayer Circle's meetings begins their ongoing attempt to cultivate fellowship, intimacy, and spiritual development. It continues with their practice of Bible reading and interpretation. In chapter 2 we saw the ideological principle of biblical relevance and the resulting strategy of applying scriptural texts to the everyday life of the reader. The LCMS Men, along with most other project groups, moved between this and other interpretive styles. They read (and refused to read) scripture as promise, created intertextual linkages, set up apparent contradictions to be resolved, explored the inferential gaps of texts, dwelt on individual words and figurative meanings, recounted biblical history, and composed intricate allegorical parallels. The Prayer Circle, however, was far more restricted in their reading of scripture.

In eleven group meetings they studied ten different biblical texts: James, Ephesians, Philippians, Colossians, 2 Timothy, Habbakuk, Psalm 119, Hebrews, 1 John, and Acts. During these meetings there was a total of seventy-three "sharings": discrete contributions from individual participants, such as Julie's from above. Of these, only eight (around 11 percent) included any consideration of textual meaning outside the range of personal application. In all eight cases the question was handled promptly and discussion proceeded to matters of relevance. For example, in their second meeting following the revised format they read the New Testament Epistle to the Ephesians. The meeting began with the following exchange between Darren and Matt:

> Darren: I think 1:4-5[2] says something about pre-destination.
> Matt: [[Laughs]] I'm gonna skip over that part.
> Darren: Okay, probably a good idea.
> Matt: It is one of those passages that, it's one of the things, I was raised Calvinist and made the change back in 1999/2000 [to] come over to [RMC].
> It's one of those issues of the Bible, is the free will versus predestination that I struggled with and see support texts for both sides; still a little on the confused side on both.

Matt then began to talk about two verses that he "always come[s] back around to" and that "always amaze" him. In doing so he leaves behind the complex, historically significant theological problem of predestined salvation. One can imagine a lengthy discussion about Calvinist and Armenian soteriologies, the proof-texts for each, and the tensions it causes in Christian communities and individual psychologies. After all, the two participants are both well versed in these distinctions; one is an ordained minister and the other is a church elder. Instead, it garners only a hesitant laugh and a nod to its divisive potential.

Several meetings later, during their reading of 2 Timothy, Julie expressed confusion about a metaphor for righteousness used in 2:20–21:[3]

> Julie: And then the other thing, and I could just use, I read this a couple of
>   times and probably didn't spend as much time trying to figure it out, is
>   2 [Timothy] starting with verse 20. [[Reads 2 Timothy 2:20–21]] And I
>   really felt like I needed to sit to think about that. And a couple of times
>   that I, I started to feel like I could get wrapped into it, and then I'd be like,
>   [[shakes head in frustration]].
> Mary: You know, I looked at that as well.
> Jenny: I did too.
> Julie: And I should have gotten . . . I have a Nelson's Study Bible. And I meant
>   to take that down. You know, because you got a different, and then to see
>   what it said there about it. And I never got to that point. But I read it in
>   both the NIV and the King James Version, you know, trying to figure out
>   what it said. And I don't know. So, I guess I would really appreciate any-
>   thing anyone has to say about it.
> Jenny: I have a Study Bible right here.
> Julie: Do you? What does it say about it?

After Jenny reads the footnote, the group, led by Julie, praises the explanation for being "right on." Instead of first venturing some ideas about
the text's intended meaning, they defer immediately to the footnote and
accept its interpretation without question. Bible footnotes are often consulted when groups face difficult interpretive questions, but they are uniformly detached from the principle of authority assigned to scripture itself.
In other groups, footnotes were frequently challenged, if not dismissed
altogether. When other groups did agree with a footnote, they would not
dispense with considering alternative interpretations. Rather, they would

use it as a springboard to their own preferred readings. It is striking, then, how quietly this text enters their discussion and how quickly it passes through.

In a third example, the group makes somewhat different use of a footnote. Beverly was the last to share for their reading of 1 John:

> Beverly: Well, I have to confess, there were many things that I noted. But I never wrote anything down. But back on chapter 5, I thought verse 6 was interesting: *This is the one who came by water and blood—Jesus Christ. He did not come by water only, but by water and blood. And it is the Spirit who testifies, because the Spirit is the truth. For there are three that testify: the Spirit, the water and the blood; and the three are in agreement.*
>
> Julie: I didn't understand *the water.*
>
> Beverly: Is that referring to baptism?
>
> Julie: That's what I was wondering. Or, is it referring back to Noah and the flood?
>
> Darren: No. Sometimes when you talk about coming by water that's physical birth. But I believe that he's talking about a spiritual birth here, which I do believe is baptism. If you go back in the Gospel of John, especially in the third chapter, he talks about a similar thing.
>
> Julie: I'm glad you pointed that out, Beverly, because I had that stuck in my head and I forgot about it.
>
> Matt: The commentary makes another possibility. "[Jesus] came by water and blood. The water, his baptism, was the beginning of his ministry and his death was the end of his ministry. *He comes by water and the blood,* is the length of time of his ministry on earth."

In reading his footnote, Matt introduces a second interpretation of this text from 1 John. Is it referring to baptism or is it an analogical statement about Jesus' ministry on earth? The group devotes no energy to untangling the two possibilities. After Matt finishes reading, Darren closes the meeting. This is precisely the type of situation in which other groups would employ different hermeneutic strategies, thereby exploiting the polysemy and richness of scriptural meaning. The Prayer Circle, however, shows little inclination to indulge discussions removed from the process of personal application.

In all three of these cases, as with the remaining five, various problems of textual meaning are given only the briefest attention. Why not spend a moment hashing out the question of predestination? Why not capitalize on the Bible's rich use of metaphor and imagery and muse on its implications? Why not affirm one reading over another and refuse to let multiple interpretations linger? The answer, I believe, is found in the power of the frame of intimacy and the hold it has on this group's conduct. Anything not directly related to nurturing relationships is set aside for individuals to consider on their own or perhaps in a different set of Christian company. But while in the confines of this setting, the focus should stay fixed on cultivating intimacy through connecting the Bible to everyday life.

In addition to this rather bounded situation of collective reading, certain literacy and interpretive procedures were dismissed that outsiders might think to be taken for granted. For example, there was a freedom from following the sequential order of biblical passages. Prayer Circle participants combined verses from different chapters of the same book as if they appeared back-to-back, to articulate a common narrative of relevance. Julie was the fifth person to share from the book of James. Finding various points of connection, she read aloud and commented on 1:19, 2:13, 5:9, 4:6, and 3:1. The other members similarly avoided the sentence-to-sentence progression as presented in scripture. Instead, they connected separate texts, ignoring the verses in between. Mary was the first to share for the second meeting on Hebrews. She read verses 22 to 39 from chapter 10, interspersing her own commentary. In doing so, she skipped over verses 25, 27 to 28, 30, 32 to 34, and 37 to 38. However, none of these interpretive strategies are problematic, because the entire activity of reading scripture is bound together by a common search: "How is God speaking to me through His Word?" It is perfectly within God's prerogative to highlight isolated verses, and not others, for the individual who is reading. As a result, elements such as narrative context become subsumed by the search for personal application.

Counterintuitively, Prayer Circle participants did not hesitate to repeat verses that had already been discussed. It is easy to imagine a scenario in which readers avoided commenting on texts that had already been raised, both to fight against tiresome duplication and to exhibit some originality in their contribution. However, this, too, poses no trouble because God can use the same verse to speak to each person in different ways. In fact, such repetition ensures a clear demonstration of the ideological principle of relevance—where the same words find new expression from reader to reader.

This rearrangement of hermeneutic norms buttresses the central purpose of cultivating intimacy. Patterning human relationships on the model of a close, personal relationship with God is accomplished best by establishing the relevance of biblical texts, not pursuing other questions of meaning. The lessons of God's Word are most easily seen through their manifestation in individuals' life circumstances, not through examining the semantic, stylistic, or generic properties of the text. Although interesting, such questions are more of a distraction from their primary aim of meeting together. Darren's treatment of Bible translations provides a final example of this single-minded interpretive environment.

Julie had a fond attachment to her copy of *The Extreme Word* (2001). It was the Bible she bought several years ago when she began "taking her faith seriously again," and has accompanied her on ministry trips to Vancouver and Ireland. It was well worn, with dog-eared edges, a crinkled cover, highlighted verses, and jottings throughout the folded and slightly torn pages. She liked its study notes and chapter summaries, a feature that aided her personal Bible study. *The Extreme Word* is a New King James (NKJV) translation—a "literal" translation in which the language is generally thought to be aesthetically pleasing but conceptually difficult (Dewey 2004). Julie often brought this and other NKJV Bibles to group meetings. Just as often, Darren teased her about not using a Bible written "in English." During their study of Colossians, the following exchange occurred as she read Colossians 3:12–14:

Julie: *Therefore as the elective God, holy and beloved, put on tender mercies: kindness, humility, meekness, longsuffering, bearing with one another, and forgiving one another. If anyone has a complaint against another, even as Christ forgave you, so you also must do. But, of all these things, put on love, which is the bond of perfection.* I like that a lot, *the putting on the love.*

Darren: Wait a minute: *Above all these things, put on love, which is the bond of perfection.* What does that mean?

Julie: Well, the way that I thought about it, like for several months, probably, for close to a year, I've been praying a lot about learning to love God the way He loves me and learning to love His people the way He loves them.

Darren: Well, with that version you have to translate it into understandable English, because that sounded kind of mysterious: *the bond of love*, or, *the bond of perfection*, or whatever.

What strikes me about this exchange is Darren's description of the text as "mysterious." In other groups, awkward translations were described as "ambiguous," "confusing," or other terms that indicated a problem in understanding the referential meaning of the text. Darren's reaction, however, approaches the difficulty of the translation from a different vantage point. For him, an appropriate translation should not be "mysterious" but obvious in its relevance. Translations, much like theological debates, should not disrupt the process of seeking application and, in turn, the continued effort of building relationships with each other. Along with their meeting structure, then, the Prayer Circle relies on a specific set of Bible reading practices to uphold their frame of cultivating intimacy. Defining what the Bible study experience is all about is partly a matter of establishing what forms of hermeneutic activity are acceptable and which are impediments to achieving this spiritual goal.

Prayer

In her analysis of Evangelical intimacy, Tanya Luhrmann stresses the integral role of individual prayer as well as discussions of how to pray in developing an experiential spirituality. For the Prayer Circle, the collective performance of prayer is equally a part of their overall effort to cultivate intimacy. I previously described the Prayer Circle members' method for praying at the end of each meeting. This, in itself, speaks to the value they place on building relationships. Their prayer requests and praise reports were often extensive and the subject matter very personal. Among other matters, participants raised issues of emotional turmoil, spiritual struggle, troubles with romantic relationships, and difficulties with their children. The level of trust infused in these exchanges is heightened by the fact that everything they say is written down by everyone else, documented and recalled from week to week. The place of prayer in the life of the Prayer Circle and its role in fostering intimacy is crystallized by another change of format suggested by Darren.

For the group's sixth meeting they read the book of Habakkuk, a minor prophet in the Old Testament. Julie was the first person to share. She went about this in the manner she had become accustomed to in the previous five meetings. Once she finished, Darren asked, "So, I had this idea, can we turn that into a prayer request somehow?" He wanted each person to connect what God taught during their reading with their prayer requests, integrating the discussion and prayer portions of the meeting. Julie adapted effortlessly, transitioning without pause into what she had prepared to raise for prayer. The other six members present that night followed suit, making direct connections between the application they found in scripture and the requests they had for prayer. They continued with this slightly adjusted format for the remaining five meetings in my fieldwork. However, with each new meeting, members devoted less and less time to sharing their reflections from Bible reading and more and more time to talking about their prayer requests. By the final meeting, in which they read the first half of the New Testament book of Acts, it was common for a single Bible verse and a few sentences of commentary to be followed by five minutes or more of prayer requests.

Consider the very tangible comparison between the number of typed transcript pages that resulted from their discussions of the Bible in their first few meetings versus their last few. The first three meetings required twelve, seven, and nine pages, respectively, while the last three meetings were all less than four pages in length. These last three meetings were no shorter in length, they simply reflect a lack of interest in discussing the text in favor of praying.

This inclination toward prayer confirms the dominance of the frame of intimacy. While Bible reading undoubtedly helps the effort to cultivate interpersonal relationships, it still requires the medium of the text and the mediating process of reading and study. Prayer requests and praise reports are a more direct means of inviting others into one's personal life and thus a more direct line to satisfying the guiding expectations about the Bible study experience.

The prevailing notion of what group Bible study is all about for the Prayer Circle is clearly that of cultivating intimacy. Their expectations for this social encounter are rather unambiguous: they desire an increased closeness in their personal relationships with each other, ultimately strengthening their relationship with God. They create this by sharing the personally rewarding and personally troubling aspects of their private lives with one another. Toward this end, they structure their biweekly meetings so that the maximum amount of sharing occurs. They organize their Bible reading so that they do not get distracted by questions of semantics or textuality and can focus instead on making their worries and joys explicit by matching their experience with biblical texts. Last, they prioritize the role of prayer, elevating it above biblical commentary in the amount of energy they devote to each activity during their time together. The Prayer Circle's strict adherence to this frame of intimacy is crystallized by Darren's response to the church Bible study director's request that the group accept several new members who wanted to join a group. He suggested that the Prayer Circle cap their size to ensure their progress toward building closer relationships would not be disrupted. The other participants eagerly agreed, recognizing the potential hurdle to spiritual growth posed by newcomers unaccustomed to this level of intimacy or not willing to openly share in the same way. An exchange at the close of the sixth meeting between Darren and Mary summarizes the framing of Bible study as a matter of cultivating intimacy:

> Darren: I think it is so healthy, spiritually, for Beverly and I to be a part of this group. You allow us, and we do the same for you, to come here and say, "Phew. This is what's going on in my life. This is what we need to have you pray for." I mean, *this* is Christianity.
>
> Mary: That's what Matt and I said, too. This is a very unusual group. You know, so many groups you're a part of you never break the surface. You guys share a lot of things that wouldn't always be spoken.
>
> Darren: Yeah. You know, life is too short not to be involved in that type of Christianity. And I hope our group never changes to the superficial stuff.

Intimacy with a History

The life of the Prayer Circle illustrates well how deeply the want for greater intimacy is embedded in Evangelical culture. The "problem of presence" (Engelke 2007) that pervades Christian culture is met head on in the context of American Evangelicalism, as Evangelicals promote a spirituality that is defined by intimacy with God and intimacy with fellow believers. Every group decision, every group practice, seems to be oriented toward nurturing this type of spiritual environment. Moreover, the example of the Prayer Circle clearly demonstrates that group Bible study is a primary site of learning for this approach to religious life. More so than isolated practices of reading, worship, or prayer, Bible study provides an ideal space to cultivate this attitude through combining various practices and performing them collectively.

I used the concept of "interactive frames" (Tannen 1993) to draw out the many ways Prayer Circle participants achieve this goal and define what this event is all about. As Evangelicals seek out a Bible study group to join, choose among the available groups in their congregation, and decide whether or not to continue attending a particular group, they are guided by their expectations for what a group should be like. What do I want from my participation in a Bible study group? What should we do together? How should the meeting time be organized and prioritized? Why opt for certain practices at the expense of others? For many Evangelicals, as represented by the exaggerated case of the Prayer Circle, the answer to these questions continually returns to intimacy. Through the course of designing a specific format, reading the Bible, and praying, the Prayer Circle participants have made a clear statement to themselves about how they understand the experience of Bible study and what they want from it.

In concluding her 2004 essay, Tanya Luhrmann asks the all-important question, "Why now?" (526). Why are we witnessing a profusion of this form of spirituality among Evangelicals at this moment in American history? She proposes two preliminary answers. First, the rise of modern media—from television to the Internet—has altered the perceptual tendencies of Americans. More than ever, due to the constant stream of images, words, and sounds, we are inclined to lose ourselves in states of inner subjectivity. Luhrmann cites the rather mundane but quite compelling example of a lone traveler set apart from her social surround and engulfed in a world of music through headphones. Second, Luhrmann argues that the set of social relationships that Americans experience has become both sparse and superficial. We are "increasingly disconnected from friends, family, and neighbors through both formal and informal structures" (527). Here, she appeals to Robert Putnam's *Bowling Alone* (2000), a widely cited sociological work that attempts to identify exactly what those "formal and informal structures" are. While I am not in a position to refute or support either of these claims, I would like to close this chapter by commenting on both and presenting yet a third possibility for why Evangelical spirituality looks the way it does as the 21st century gets underway.

On the whole, I find Luhrmann's two explanations intriguing but not thoroughly convincing. Cultural changes in perception and subjective experience due to media and technology could account for religious practices such as trance, which involve an altered state of consciousness. Perhaps it is the case that the cultural training our bodies and subjectivities experience as Americans helps create an environment in which religious expression follows suit. However, this proposition fails to account for the intricate notions of intimacy and relationships that actually define Evangelical spirituality. This explanation seems to conflate the experiential-bodily element of spirituality with the cognitive-emotional model of intimacy.

We have, then, the appeal to the American societal trend of a decreasing quantity and quality of interpersonal relationships. In this formulation, Evangelicals are reacting to a broader cultural change, seeking a sense of community among themselves because there is none to be found elsewhere. A debilitating problem with this explanation is one of time. Assuming that American society has experienced a steady decline in interpersonal support over the past half-century, this social fact is at least contemporaneous with (and more likely predated by) an Evangelical spirituality defined by intimacy. If this explanation was spot on, we would expect to see Evangelicals responding some years after the social fact of isolation had set in among Americans. This is simply not the case. And for both explanations—perceptual and interpersonal change—we are asked to look to the wider cultural surround of which Evangelicals are a part, not to Evangelicals themselves.

How might we explain the intimate, relational spirituality of Evangelicals—and of groups like the Prayer Circle—by appealing to the history of Evangelicalism? The third possibility I raise here does just that. Dating to at least the late 18th century in America, Evangelical movements have constructed discourses that advocate a "return to first-century Christianity," and a "restoration" of New Testament church life (Conkin 1997: 1–56). These American "restorationists" (note: not "reformers") advanced both theological and ecclesiological changes: opposition to Episcopal hierarchy, rejection of strict denominationalism, and hesitancy toward charisma (Conkin 1997: 1–56). More than anything, though, these Christians wanted their everyday religious lives to be defined by deep, spiritually rewarding, and intimate relationships, both with other believers and with the God of the universe. The descendants of these restorationists are many and varied, but most all have moved from small sectarian interests to internationally established organizational structures. One outgrowth of these early American roots, in fact, is the denominational home of the Prayer Circle: the Restoration Movement Church in America. My suggestion, then, is this: between the late 1700s and the late 1900s, the notion of an intimate, relational spirituality became infused in the religious imagination of all streams of Evangelicalism. At various points it has become crystallized in unique movements such as the neocharismatic Jesus Movement of the 1960s and 70s (Miller 1997) and the ecumenical emerging Church "conversation" beginning in the late 1990s (Bielo forthcoming). Enveloping all of these individual trajectories, the idea of an intimate spirituality has become habitual in storefront churches and middle-class, suburban megachurches. It is this longstanding conviction that may best explain why Evangelical spirituality looks the way it does—and why the Prayer Circle was so excited to read the book of James every day for two weeks.

* 4 *

Integrating Participant Interests

Janet Simmons is the small group director at a suburban United Methodist Church. Once a month she holds a leadership "huddle" after the second Sunday morning worship service. The monthly huddle is a gathering
of the church's Bible study facilitators, usually between ten and fifteen individuals. The primary goal is to have facilitators exchange updates about
their groups, discuss ideas for improvement, and trade potential study
resources. Ethnographically, it was a convenient way for me to moni-
tor what each group was doing. More important, it was an opportunity
to hear evaluative commentary from the facilitators of groups I was observing. At the February 2005 huddle, I was especially interested in what
Charlie would say.

Charlie is a very handsome man in his early fifties with curly, silver-
streaked hair and a well-managed physique. He was also among the most
articulate and energetic facilitators I had encountered, and I realized early
on in my fieldwork that he spoke his mind freely, without hesitation. During our conversations before and after group meetings, he was perfectly
willing to evaluate the other Bible study members: their personal backgrounds, theological positions, and roles within the group. Most of the
facilitators at the huddle were reluctant (or unable) to say much of substance about the dynamics of their group. However, when Charlie's turn
arrived, he met Janet's inquiries head on:

> Really, the group is a collection of pseudo-rebels and iconoclasts. They
> are extremely studious and intense. They don't want anything to do with
> popular culture, and they love to nibble on controversial topics. Right
> now we're reading Philip Yancey's *The Jesus I Never Knew* [1995], which
> we love. We did the Ortberg [2001, *If You Want to Walk on Water, You've
> Got to Get Out of the Boat*] and Warren [2002, *The Purpose Driven Life*]
> studies before that, which none of us could stand.

The "Ortberg and Warren studies" were both congregation-wide programs selected by Janet and the church's senior pastor. I came to learn that this type of unapologetic evaluation is vintage Charlie.

Despite Charlie's group's aversion to her choice of study materials, Janet was quick to recommend his group to me during my first meeting with her in September 2004. She (correctly) suspected that the group would be eager participants in the project. I remember my first presentation of the research to them and the absence of any skeptical or tentative reactions. Their initial response, in fact, was to be "the best group in the project." They laughed and warned me of their competitive streak. As usual, Charlie found a way to synthesize everyone's comments: "If all the other groups bring in fifty cans of beans [to the food drive], we'll bring a hundred."

Charlie's group, "The Iconoclasts," are a collection of five married couples and two single women. Most of the group was in their late forties and early fifties, though the youngest couple was in their early thirties and one of the women was in her early sixties. They met every Sunday evening in Charlie and Diane's living room: an open space, always immaculately clean, with tall ceilings and neatly arranged furniture. The group began meeting in 2002 when Charlie facilitated one of the *Forty Days of Purpose* home groups. Much of Charlie's adult years were spent in the neocharismatic Vineyard Fellowship, where his most profound spiritual memories are tied to Bible study groups. When the opportunity arose in 2002 to facilitate a group at this church, he anxiously volunteered. Half of the twelve members were in a Sunday school class together several years earlier, which Charlie also led. While they did not share the same level of intimacy as the Prayer Circle, they were clearly fond of each other and spent time before and after meetings talking, laughing, trading books, and planning social events.

The group is well educated, with nearly everyone holding a bachelor's degree and several with advanced degrees. Charlie and Diane own a private consulting business for large, pharmaceutical corporations. Others' occupations include an ex-Olympic weightlifter/part-time community college instructor, several elementary school teachers, a church music director, a geologist for the state, and a social worker for the state prison system. The group's twelve members also hail from a variety of Protestant backgrounds. Before his years with the Vineyard, Charlie grew up in a fundamentalist, independent Baptist family. Others had significant experiences with Lutheran, Brethren, and American Baptist denominations, and several were lifelong United Methodists. Despite this mixed set of religious backgrounds, the group adhered closely (though, not dogmatically) to conservative Evangelical doctrines. Linda—the unmarried woman and the oldest member—was a notable exception. Aside from Charlie and Diane, Linda was the most faithful in her attendance, only missing one of sixteen meetings in the study of *The Jesus I Never Knew*. Linda had actually stopped attending worship services at the United Methodist church, but her enthusiasm had not waned for the Iconoclasts. Yet, her nonorthodox theological comments were a blatant anomaly, and they were ignored or quickly refuted by the other participants. On one occasion, she denied the exclusivity of Christ for salvation, arguing for a universalist soteriology. On another, she denied the Bible's complete divine authorship, arguing that the early Catholic Church had wrongly (insidiously?) canonized scripture. The others' comfort with Linda despite her theological differences likely emerges from their status as "seeker" Evangelicals (Roof 1999), namely their conviction that doubting and questioning are helpful (often necessary) for an individual's spiritual "journey."

Similar to the LCMS Men, the Iconoclasts always enjoyed lively discussions. Their general interactive frame was more about intimacy than textual analysis but certainly not to the extreme degree of the Prayer Circle. Charlie's dynamic leadership style combined with the eager participation of several members to make silences rare. Brief bouts of intellectual sparring, often around controversial topics, were reliable as well. During the course of reading *The Jesus I Never Knew*, the group devoted extended discussion to historical and textual proofs for the veracity of the Bible, the problem of theodicy regarding the 2004 Asian tsunami, Wesleyan theological ideals of purity and holiness, New Testament statements about women, and the proper relationship between scientific knowledge and religious faith. The Iconoclasts' reading of *The Jesus I Never Knew* demonstrates an important theme in Bible study life: the structuring force of participants' shared interests on religious reading.

Subtexts for Reading

The act of reading is a thoroughly social one. Even when we read alone we do so with a host of culturally informed notions about what we are reading, how best to read, and what the very activity of reading entails (Long 1993). Group Bible study exemplifies the claim that "not only is all reading socially embedded, but indeed a great deal of reading is done in social groups" (Boyarin 1993: 4). This raises the issue of how the act of reading socially compares with being a solitary reader and what can be gleaned from examining contexts where collective reading occurs. Echoing Stanley Fish (1980) and other reader-response theorists, Elizabeth Long (2003) argues that the ethnographic study of reading ought to shift its attention from being a writer-centered to a reader-centered (22) enterprise. By relocating the focus from writers to readers, we are effectively imagining "reading as one kind of cultural practice, a form of behavior that performs complex personal and social functions for those who engage in it" (22). This is particularly resonant in contexts of collective reading, in which there are multiple interactions managed among readers and between readers and their texts. In the case of the Iconoclasts, we might ask why they read *The Jesus I Never Knew* the way they did and not otherwise.

To answer this question I take a cue from Elizabeth Long's historical and ethnographic work with female book clubs (1993; 2003). Long spent several years locating and observing a variety of female reading groups in the Houston, Texas, area with the hope of understanding why this social phenomenon is so significant for "everyday readers." She makes the astute observation that reading groups often form, stay together, and look past potentially severe differences because they have a "subtext" (1993: 194): some intersection of shared values, interests, or passions that bind them into a cohesive social unit. This subtext of mutual interests and common social ground structures much of what happens within group life, namely what they choose to read and how they go about reading it. Long gives the example of a "feminist group" to illustrate how "sociopolitical allegiances condition engagement with books" (202). She describes how the group members' concern with feminist epistemology distinguished their reading practices from other groups, creating an environment that is recognizably "focused and academic" in tone.[1] The subtexts for reading that Long presents, ultimately, are a concrete means of applying reader-response ideas regarding interpretive communities (Fish 1980). If we are to argue that reading is a culturally embedded activity and that readers arrive at shared interpretations through shared hermeneutic avenues, then we must be able to map the actual processes that give life to these assertions. An analysis of subtexts in situations of social reading does just this.

Much like other contexts of collective reading, Bible study groups coalesce and continue meeting because individual members share certain passions with one another. Groups bond, in part, because they are participants in the same religious tradition but also because they are able to relate and connect to one another for other reasons. The subtexts for reading in group Bible study, as with Long's female book clubs, provide a filter through which texts are chosen, read, interpreted, and debated.

In chapter 2 we saw that Evangelicals relied on a shared textual ideology surrounding the Bible to structure their scripture reading practices. Here we shift the focus from deeply ingrained presuppositions about the nature of a text itself to the type of common social ground entailed in the concept of "subtexts." We do so for the purpose of analyzing the Iconoclasts' reading of *The Jesus I Never Knew*, not a sacred text for Evangelicals and therefore not a text afforded the type of ideological attention that scripture receives. Yet, reading this text was still religious reading and so remained a vital medium through which these Evangelicals imagined and reflected on who they are and what they do.

This is a particularly important shift of attention because it reaches outside the confines of a strictly religious imagination. In the case of the Iconoclasts, their reading of *The Jesus I Never Knew* is organized by a devotion to "history" as a category of knowledge. Of course, venerating this particular knowledge source is not terribly surprising given the cultural capital of history in contemporary American society. One need look no further than the success of David McCullough biographies, History Channel hysteria, or the size of the history section in the nearest Barnes & Noble to see the popularity of this discourse on a national scale. As Charlie and Dave (the husband of the youngest couple) were fond of joking, "Heaven has gotta be like perpetual History Channel and *Band of Brothers* movie night." The group's mutual love and appreciation for history—rather than anything that is solely religious, Christian, or Evangelical—is what grounds the hermeneutic work they do with Yancey's book. Yet, as we will see in the group's interactions, members use the subtext of history to reach back into their religious imagination, illuminating themes of Evangelical theology, language, and ideology. In short, this analysis of history as the Iconoclasts' subtext for reading is ultimately an analysis of Evangelical culture. We begin with their text of study: Philip Yancey's *The Jesus I Never Knew*.

The Jesus I Never Knew

When I first met the Iconoclasts in October 2004 they were finishing a book-video series selected by Janet and the church pastor: John Ortberg's *If You Want to Walk on Water, You Got to Get Out of the Boat* (2001). Ortberg is a widely published Evangelical author who originally came to prominence as a teaching pastor for Willow Creek Community Church (see chapter 1). His books are frequently used in Bible study groups, and several have achieved a wide circulation within this local United Methodist Church. As part of a church-wide initiative, all of the home groups were reading the same material and, ideally, reading at the same pace. The premise of this approach, according to Janet, was to foster a greater sense of community belonging and common purpose within a rapidly growing congregation.[2] However, aside from ridiculing the "corny" beachside setting of the study videos, the Iconoclasts found little enjoyment in Ortberg's lessons. When I asked Charlie why the group responded so negatively to the material, he said that it had "little of substance" and was a good example of "pop psychology for Christians."

This was the second consecutive study chosen by Janet and the pastor that the group disliked, and they unanimously decided to choose the next book themselves. During the final meeting of the Ortberg series, Charlie offered a suggestion. Several years ago Diane had read *The Jesus I Never Knew*. She immediately recommended it to Charlie, and he has since read the book twice. He described it to the group as "easily one of [his] top-ten books of all time." Charlie and Diane's glowing recommendation excited the group and they quickly agreed to purchase the book before their next meeting. In early November 2004 they began Yancey's book, a study that would take sixteen meetings to complete and would not conclude until late May 2005.

Philip Yancey is a best-selling Evangelical author several times over. *The Jesus I Never Knew* received critical acclaim as well, winning the Evangelical Christian Publishers' Association's "Gold Medallion Christian Book of the Year Award" in 1996. The following quote from the book's introduction gives a good sense for its basic aim:

> That . . . is the problem with most of our writing and thinking about Jesus. We read the Gospels through the flash-forward lenses of church councils like Nicea and Chalcedon, through the church's studied attempts to make sense of [Jesus]. . . . In this book I hope to go back beyond those formulations. I hope, as far as is possible, to look at Jesus' life "from below," as a spectator, one of the many who followed him around. If I were a Japanese filmmaker, given $50 million and no script but the Gospels' text, what kind of film would I make? (1995: 24)

In 250-plus pages, Yancey expounds on Gospel texts, shares personal experiences, raises questions, and connects his reading of Jesus' life to

American society at the end of the 20th century. He divides the book into fourteen chapters and three sections: "Who He Was," "Why He Came," and "What He Left Behind." Yancey writes in an accessible, largely anecdotal style. He presents a highly polyphonic (Bahktin 1934) work, incorporating lengthy excerpts from the four canonical Gospels, quotations from famous Christian writers such as C. S. Lewis, Dorothy Sayers, and G. K. Chesterton, and literary references from Shakespeare, Voltaire, Frost, and Dostoevsky, among others.

The group expressed great admiration for the book, much as Charlie and Diane predicted. Each week they met to discuss one chapter, though on two occasions they devoted two meetings to one chapter because their discussions proved lengthy. To organize these meetings, Charlie distributed a list of six to fourteen questions for each chapter. Each question was accompanied by a one- to three-paragraph excerpt from the book, which was read aloud prior to anyone responding to the question. The group was never strict about addressing all of the questions, and Charlie took the lead in deciding which ones they would discuss first and which might go unexamined.

The Iconoclasts and History

The category of "history" served as the Iconoclasts' subtext for reading *The Jesus I Never Knew*. By this I mean simply that the group shared a continual interest in knowledge about the past. For these individuals, this was not a recent or sporadic interest but a longstanding passion that stayed at the forefront of their attention. Participants varied in their particular historical fetish, though everyone confined their gaze to the Western world. They drew associations with slavery and civil rights in the United States, Native American colonial struggles, Nazi Germany, American Anabaptist groups, ancient Rome, the Spanish Inquisition, biblical archaeology, American military history, and a host of other eras, personalities, events, and places. This thoroughly historical interpretive imagination was not one that continually sought to establish connections with particular events or individuals. Instead, their discussion of Yancey's book was dominated by a near-automatic inclination to situate texts into a historically oriented framework, sometimes specific, sometimes generic, but always focused on the past.

The Iconoclasts' bent toward history was evident from their very first meeting. This initial gathering was not devoted to chapter one of the book but to providing a general introduction and orientation to the book using questions designed by Charlie. The first question prompted each member to "list three images you have of Jesus." Following several responses, Tom (a lifelong Methodist, pastor's son, and pharmacist in his late forties) entered the discussion. He imagined Charlie's question as a historical problem and reasoned through it as such:

> I always thought of [Jesus] as being very muscular, strong, and athletic with the idea that he would have been a carpenter at a time when there wouldn't have been, you know, the tools that are available now. So, I thought he had to have been very strong to do that, plus with all the walking that they would do from place to place and as much traveling as he did. I just always pictured him as being, I'll say almost an athletic type of build in order to be able to do the things that he did.

In a manner typical to his participation style, Tom sat quietly and listened to others' contributions before offering a cogent comment of his own. His response to Charlie's question begins to show how history is used as a subtext of reading. He integrates his presumed knowledge of a specific time period (the 1st century a.d.) to contextualize the question and piece together a scenario based on historical probabilities. Linda performed a very similar interpretive act at the beginning of their second meeting. Charlie began the discussion by reading the following excerpt from the book:

> The more I studied Jesus the more difficult it became to pigeonhole him. He said little about the Roman occupation, the main topic of conversation among his countrymen. And yet he took up a whip to drive petty profiteers from the Jewish temple. He urged obedience to the Mosaic Law while acquiring a reputation as a lawbreaker. He could be stabbed by sympathy for a stranger, yet turn on his best friend with the flinty rebuke, "Get behind me, Satan." He had uncompromising views on rich men and loose women, yet both types enjoyed his company. As Walter Wink has said, "If Jesus had never lived, we would have never been able to invent him." (1995: 23)

Charlie then picked up on the reference to "petty profiteers"—the Gospel text of Jesus and the moneychangers[3]—and suggested that a similar reaction would be directed at their congregation's own bookstore and the fact that the church makes a profit from it. He thought that if Jesus were to come back now, this is precisely the type of scene that would infuriate him. Linda objects to Charlie's analogy, mimicking Tom's historical logic:

But I think the reason he was upset with the moneychangers was not so much that there was transaction, commercial business on the temple grounds, but the fact that they were cheating the people. Because you had your sin offerings, and so you know if you did this sin you had to give a chicken or the blood, and then on and on. And so, where was it in Leviticus it lists all the sin offerings? And so, these were the moneychangers saying, "Okay pay me fifteen rubles for this chicken, pay me twenty for this pigeon, give me fifteen for this lamb." And because you had so many different currencies, you had the Roman currency, but you probably had some local currencies and converting it that it could only be in the currency of the temple. So, I mean, so there was a lot of possibility for defrauding the people and for cheating them, which would have been a way for the temple to make money or if the moneychangers did, they probably had to give a percentage to the temple in order to set up shop there.

Linda's explanation of currency and Tom's vision of 1st-century fitness provide examples of individuals responding to an isolated question under collective consideration. Their shared method clues us into the group's use of history as subtext and sets the stage for a lengthier encounter. The following example, also from the second meeting, provides a more elaborate illustration of their historical imagination. It begins with Charlie reading another excerpt from Yancey:

Charlie: "Nine months of awkward explanations, the lingering scent of scandal—it seems that God arranged the most humiliating circumstances possible for his entrance, as if to avoid any charge of favoritism. I am impressed that when the Son of God became a human being he played by the rules, harsh rules: small towns do not treat kindly young boys who grow up with questionable paternity. . . . Often a work of God comes with two edges, great joy and great pain, and in that matter-of-fact response Mary embraced both. She was the first person to accept Jesus on his own terms, regardless of the personal cost." [32]

Linda: I think he's losing a lot of Joseph's role in this whole dynamic because Joseph was pledged to Mary; at least Mary was betrothed to Joseph. So, it was already preplanned that they were to be married. And he stood up for her and said, "I will accept you as you are," once she told him she was pregnant.

Charlie: Yeah, once he was told in a dream by the Lord. He was actually going to put her away quietly.

Linda: Okay, so he had the intervention from the Lord to say, "Hey, she's on the up-and-up level, she is carrying my child." So, then he had that extra role of standing up to the community to say, "This is my betrothed. This is my wife. This is my child. He is my son."

Charlie: Yeah, it's real interesting, Joseph and Mary, these were not people of high social status.

Linda: And when did he, when did they finally get back to their home community? Because, okay, they go off to Bethlehem because of the census, so he's leaving his home community. And then they go off to Egypt for a couple of years. So, I mean, so it's got time for the scandal to really die down by the time they would have circulated back to their home territory.

Lori: Yeah. And not only that, they're moving back to Nazareth. And Nazareth was like the south side of Chicago, like the slums.

Linda: But he was a skilled craftsman. So, at least he could provide for his family. He had the means; I mean it wasn't that it was all poverty. He had a good income for the community that he lived in.

Joanne: He had to move so people wouldn't kill him.

Linda: And actually, to have the baby born in the stable was the cleanest place he could have been born. Because it was clean straw and I mean, like with all this ingathering of all these people that have been spread out for this census purpose. It would have been a filthy, dirty place inside the inn. The stable was actually the cleanest place to be.

Lori: But what was the society like then? Would it have really been that big a deal if, I mean, you kind of assume that everyone thinks this is Joseph's kid.

Tom: Right.

Lori: This is something, so, the only two people that have to know anything different about it are Mary and Joseph. Everyone else is going to think it's Joseph's. So, I mean, you really only had two people that had to really know what it was. So, I'm not sure it was even all that big a deal. I mean, how many young girls became pregnant back then? I imagine it was very similar like it is today.

Charlie: Yeah.

Lori: So, they were poor and they were a lot of things. But whether it was she was going to get put off in a loony bin I guess would depend on, you know, did she go around saying this or was it just, other than Elizabeth?

Linda: And even betrothal at that time was a much deeper commitment than just being engaged is in today's society.

Linda and Lori led the historically charged critique of Yancey. They rely on suspected details of historical context to understand the circumstances surrounding Christ's birth. In particular, they focus on betrothal, the lifespan of rumor, carpentry as an occupation, sanitary stables, and teen pregnancy as proof against Yancey's assertions. They invoke these sources of evidence in an effort to reason through the question of Mary's acceptance into her community. It is striking how certain the participants are in their interpretations, as though they were speaking from personal experience and not historical inference. This is a particularly compelling example because it is one of the only occasions in all sixteen meetings in which the group disagreed with Yancey, not to mention with such immediacy and uniformity. Departing from the unified praise of Yancey might, in fact, index the authority they invest in history as a category of knowledge. Challenging Yancey requires good reason for doing so, which history never ceases to provide. In all three examples, history provides an organizing narrative—a shared interpretive backdrop that orchestrates reading and discussion.

The group's use of history as a subtext for reading does not end with the application of historical logics to individual questions. In a more fundamental way, the principal hermeneutic activity the Iconoclasts engaged in while reading Yancey was itself historically grounded. Their guiding hermeneutic begins with the question: are we practicing Christianity the same way Jesus and his followers did in the Bible? This question assumes an ideal type of Christian life described in the New Testament that is available for imitation. Some details of this ideal life are captured in Charlie's laudatory description of early Anabaptists in America:

> The Gospels themselves are just revolutionary and life changing. They talk about a much different faith. And when you read a lot of history and everything, you read times and places where people have really latched on to that. They take a lot of heat for it. There was this one group called the Anabaptists and they were forerunners of the Baptist church. And these guys were big in . . . I think they started off in Moravia. But they took their faith seriously and they were persecuted out of Europe for it. All they did was take down a lot of the structure and take down a lot of the pretense, and care about each other, and love one another, and practice basic, primitive, 1st-century Christianity. And they were run out of Europe for it, same way with Puritans and the Quakers. The Puritans set up their little zone; they had their little ways of doing church and all that.

Quakers show up and have get-down "charismaniac" church services. Can't have that—"You guys go down and quake, do that quake thing"— they sent them to Rhode Island and Connecticut.

It is hard not to recall in these words the restorationist attitude that imbued the life of the Prayer Circle. "Structure" and "pretense" are foregone in favor of "loving one another," a clear sign for Charlie of "1st-century Christianity." He looks to the religious life of early America for his illustration, signifying a clear divide between Christianity as it should be practiced, has been practiced, and currently is practiced.

The ongoing assertion of this ideal Christianity is a prelude to their guiding hermeneutic. The Iconoclasts continually established a problem of dissonance between this ideal and the religiosity of their own lives and their surrounding Christian culture. As part of this interpretive claim they sought to identify the institutions and practices that failed to emulate the words and actions of Jesus and other New Testament figures. They performed this moral-spiritual criticism in the context of their own lives, the life of their local congregation, and the status of American Christianity more broadly. Charlie consistently and articulately stated this ideological position beginning in their first meeting:

> We've taken Jesus and we've compartmentalized and put him in a spot that we're comfortable with. And when you look at what Jesus says about himself and the things he does in the Gospels, many times in the church we do exactly the reverse. Jesus said, *Judge not less you be judged.* And we judge *people every* single day that go wandering into our lives and into the church. That's why I was just so blown away when I read the Gospels this last time around, because the reverse culture, the *upside down* world that Jesus talks about we don't do. We put together our little systems, our orders, and we go about our business.

He continued several minutes later among nodding heads and affirmative sighs:

> The thing that it's all about, at the end of the day, is what's presented in the Gospels. The Gospels are so revolutionary compared to how we live in our society. Give you an example: *the last shall be first and the first shall be last.* That's out of the Beatitudes. In our society, the first shall be first. Those who die with the most toys win. In God's economy, those who

have died with the most toys have a lot of toys on earth, but you ain't got nothin' when you get to heaven.

Here, Charlie responds to a passage from Yancey that discussed the enigmatic quality of Jesus' life: the company he kept and the sins he chose to address (23). The underlying logic of Charlie's words, however, is abundantly clear: there is a great and wide separation between what Christianity is really about and how it is practiced in 21st-century America. This species of hermeneutic activity, this attempt to establish dissonance, was repeatedly asserted by Charlie and the other members. It was clear to me after several meetings that this was an ideological position they brought with them to their reading of this text and something they were only finding support for in the words of Yancey. The question I am concerned with is how does the group's commitment to history maintain this interpretive practice?

To answer this question I must introduce a third discursive-ideological presence among the Iconoclasts. The group was very certain that the failure of American Christians to truly live out the Christian faith is not unique or surprising. They were quick to identify similar failures throughout history. Rather, this dissonance is a predictable consequence of a fallible human nature. Consistent with the orthodox Christian doctrine of original sin, the Iconoclasts were committed to the belief that human beings are innately sinful and separated from the righteousness that defines God.[4] This nature has remained unchanged through time and is only alterable in the individual life through the decision to accept Jesus Christ as the universal Messiah. The recognition of a fallen humanity appeared throughout the group's study of Yancey's book and in response to a variety of specific concerns. It was often introduced to reinforce the reality that human actions and motivations have been stable across time and to contextualize discussions of seemingly unfathomable human problems and decisions. Two interactions from the Iconoclasts demonstrate how this assumption is used to explain the problem of dissonance.

The first example comes from the group's seventh meeting, in which Charlie asked the group to reflect on the concept of spiritual "purity," a recognizable theological query for these Wesleyan Methodists:

Charlie: So, the reason I put that paragraph in there, the reason I stopped at
    that paragraph is I thought, "Ah, purity. That's like that word 'holiness.'"
Chrisann: Hmm.

Charlie: That's like nothing you ever hear in church anymore. You don't hear that and there's not an emphasis on it. Because it is, in our society, a politically incorrect term, because we're not supposed to judge others. But I thought, "Ah, this would be a great controversial topic in a group like this. We could really stir it up." And yet, you can't read the Bible and you can't read the scriptures without seeing that. Now, I'm not saying that, I'm not judging other people for where we've all been in our lives. What I'm saying is when you talk about really what God wants us to be. I was reminded of a verse in Ephesians that says *God wants us to,* as we come along and as we become mature in Christ, *he wants us to come out of the darkness and into the light.* And [this] is always equated with what the Bible listed off as a whole series as impure acts, which, by the way, having a bad attitude is one of them, too. Having a bad attitude is like at the top of the list. But I thought, that's interesting, the whole impurity and purity thing, especially in the time and place we live in. The great example of our time, our fascination and our saturation with sex. Everything's sexual. Tough stuff. Can't hide your kids from it. It's everywhere.

Fred: Companies sell their . . . it's driving all the sales of everything.

Charlie: Oh, absolutely. Yeah. Absolutely. . . .

Charlie: Impurity is not only sexual. Purity is other things. Purity is our attitude towards money. It's our attitude towards others. There's lots of ways to be impure. We just think about sex all the time because that's what we do in the United States. But it's many ways, having a pure heart. It's like if you obsess on anything else. Maybe this is a good working definition: if you have an obsession you can't see God clearly because you're thinking about that other thing.

Lori: But part of the problem with that is mankind was built with that innate urge to continue to multiply the whole thing.

Charlie: Mhmm.

Lori: It's not something that's just now. If you look back in history to the things that went on, we maybe didn't have the media, but there were a lot of other things that went . . . [[interrupted]]

Charlie: That's Diane's point. Diane tells me that all the time.

Lori: You go back and you read, the Vikings when they came in. What were they going to do? Rape and pillage.

Chrisann: *It's nothing new under the sun.*

Diane: Man and evil and temptation and all those things that have been around forever.

The themes of sin, cultural critique, and historical precedent that organize this exchange are repeated in the second example. In their fifteenth meeting, Charlie read a passage from Yancey describing Jesus' refusal to use "coercive power" (246):

> Charlie: Jesus consistently refused to tell people, "You gotta do this or I'll," you know. And he could have. He was God. If God really wanted people to behave, all he'd have to do is line up a demonstration.
>
> Dale: What would it have mattered? I mean, what did . . . people got freed from Egypt.
>
> Lori: Wouldn't have mattered.
>
> Dale: Out in the middle of nowhere, they got food out of nothing. And they are still casting gold calves and stuff to worship.
>
> Lori: Right. And the miracles that Christ did. Some people it was odd and moved them, and others just wanted to know what kind of trickery and who, you know, it was done by the devil.
>
> Charlie: Yeah. Ravi Zacharias, on the radio the other day, said exactly the same thing. He quoted a scripture of, I think it was John, where Jesus said, *I sent you the prophets. You didn't listen to them. I sent you John the Baptist. You wouldn't listen to them. So, what makes you think you're going to listen to me?* Because we always want to do what we always want to do, and we always want to get what we always want to get. We want to believe what we want to believe.
>
> Lori: Even after having proof right in front of you. I mean, how many times have you tried to prove to someone that what, whether it's wrong, and you have undeniable, it's proof, and they still won't believe you. It doesn't matter to some.
>
> Charlie: Years ago we had a family member staying with us and they had a little boy named Jack. Jack was at the house, and he was not obeying his mom. And his mom said, [[angry tone]] "Okay. That's it. I'm taking you up the stairs." And all the way up the stairs he goes, [[defiant, obnoxious tone]] "No. You're not in charge of me. I'm in charge of myself. You're not in charge of me." And I looked at him going up the stairs and said, "That's us. That's all of us."
>
> [[Laughs]]
>
> Charlie: I had just finished reading something in the Old Testament about God calling the Israelites *a stiff-necked person*. If you ever want to read what you are like as a human being, what we're all like as a human being,

read the Old Testament. Read the New Testament. It's all there. Every little
trick, every little devious evil thing, we can all do it.

In the first example, Charlie gives a lengthy account of holiness as a
spiritual ideal and the many ways it is not apparent in the life of the modern Christian. Lori—with support from Charlie, Chrisann, and Diane—
generalizes Charlie's claim to suggest that the problem is not with Americans but with humans. Chrisann's contribution is especially noteworthy
for its recontexualization of the well-known text from Ecclesiastes, en-
dowing Lori's interpretation with clear scriptural legitimacy.

In the second example, Dale introduces humanity's fallen nature much
earlier in the discussion in order to explain the problems of disbelief and
defiance. Lori and Charlie take up this notion and identify their own biblical examples.

Both of these interactions are organized by the discursive-ideological
subtext we have been considering. The appeals to human nature help the
Iconoclasts understand the problem of dissonance between 1st- and 21st-
century Christianity. And all of this is performed with a historical logic in
mind: the best way to demonstrate humanity's failure is through humanity's
past. In this way, the category of history extends its impact on the Iconoclasts' reading practices to comprise a guiding hermeneutic imagination. It
is striking in these two examples how far the group travels from their starting point in Yancey's book. As suggested by Jonathan Boyarin (1993: 222),
ethnographies of reading are uniquely positioned to demonstrate how texts
are not solely "records of dialogue," but also "occasion[s] for dialogue."
These readers are not passive, but active, casting themselves into the narratives they encounter. What these two examples make clear is that the Iconoclasts' involvement with Yancey's book is not lacking in direction. Their
reading is organized by an integrated certainty about the value of history,
the problem of dissonance, and the theology of original sin.

The Iconoclasts' commitment to history was crystallized in their choice of
text following *The Jesus I Never Knew*. With three meetings left, they began talking about their next study topic. Diane mentioned "a video series
that has a lot of archaeology" that some other groups in the church had
used. The following Sunday, Diane brought a description of the series and
a sample of study questions that provoked unanimous agreement from the
group. The video series is titled *That the World May Know* (1995) and is
produced by Focus on the Family.[5] The series is led by Ray Vander Laan, a

"historian and biblical scholar." In each video, Vander Laan teaches a lesson about biblical history to a group of students at or near the physical site included in the teaching. The series markets itself on this unique design, advertising Vander Laan as a "renowned" scholar who teaches "about the Holy Land from the Holy Land." As anticipated, the Iconoclasts loved the study and continuously praised Vander Laan for his historical acumen. Aside from its other appeals—namely, a conservative Evangelical resource being studied by an Evangelical group—it is clear that the Iconoclasts' initial attraction and ultimate admiration for this series was grounded in their passion for history.

Textual Economies

For sixteen Sundays between November 2004 and May 2005 the Iconoclasts met in Charlie and Diane's living room to discuss Philip Yancey's *The Jesus I Never Knew*. Much like other collective reading situations, Bible study functions partly on the basis of shared interests. Following Elizabeth Long (1993), we can assume that any collection of readers—no matter what else brings them together—will coalesce around some commonality, providing a "subtext" (194) for their reading practice. In the case of the Iconoclasts, this meant a reliance on the category of history. This appreciation for the past infused explanations of individual questions but was also more deeply embedded in the group's interpretive logic. Ultimately, we saw how the subtext of history reveals some of their fundamental assumptions about the nature of humanity and Christian spirituality. Unlike the analyses of the LCMS Men and the Prayer Circle, the view of American Evangelicalism provided by the Iconoclasts occurs through their reading of a nonscriptural text. This case study thus draws attention to an important theme in Bible study life as well as in the broader culture of American Evangelicalism.

Throughout my research with Evangelical Bible study groups I returned to a curious social fact: these Christians are voracious readers with a hunger for all manner of texts. Individuals pride themselves on how well read they are, not just in scripture and scriptural commentary, but also in books such as Yancey's that use scripture as a springboard into all topics imaginable. Books are central to many of the processes and activities that define Evangelical life, such as attempts at conversion. A favored method of witnessing among Evangelicals is to give theological, fictional, and inspirational Christian books to those who are not "saved."

The international discourses that Evangelicals participate in (for example, prosperity theology, missionization) are also frequently enacted through books and other textual genres. American Evangelicals (along with much of Western Christendom) are not only people of the Book, but are people of books (cf. Brown 2004; Jeffrey 1996).

There is little doubt about the historical basis for this phenomenon. We might begin with the 1st-century Church, and the close familiarity of Jesus' first followers with the Hebrew scriptures. While theologians might locate the first theory of Christian reading in the Bible, more sociologically minded scholars look toward Saint Augustine of Hippo at the end of the 4th century (Stock 1996). Augustine was the first to break with the strict convention of oral, public literacy, finding in the act of private, silent, contemplative reading a means of nurturing one's relationship with God. Attention to texts and reading continued in Western Christianity, taking on renewed significance in the 16th-century European Reformation (Cummings 2002; Gilmont 1999; Jeffrey 1996). Along with the call by reformers that all people should have the ability and opportunity to read the Bible, this era saw the advent of the printing press. This new technology received mixed blessings: it was simultaneously viewed as a divine gift from God for sharing His Word in an unprecedented fashion and a devilish tool perfect for spreading heresies (Cummings 2002). Ultimately, though, the Reformation birthed an unceasing hunger for texts: "Writing was a guarantee of authenticity. What had been true in the early centuries of the Church was equally true in the 16th century. Moreover, the authority naturally invested in the Bible was transferred to other forms of religious writings" (Gilmont 1999: 233). David Paul Nord (2004) and Candy Gunther Brown (2004) have both observed the central place of texts and reading in the religious life of early America. Since at least the early 1800s, conservative Evangelicals have fashioned themselves as religious readers, firmly convinced of the transformative power of words and the Word (Brown 2004). Yet, despite the profusion of historical accounts, we are in need of some analytical tools to make sense of this phenomenon as it persists among American Evangelicals. Perhaps there is some banality in this social fact—the obviousness of text in Christianity—that has facilitated this lack of adequate theorizing.

Toward this end I offer the concept of "textual economies" to capture the relationship Evangelicals sustain with books other than the Bible. A working definition might read: the differential social capital Christian communities invest in the category of text, individual authors, individual works, and distinct genres. Unlike scripture's textual ideology, the absence of well-formulated ideas about other forms of religious reading provides a fluid textual economy in which value is constantly reevaluated, and texts and authors move in and out of favor. In the case of American Evangelicals, this prompts four initial observations. First, a select few authors and works have achieved a unique place in this textual economy, garnering an authority second only to scripture itself. The best example of this is probably C. S. Lewis, whose fictional, apologetic, and autobiographical work constitutes a canon of reliable texts that Evangelicals return to themselves and also use to reach others. Second, specialized genres have accrued widespread popularity. In their own ethnographies of reading, Amy Frykholm (2004) and Lynn Neal (2006) have highlighted the pervasiveness of apocalyptic and romance fiction among Evangelical readers. Frykholm and Neal both do well to argue that entertainment is but one outcome of this new literacy and a marginal one compared to the ideologies and interpretive practices encouraged by these books. In the case of Evangelical romance reading, we see a moment of overlap between this textual economy and a more general one in American society, where stigmas transfer along with textual styles and narrative structures. Third, there is an undeniable pedagogical element to this textual economy. Books—such as Yancey's *The Jesus I Never Knew*—have become the primary way that Evangelicals learn and reproduce core Christian doctrines, as well as matters of orthopraxy. Instead of relying primarily on their local clergy, lay Evangelicals look to a cadre of published teachers for theological and moral instruction. Fourth, in her study of early American religious reading, Candy Gunther Brown argues in step with Benedict Anderson's work on nationalism: "The idea of a textual community provided an alternative to viewing the Christian church as centered in the local congregation. . . . Evangelicals used texts to envision themselves as belonging to the church universal, which included Christians from all time periods, countries, and denominations" (2004: 12). The type of imagined community emerging from the shared textual economy that Brown describes is still visible among American Evangelicals. Reading the same books has the ability to generate, quite immediately, a shared sense of belonging and Christian identity for individuals who have never met or might otherwise have no binding social ground.

Evangelicals continually rework this textual economy in a variety of contexts, namely group Bible study. The Iconoclasts, in not studying directly from scripture, are actually more representative of the project sample than the other case studies presented in this book. For a variety of reasons, groups frequently prefer to read nonscriptural texts together. Pastor Dave of the LCMS Men connected this to the issue of textual ideology when explaining his preference to the group at the end of their second meeting in the study of Proverbs:

> One of the things I think happens when we read the books that's helpful is that I believe we're more free to disagree with the books because we know it's not God's word from beginning to end. And we often feel intimidated understanding the scripture and sharing the scripture, and we're afraid we're going to get something wrong. But when we're reading a book, I think we have a little greater freedom of, "Well, I think I can have an opinion on that."

Dave's sentiment, of which I heard different versions in many of the other groups, is that nonscriptural texts are often better for provoking discussion because individuals are not as likely to be stymied by an overwhelming authority. Because texts like Yancey's are so prevalent in group life, Bible study has become a site where texts and authors get consumed in bulk, evaluated, and incorporated into Evangelicals' textual economy. And as the example of the Iconoclasts attests, nonscriptural texts can be a powerful vehicle for coordinating group life and eliciting central assumptions in the Evangelical imagination.

✳ 5 ✳

Preparing to Witness

Since 1992, the Tuesday Men have gathered weekly at 7:30 a.m. at Inner-City United Methodist Church (IUMC). The church building is located in the heart of the city at the corner of two high-traffic streets. The surrounding neighborhoods are ethnically diverse and predominantly working class, though a large number live below the national poverty level. Established in 1912, the building barely reflects its surroundings or its age. It is a two-story, red-brick structure that is neatly kept, with several newly refurbished sections. The group meets in a second-story classroom overlooking the rear parking lot. Four fold-out tables are arranged to form a large rectangle. Every week the men take the same seats, evenly spread out, minimizing the vacant space.

Four of the seven members have attended since the group's beginning thirteen years ago. The pastor at the time was experiencing personal difficulties and started the group for emotional support as much as scriptural study. When Pastor Bill arrived at IUMC in 2002 he took over the role of facilitator. Along with two additional participants, the group's membership has remained constant for the past several years.

Bill is very much an authoritative voice in the group as well as the youngest member at fifty-one years old. He often spoke at length, and the other members relied on him when difficult questions arose. Bill was educated at Asbury Theological Seminary and is theologically conservative, though he is quite progressive in his politics and approach to congregational life. He is often at theological odds with the more ecumenical pastors in his regional United Methodist district but is recognized for his creativity in rethinking church worship. The remaining six participants uphold Bill's theological tone but sometimes struggle to understand his ethos on other matters. Eddie is the oldest member at seventy-two years old. He is a retired United Methodist missionary and chemistry teacher who worked for several decades in India. He now volunteers full time at the church as the coordinator for a growing population of Middle Eastern and African refugees that have joined the congregation. Bill clearly values Eddie's contribution to the group, often consulting him on controversial issues and questions that benefit from his international experience. Ron and Jerry are brothers, cofounders of a (very profitable) local business and lifelong members at IUMC. Jerry was reserved in his comments but had a knack for raising astute observations and questions that kept discussions moving. Ron was often the first to answer questions and was fond of asking others to elaborate on their responses. Bob is a retired engineer and a newcomer to the congregation. Along with Roger and Lynn (both retired), these three men comprised a cohort of attentive but mostly silent participants.

The group's meetings were always amiable. Even when disagreements arose they were sorted out with good humor and mutual curiosity. However, the type of dynamic exchange that characterized the LCMS Men and the Iconoclasts was somehow rearranged among the Tuesday Men. Their conversations were fluid but maintained a distinctly calm feeling. Each meeting contained lengthy silences as the men thoughtfully pondered study questions. During my fieldwork, the group studied the New Testament book of Acts.[1] They used the Life Guide series published by InterVarsity Press to structure their weekly readings. The series has study guides for all sixty-six books of the Christian Bible. The series is a favorite of Bill's and one he has used in a variety of other groups. The men used one study sheet each week, which included a brief narrative introduction to a reading from Acts followed by ten to twelve questions about the text. The questions ranged from straightforward descriptions to fairly complex exegeses and personal applications. The men spent two or three meetings reading each text and completing the questions. Bill always passed out the upcoming sheet a week ahead of time, giving the men a chance to complete it beforehand. Without fail, they arrived to the following meeting with responses, often multiple paragraphs worth, for every question. The Tuesday Men provide a case study for how groups remember, reflect on, and rehearse acts of witnessing during Bible study.

Bible Study as Backstage Witnessing

For many Evangelicals, their most memorable social encounters are those understood as acts of "witnessing." Broadly conceived, witnessing encompasses any interaction between a Christian and a nonbeliever in which the spiritual faith of the former is demonstrated (intentionally or unintentionally) for the latter. The goal of witnessing is sometimes immediate conversion but is more often to "plant a seed" to give nonbelievers a reason to want to know more about the Christian life. "Sharing the Gospel message," "reaching out to the lost," "sharing's God's love," and "winning people for Christ" are examples of the many ways Evangelicals describe this type of interaction. My aim here is to ask how Bible study provides a space to create a preparatory discourse for Evangelicals' lives as everyday evangelists.

Perhaps the most well-known analysis of Evangelical witnessing comes from the anthropologist Susan Harding (1987; cf. 2000). In a now-seminal article, she examined the "rhetoric of conversion" (1987: 167) among North American fundamentalists, using her own interview-turned-witnessing encounter with a Southern Baptist minister as empirical data. Anyone familiar with the article can easily recall the discursive acumen of its central character, Reverend Milton Cantrell. He immediately reframes Harding's ethnographic visit into a spiritual one, methodically progressing from one narrative event to another. He stuns Harding with the dramatic story of killing his own son with a moving crane, only to accept the tragedy with an unquestioning peace. In Harding's account, Evangelical witnessing is a highly structured, finely tuned, and strategic verbal display, rife with tropes, turns of phrase, images, and intertextual references that populate Evangelicalism writ large.

The witnessing encounter is thus firmly entrenched in the Evangelical linguistic repertoire and a paradigmatic example of a "performance genre" (Bauman 2004). All cultural groups have such ritualized forms of communication; ways of speaking that require a certain competence of what to say, how to say it, and what is expected from the act of saying specific things in specific ways. Witnessing—much like other performance genres such as preaching, prayer, or prophecy—signifies membership in the Evangelical community and helps to reproduce important elements of Evangelical culture. Performance genres are vital for this very reason: they act as bearers of social tradition and as vehicles for supporting or challenging widely held assumptions about the nature of everyday affairs.

For Evangelicals, witnessing is closely bound to their sense of identity and purpose. More than any other religious activity, the foremost duty of Evangelicals is to "reach the lost." Among the most widely circulated biblical texts within Evangelical communities is the so-called "Great Commission" at the end of the Gospel of Matthew: *Go and make disciples of all nations, baptizing them in the name of the Father and of the Son and of the Holy Spirit.*[2] "Sharing the Good News of Jesus Christ" is a central motive in the Evangelical life and has always been a distinguishing trait of the movement in America (Noll 1992). The receptivity of non-Christians is rather inconsequential in the witnessing encounter. The guiding theology suggests that "God is using" the witness to "reach" the nonbeliever. No matter what their stance is toward Christianity, they will eventually be overcome by "the Truth" and convert. Evangelicals have no shortage of ideas about the witnessing encounter. It is common lore to assure a fellow Christian, after a seemingly failed witnessing attempt, that "most people" hear the Gospel message "x-number" of times "before they accept Jesus." During my fieldwork I heard this formulaic scenario voiced in several groups (including the Tuesday Men), though the exact number of witnessing attempts varied among speakers from nine to twenty-seven. Without fail, this potentially disheartening scenario is framed by the uplifting biblical trope of seed planting—"they may not have converted right away, but you planted a seed that will stay with them." In short, there is no such thing as an unnecessary or ineffective witnessing encounter for Evangelicals. There is, by extension, every reason to always witness.

As Harding indicates, Evangelicals are exposed to plenty of formal training venues where they can hone their "soul-winning techniques" (1987: 171). These range from instructional pamphlets to book-length studies and weekend seminars. A best-selling example, and one used by IUMC soon after Bill's arrival, is the six-week congregational campaign *Becoming a Contagious Christian* (1994). Produced by the Willow Creek Community Church, and coauthored by its founder and senior pastor Bill Hybels, the *Contagious Christian* program is a detailed guide for being a more effective witness. The book and its accompanying program typify "relational evangelism," a witnessing style that prioritizes one-on-one interactions with non-Christians and the sustained attempt to build meaningful relationships with "the lost." (We might contrast this with visiting strangers door-to-door or distributing Bible tracts on street corners.) By its own description, relational evangelism is not primarily an exercise in exhorting people about their sins, "turn-or-burn" speeches, or detailed apologetics of Christian theology and history. As advertised on the book's back cover, it promises to help "discover your own natural evangelism style; develop a contagious Christian character; build spiritually strategic relationships; learn to direct conversations toward matters of faith; share biblical truths in everyday language." Like hundreds of other Evangelical products, the goal of *Becoming a Contagious Christian* is to craft an individual's witnessing proficiency. In doing so it plays on several widespread Evangelical tropes, such as "building relationships" and "biblical truth."

In the study of Evangelical culture, then, witnessing is a crucial topic. Unfortunately, because it is an emergent performance event, it is difficult to empirically document witnessing encounters as they naturally occur. In listening to dozens of retellings throughout my fieldwork, most witnessing encounters of which Evangelicals speak occur spontaneously in situations that they had not planned the opportunity to arise. (This, in itself, is part of the guiding theology of witnessing: "God uses us when we least expect it.") This difficulty is amplified in cases like mine, where the researcher counts themselves a Christian and cannot, like Harding and others, rely on being the target of witnessing.

Rather than try and defeat this empirical problem, this analysis shifts attention away from the witnessing performance itself to the preparation for witnessing that occurs in group Bible study. As we have seen throughout the previous chapters, Bible study is a crucial dialogical space for Evangelicals. The practice of collective reading provides a medium and forum for reflecting on habitual thoughts and actions, modes of subjectivity, and the broader discourses in which groups and individuals participate. When focused on events outside the group context, like witnessing, Bible study becomes what Erving Goffman (1961) famously termed a "backstage encounter." According to Goffman, social interactions can be divided into two basic classes. Public interactions—such as witnessing, in which performers (Evangelicals) and their audiences (non-Christians) are both present—function as "frontstage encounters." Here, the performance event counts—that is, the full set of social responsibilities and consequences entailed in the performance are in effect. Every frontstage encounter is likely to have at least one backstage encounter—a corollary event in which only performers (Evangelicals as previous and potential witnesses) are present. Such backstage encounters have immense social significance because they allow individuals to rehearse, reflect, and otherwise prepare for their next frontstage performance. Studies of verbal performance have reiterated Goffman's claim by arguing that performance rehearsals—often taking place away from public view and sometimes as a solitary act by the performer—are equally implicated in the cultural work accomplished in the actual frontstage performance (Graham 1995). Backstage encounters reveal with little doubt the social fact that individuals often operate as strategic cultural actors, consciously invested in their social practice (Murphy 1990). We can ask, then, what happens in the backstage discourse of group Bible study regarding witnessing? And what can these preparatory conversations tell us about how witnessing figures in the Evangelical imagination?

The notion of linguistic indexicality helps us understand this backstage discourse. As explained by Ochs (1992), various features of language are used to encode cultural ideologies. By studying the social circulation of narratives, words, pronunciations, and grammatical structures we can see how meanings are mapped on to these discursive vehicles. This often occurs through second-order linkages or indirect indexical chains in which the ideological association is less explicit. For example, everyday behaviors for Evangelicals thought to be "biblical" are often defined as "clearly part of a positive purpose." In turn, linguistic activities such as swearing or speaking in a derogatory manner are decidedly "unbiblical" because of their negatively valued qualities. This process of linguistic indexicality—of creating transitivity between ideologies and language—is central to the process of communicating social meaning. Gabriella Modan (2007) demonstrates how indirect indexical chains are used to build cultural dispositions through ideological contrasts. In her ethnography of place and identity in a Washington, D.C., suburb, she argues that local identity is organized around a series of contrasts reflecting the self/other separation between cities and suburbs (106). Neighborhood residents rely on categorical oppositions such as multiethnic/white, filthy/clean, noisy/quiet, dangerous/safe, and public/private to situate events and actions within an ongoing narrative that distinguishes "living in the city" from "living in the 'burbs." Using this analytical method, I argue that the backstage witnessing in group Bible study is structured by a base ideological contrast of "effective" versus "ineffective" (or, simply, "good" versus "bad") witnessing.

Preparing to Witness

Throughout their reading of Acts, the Tuesday Men continually focused on the opposition of good/bad witnessing, evaluating various forms of semiotic action as examples of how best to "share the Good News." Within the context of the other project groups and their texts of study, this is a striking observation. As evidenced by the LCMS Men and the Prayer Circle, despite the presence of a widely shared textual ideology, Bible reading can be carried out toward quite different purposes and in quite different manners from group to group. Reading Acts with an eye toward witnessing—as opposed to, for example, individualized relevance or the exegesis of scriptural genres—clues us into the priorities and concerns of the Tuesday Men. The following interaction provides a good introduction to this backstage discourse. The group's sixth meeting marked their entry into chapter 3 of Acts, a twenty-six-verse narrative of the apostle Peter's healing and sermonizing. The meeting began with an open-ended question from their study guide: "What causes non-Christians to be open to hearing about Jesus?" Bill started the exchange by reframing the question and resituating the agency under consideration:

Bill: What kinds of things cause us to be attractive?

Ron: Being happy, joyful people.

Bill: Okay. Yeah. I think another word I'd use is "vulnerable." I think if we come off as being better than somebody else, if we give the impression that we think we're better than everyone rather than expressing the grace of God. I think that turns people off pretty quickly. And I think that happens a lot.

Ron: Yeah. You say you think that happens a lot?

Bill: Yeah. I think that's a struggle for people. I think people, rightly or wrongly, see the church as people who think they're better than others.

Ron: Yeah.

Eddie: Along that line, I was trying to think of the theologian, but I can't remember his name, who said, "Witness is one beggar telling another beggar where to find bread." In the theme of *Jesus is the bread of life*.

Bill: Yeah. I heard that as a definition of evangelism. And I heard it as E. Stanley Jones.[3]

Bob: I think you see Christians thinking they're better than everybody else on TV quite a bit.

Bill: Sure.

Bob: I don't watch a whole lot of those kinds of programs on TV. But every now and then you do. If you're channel surfing you know exactly, without even hearing what the man's saying, you can tell exactly what the subject is, that it's a religious station, just by the way he's talking. They speak in a way that is speaking down.

Jerry: Condescending.

Bob: Yeah, just their tone of voice. That's my impression.

Eddie: I think it's very hard because, like you're inviting someone to church. "Come, because we have something you don't. There's something here that you need that we have that you don't have."

Bill: Of course, it's the same thing that Wal-Mart does. They tell me that and I can receive it from Wal-Mart. "They got stuff I need. Wow!" So, I'm not sure it's a matter of that issue per se. It's a matter of how we go about it.

Eddie: Yeah. But how can you present it without giving that idea? For Wal-Mart, I think it is okay. If Christians are going to be vulnerable then it's not okay for Christians to do what Wal-Mart does. I mean, you've got to do it in a different way. I mean, you can't just say, "Come on. We've got it and you need it." Otherwise, we're not being vulnerable.

Bill: Well, I'm not sure I agree with that because I think I can be vulnerable in saying that. I think the vulnerability comes in where we say: "Look, this is not something that I figured out or I created. I've been blessed by the reality of God in my life. I didn't deserve that. I didn't earn it. But through the grace of God, I've discovered it, and I want that for you, because we all need that." That's what I meant by vulnerability. I don't think it's a denial of the message so much as it is the need that everyone has for that grace. It's just the way in which we approach it. I think some folks kind of approach it from the perspective of "I've arrived, and I've got this thing that you better get. And I've got it." There's a difference there.

Eddie: Yeah, there's a difference I think. But are you including what E. Stanley Jones suggested? Are you that vulnerable?

Bill: Well, I think so. Again, as we identify ourselves as, "I'm a beggar too. I need the grace of God just as much as anybody else. We all need it. So, here's where to find it."

Eddie: Yeah. I guess I'd just give the alternative, which would be: "Come, we need you too, to help us go forward together." "We need you," not "You need us." "Because without you we're incomplete and we can't get the job done of going together to the Lord." Now, that makes it corporate rather than just individual. It's something I've struggled with, because I don't think we do it intentionally and we even may say we're not doing it. But how do we really let them know?

Bill: Well, I think, I guess the bottom line is I do believe everybody needs what we have. And so, offering that in a way that is attractive seems to me to be the goal, the desire, to help people find their way to Christ. Certainly, we need them as well, and they have gifts to bring to the whole. And we look forward to that sharing that takes place between us.

The organizing contrast of good/bad witnessing appears here as attractive/unattractive. The group indexically links "good" with being joyful, staying vulnerable, and being corporately oriented, and they link "bad" with being arrogant, condescending, and overly individualistic. In this particular encounter, their discourse around witnessing is given to tension rather than continuity. Bill and Eddie lend significance to the same category ("vulnerability") but cannot seem to agree on its boundaries or proper definition. In other exchanges, the men were more uniform in their opinion and their reading of Acts, but throughout they remained highly invested in the basic question of what makes good witnessing good.

In twenty-three meetings, thirteen lengthy interactions, as well as several dozen more abbreviated references to evangelism, occupied the bulk of their attention. Individuals recounted narratives of their own witnessing encounters. They relayed stories of witnessing encounters that they had observed or been told about. They referenced witnessing encounters they knew of from events and personalities outside their firsthand social network. They created hypothetical scenarios of likely witness encounters. And as in the above example, they reflected in a theoretical manner on the principles and processes that make for successful witnessing. All five of these interactional types were organized by four sets of ideological contrasts that articulated, each with a different emphasis, what it means to be a good Christian witness.

Four Ideological Contrasts

Relevant vs. Irrelevant

This opposition represents a prevailing concern among American Evangelicals: bridging generational and cultural divides when communicating the Gospel. A great deal of Evangelical discourse concentrates on keeping (or, in many cases, getting) "young people" "focused on Christ." This usually begins and ends with the concept of "relevance": finding ways to translate Evangelical theology into terms and mediums of interest to individuals in their teens and twenties. The most audible instantiation of this struggle is the widespread popularity of contemporary praise and worship music (Hendershot 2004: 52–84). The strangeness (read: irrelevance) of organ-based hymns—typically penned in the 18th, 19th, and early 20th centuries—has steadily been replaced by the electric, pop-infused, percussion and guitar-driven style of the praise band. The shift in Evangelical congregations from traditional to contemporary music is carried out largely in the name of being relevant to the surrounding "culture." We can see below how this same cultural model helps structure the Tuesday Men's imagining of witnessing. Take, for example, Bill's lengthy response to Acts 8:26–40, the story of the Apostle Philip's encounter with an Ethiopian eunuch:

There's so much in that story. I mean, what chariots are we standing by and where are the chariots today that we might stand by? Where might we find those chariots with people in them who are reading stuff or watching movies or listening to music that God is using in some way? One of the things I was listening to lately, there's a band called Coldplay. They have a song that closes their concerts called "The Gospel." And it's not the Gospel that we know. It doesn't talk about Jesus and it doesn't talk about the cross or anything like that. It talks about human situations and human life and struggles and what we hope for, what we wish for. And at their concerts, they always do it as the last song. They do it as their encore. People in their concerts, by the thousands, will stick around and sing the chorus of that. Some of it's almost like a psalm. See, we have two ways of approaching that, I think, as the Church. And the first way is what we often do: "That's not the Gospel. That's not the Truth." We just crush it. And people respond to that pretty poorly. The other way is to say, "Man, here's somebody in the chariot who's seeking. They don't know about Jesus. They don't know anything." That's what this guy's position was. And Phillip knew about Jesus. He knew what this was talking about. But we've got people all around us in chariots who don't know, who don't have any concept like this kind. But they're seeking. And what we need to do is stand by the chariot long enough to understand, to listen and to hear that seeking in ways that I think the Church hasn't very often. We tend to just kind of come down hard in a judgmental sense because it's not perfect. It's not just right, and people are seeking the wrong thing so we need to set them straight and get them to the truth. And I don't disagree with that. We do need to do that. But unless we're willing to listen to what their heart's cry is and help them in relationship to understand that their heart's cry and the offering of Jesus match up, then, we just sound judgmental. We sound like we've got it all together and they don't. And that's not what Phillip did. That's not what successful people do in places where people are really finding their way to Christ. One of the books I just have bought recently, I haven't read yet, is entitled *The Gospel According to Tony Soprano* [Seay 2002]. Maybe you know who Tony Soprano is. He's the lead character on an HBO mob show, has lots of sex, lots of violence. Again, how can we be somebody standing by the chariot of that show, which is extremely popular in the culture? The guy that wrote the book was saying one of the reasons he started watching the show was everywhere he went, like at the gym and everything, people are sitting around talking about this show all the time. And so, to look at this guy's life and the struggles that are going on there and to put those in the context of the Gospel then and the struggles of the Gospel is what he was trying to do and trying to relate then that situation to the good news of God and to listen to Tony Soprano and some of the positive things that are there. I mean, family. The mafia, you know, family's really important. And basically relationships and stuff, and here's a guy that, he's messed up and he's in many ways horrible. And yet, there's these other things. Just to try and relate that to the Gospel in a culture where that's very popular. What is it that draws our hearts into those kinds of things? What is it that makes those kinds of things popular? And it's not always things you can relate to, but often it is. But we gotta stand by the chariot. I like that.

Bill's interpretation of this biblical narrative is both an exposition on proper evangelism and a critique of what "the Church" often does. He uses two examples from American popular culture—the rock band Coldplay and the HBO drama series *The Sopranos*—to suggest that good witnessing is always relevant witnessing. And relevant witnessing requires "listening" for connections between the Gospel message and the messages of pop culture, especially when they may appear to be at great odds with one another. Coldplay, in a psalmlike manner, talks about "human life and struggles." *The Sopranos*, despite its vulgarities, has "positive things" like "family" and "relationships." The goal is not to elevate these forms beyond anything other than popular culture but to treat them as a viable means for presenting Evangelical Christianity. The goal is to "meet people where they are." In Bill's formula, non-Christians are "seekers." While they may be anti-institutional, they are not antispiritual and are presumed to have a great interest in matters of faith. They are therefore receptive to what Evangelicals have to say; they simply require that it appears before them in a familiar package. Being relevant means taking the onus to make these connections and, as a result, means being a better witness.

Love vs. Judgment

This opposition returns us to the opening interaction's focus on "vulnerability" and to a pervasive tension among American Evangelicals. Bill and Eddie's distinction between vulnerability and arrogance is part of a broader distinction between maintaining a loving attitude toward non-Christians and overtly exercising judgment on what is considered a sinful state of being. How do you act in love toward someone when you abhor what they say and do? How do you share the Truth of Evangelical Christianity without completely dismissing someone's current belief system? How do you point out sin without appearing overly harsh, pious, or self-righteous? These are the questions Evangelicals pose to themselves as they evaluate previous witnessing encounters and think about their next. This opposition of love versus judgment resonates deeply because of its theological basis in understanding the character of God. Much like the model of intimacy described in chapter 3, loving and judging others iconically signifies the relationship between humans and the divine. Evangelicals talk quite a bit about God's propensity for both compassion and wrath. God can punish the wicked but can still show mercy and forgiveness. This dichotomy is ingrained so strongly in the Evangelical worldview that it produces divergent forms of faith and interpretation depending on where the emphasis is placed (e.g., Bartkowski 1996). Bill illustrates how this ideological contrast informs his understanding of witnessing in his response to the story of Stephen in Acts 7:

> Bill: I see a lot of parallels to these religious leaders. And I think it's the opposite of where we need to be. I think we need to much more be Stephens and be listening to people. Doesn't mean we have to agree with everybody, doesn't mean that everything is right. It just means that as Jesus' followers we need to love people. I heard a great story when I was out in San Diego, actually it happened in Grand Rapids. And I'll probably tell it again because I love it so much. It might even end up in a sermon sometime. How many of you know who Marilyn Manson is?
>
> [[None of the other participants know]]
>
> Bill: It's a rock singer that talks a fair bit about suicide and is quite dark. Anyway, not someone who proclaims a Christian message, as it were. Marilyn Manson came to Van Andel in Grand Rapids and there were two Christian churches that went down to that concert. One of them, group of folks, went down to protest and got into arguments with people in the lines. You know, telling them about how horrible this guy was and this concert was and how wrong it was, and shouting back and forth. I think that's the one that made the news, of course. Another group of folks went down to the same concert with big trash barrels full of ice and Mountain Dew and handed out Mountain Dew to folks in the line. And people said,

obviously, "Why are you doing this?" And they said, "Because we care about you. Because we love you. Because Jesus loves you." That's all they said. Got into many more conversations, nice, peaceful, more quiet conversations with people. One of the guys in the line was really high, really messed up, and as they talked with this guy ultimately he didn't go to the concert. Got out of the line and they took him to rehab to get help. Now, I think that's the difference between Stephen and the religious leaders. And we find religious leaders in jihads in Islam, but we also find them in the Christian Church today.

Bill uses the drastically different styles employed by Christian groups at the Marilyn Manson concert to demonstrate the crucial difference between acting in love and acting in judgment. The first group picketed and rebuked the concertgoers. The second group silently handed out Mountain Dew to those in line. The success of the latter, and the strategy of love, is made abundantly clear. The shouting and arguments of the protesters won no favor, whereas the peaceful, quiet approach elicited an open-ended question and may have saved one young man from the destructiveness of drugs. In a final move that is both subtle and forceful, Bill associates the style of judgment with Islamic jihadists. In doing so he leaves little room open to challenge this model of a good witness.

Relational vs. Superficial

The third ideological contrast reaches back into the popular discourse of American Evangelicalism to find another pervasive trope: building relationships. Recall the discussions of intimacy and relationships in chapter 3 and the significance of these cultural models for Evangelicals. They wish to emulate their familial-like bond with God in their interpersonal relationships, using this ever-increasing closeness as an index of spiritual growth. Note the emphasis in my earlier reference to Hybels's best-selling *Becoming a Contagious Christian* on "relational" evangelism. The backstage commentary on witnessing draws out in even greater detail this contrast between meaningful and superficial relationships. In the next example, Ron recounts a recent experience with his longtime veterinarian. It occurred as somewhat of a tangent from their initial study question that asked the men to apply the story of Ananias and Sapphira from Acts 5 to their own church community. Bill began the diversion by talking about an upcoming church program at IUMC:

Bill: I'm really looking forward to this Forty Days of Community[4] that we're doing, because so much of the stuff that we're talking about in here is precisely what I think we're gonna be addressing in all of those groups. I think we're gonna be challenged to grow that level of trust in our lives.

Ron: That reminds me. I had prayed, I believe it was Saturday morning, "Lord, bring that person to me that I'm supposed to invite to the new service." And we were taking care of our son's dog this weekend. It was sick. My son called from Chicago and said what was wrong and he talked to the vet and [we were] supposed to start the dog on this medicine. But he said, it's okay if I wait until Tuesday. And I got off the phone and I thought, "That doesn't make sense." If the dog's not doing well, I better go down and see the vet. Now, we've had the vet, she and her husband have been here for two Christmas Eve services, one this year and one six or seven years ago. And they've told us that "Church, it isn't our thing." So, I walked in to the vet's office. And she was glad I came because she had thought about my son's calling her. She came out and I said, "How you doing?" And she said, "I'm doing okay." And I looked at her and she didn't look okay. So, I put my arm around her and I said, "Now, how are you really doing?" And she started to open up. And I said, "This isn't a commercial or anything." I said, "I've been praying for you," because she's had some other issues. Cancer. I said, "We're starting this new service." I said, "I'd like the opportunity, when it does start, to ask you and your husband to join us." She says, "Well, talk to me." And I thought, "Wow! That's the furthest she's gone." But I was so excited to get home and tell my wife.

Bill: See, I believe that's gonna happen a whole bunch.

Ron: But I could have just let it go when she told me she was doing fine.

Bill: Sure. Yeah. That's great.

Ron: But like Eddie said, it's because I've known her for a good many years. If I had just gone in there and hadn't, I wouldn't have known whether she was looking good or wasn't.

Bill: Well, and a piece of that that I think is so important is, she was your vet. So, you were there for a service from her. And I think so often we look at the people around us like that. That's my vet. You take care of my dog and I'll pay you money, and that's the extent of our relationship. You're my waitress, or my wait-person, bring me my food. I'll give you a tip. That's it. You cut my hair. Whatever it is. Those are our relationships. When we pray, "God lead me to people," we begin to see these people around us. All these folks are people we can relate to. All these folks are people who have lives just like we have, who have struggles just like we have. And we can engage them. We can connect with them. And that's the biggest part of evangelism, is those kinds of things. So, that's really cool.

Bill sets the agenda of the discussion with his focus on trust. Following Ron's narrative, he and Bill reflect on the lessons available in this encounter with the vet. For Ron, his ability to effectively witness was contingent on his already established relationship with the vet and her husband. His previous efforts enabled him to assess her well-being, see past the vet's lip service of being "okay," put his arm around her, inquire a second time about the vet's well-being, and ultimately receive an honest response. Her moment of openness (vulnerability?) allowed Ron to extend an invitation. Bill, taking Ron's experience a step further, suggests that our day-to-day world looks very different—in particular, the types of relationships we cultivate with other people—once we begin thinking relationally. In this way, being a good witness changes one's everyday realities, altering how we experience seemingly meaningless interactions and social spaces that are not predictably spiritual. Ron and Bill both tap into the substantial social meaning embedded in building relationships, opposing it to the trouble that plagues being superficial.

Focused vs. Distracted

The fourth ideological contrast juxtaposes witnessing styles that adhere strictly to the Gospel message with those that incorporate other preoccupations. Good witnessing concerns itself only with sharing the Good News, while bad witnessing complicates matters with extraneous issues, namely political questions. The Tuesday Men were careful to point out that despite strong, biblically framed opinions on moral and politicized topics, these still had no place in the witnessing encounter. The following exchange between Bill and Jerry exemplifies this difference between staying focused and getting distracted. The interaction came at the very beginning of their seventh meeting after reading Peter's speech to the Jewish Sanhedrin in Acts 8:

> Bill: What do some of these things say to us, then? If this is what Peter did and the response that happened and all of these people responding. What are some of the principles in that that we might apply as we think about being the Church and presenting the Gospel today?

Jerry: He was very direct. I just think of today, I often think of Billy Graham—somebody that has consistently been very direct and stayed on message. He hasn't been sidelined. And I think we get sidelined pretty easily.

Bill: Okay. He has been extremely effective around the world, continues to be in many parts of the world as he is able to be. I guess I would broaden that to say that style of evangelism is effective in some parts of the world. I think it's less effective in our culture today. It was very effective in a mindset that was looking for the right answers and for truth. He did a marvelous job of presenting that in a very direct way. Today, that method may not be as effective as it was in a different generation. But it's still effective and it's still necessary, preaching I think is still necessary. It just has to be shaped a little bit differently. So, being direct is a good thing.

Jerry: Yeah, I guess I wasn't so concerned with the method as that he stayed on track.

Bill: Stayed true to the message.

Jerry: Stayed true to the message. We can get sidetracked so easily in the political side.

Bill: And those things are important. But central must be the Gospel. If we miss that central part, we miss the power part. . . .

Bill: Yeah, I don't know what Peter and John thought about. I suspect they probably thought that Israel ought not be under the control of Rome. I suspect they probably thought that. Most Jewish folks thought that. I suspect they probably didn't really like the idea of paying taxes to Caesar and all those kinds of things. And they probably spoke about that and dealt with that with their friends. But that wasn't their central message. I mean, it's like Paul. I think a lot of times when people read Paul in our day and don't put it into context of what was going on, particularly in some of the issues that he addresses around women and some of these things. Paul, he's the one that said, *there's neither Jew nor Greek, slave nor free, male nor female*. Paul understood what the Gospel did for people. But he also was not willing to comprise the spread of the Gospel for political end. And so, anything that got in the way of the spreading of the heart of the Gospel, he said, "Stop doing that." I mean, he's the guy that boldly comes before the Jerusalem Council and says, we must *not insist on these Gentiles becoming Jewish and being circumcised*. That's not *the gospel*. And he was convincing enough that they understood that that was the reality. Then, you see him with Timothy, who has a Greek background and it would have been a problem for the spread of the Gospel, and he circumcised him. That's not the issue. The issue is the Gospel. He's gonna die for that, but he's not gonna worry about all the side issues. He focuses on the central issue.

Through his question, Bill asks the group to reflect on the application of Peter's actions to their lives as committed Christians. Jerry is quick to raise the example of Billy Graham and his consistency in "staying on message." Bill agrees (though not without a brief reminder that the method of evangelism must remain culturally relevant) and proceeds to the political leanings of New Testament apostles and eventually the directness of St. Paul. There is a thinly veiled comparison here between the political interests of Peter, John, and Paul and those of contemporary Evangelicals in America. Bill effectively invites the group to replace Roman control, Caesar's taxes, and Jewish circumcision with abortion, same-sex marriage, and stem cell research. In turn, the unrelenting focus exhibited by these 1st-century Christians should be emulated by today's Christians, avoiding "side issues" and focusing on "the central issue."

The type of preparatory discourse in the Tuesday Men's backstage talk about witnessing takes shape around a series of ideological contrasts, each of which extends the contrast of being a "good" or "bad" Christian witness. Through the process of linguistic indexicality, the group articulated what constitutes effective witnessing and what signifies failure in evangelistic encounters. Through their reading of Acts, the men identify words, discourse styles, and demeanors that are directly and indirectly bonded to the ongoing question of what makes a good witness. "Good" appears as joyful, vulnerable, relevant, attentive, loving, peaceful, inviting, relational, focused, and direct. Conversely, "bad" appears as arrogant, condescending, irrelevant, dismissive, judgmental, shouting, accusatory, superficial, distracted, and sidelined. These oppositions work together to distinguish clearly between an effective versus an ineffective Christian witness. Each field of traits is substantiated by narratives of personal experience, stories of successful evangelism that circulate in Evangelical networks, and more abstract explanations rooted in theological principles. The examples of good witnessing garner authority when the men create parallels with biblical texts. They established explicit connections between these models of witnessing and the words, actions, and motivations of biblical characters. Bill's conceptualization of Coldplay and *The Sopranos* occurs as a modern version of the Apostle Philip's decision to "stand by the chariot" of the

Ethiopian eunuch. The Christian groups juxtaposed at the Marilyn Manson concert metaphorically substitute for the difference between Stephen and the Jewish religious leaders. Ron's narrative of inviting his veterinarian to church followed a lengthy discussion of Ananias and Sapphira and the consequences of the couple violating their relationship with the early Church. And Jerry's framing of Billy Graham as someone who has "stayed on message" is equated with Peter, John, and Paul. By grounding backstage witnessing in biblical authority, the group extends the chain of indexical associations. The result is an affirmed gulf between good and bad witnessing and a stigmatizing of certain actions and ways of being. The ideological contrast of good/bad is thus cast as part of a more compelling pair of distinctions: biblical/unbiblical and Christian/un-Christian. In turn, the textual ideology of biblical authority benefits from this evidentiary discourse—accruing new testimony every time this group meets to read the Bible together.

Witnessing, Relevance, and "Emerging" Evangelicalism

"Sharing the good news of Jesus Christ" is a hallmark of American Evangelicalism (Noll 1992) and a constant matter of reflection for adherents. It is no surprise, then, to see the topic of witnessing play an important role in the life of group Bible study. The question we have considered is not if it happens but how such talk is organized. Using the Tuesday Men as a case study, I have argued that backstage witnessing is concerned primarily with defining the categories of good and bad witnessing. This base contrast appears again and again through a series of secondary oppositions that speak to different matters of effectiveness. These ideological contrasts are ultimately grounded in biblical terms, widening the separation between what constitutes good and bad witnessing.

This analysis asks us to think more carefully about the general contours of Evangelical witnessing. I began this chapter with Susan Harding's seminal work, in particular her widely read account of Reverend Milton Cantrell (1987; cf. 2000). His compelling verbal display leaves the distinct impression that witnessing is a highly stylized, well-ordered, neatly structured, and (no doubt) rehearsed performance. On the one hand, this analysis has asked where such rehearsals take place and how they unfold. But the Tuesday Men also remind us that the category of witnessing is not so narrowly conceived by Evangelicals. For Harding,

A witnessing session minimally includes the gospel story . . . and a con-
frontation between the witness and his or her listener in which the witness invites or exhorts the listener to receive Christ as his or her personal
Savior. Witnesses may also tell how they and others came to know the
Lord as Savior; they may testify . . . and deliver other doctrinal exegeses."
(170)

This definition is quite fitting for the performance of personal conversion
narratives (cf. Stromberg 1993). However, this analysis of backstage witnessing forces us to recognize that the highly stylized witnessing encounter is part of a broader speech genre. Indeed, to understand witnessing as
Evangelicals do we must include the distribution of soda, inviting someone to a worship service, and connecting the lessons of popular bands
and TV programs with the Evangelical metanarrative. Group Bible study
serves as a backstage for all expressions of this genre, placing the mundane encounter alongside the finely tuned narrative performance.

The Tuesday Men's concern with witnessing is also informed by a
wider discourse within American Evangelicalism that touts a rethinking
of individual and institutional religious life. In particular, the theme of
"relevance" to the surrounding "culture" is an ideological model with considerable currency among Evangelicals. How do you attract generations
bored, or repelled, by 19th- and 20th-century church models and the divisive public personae of conservative Christians (pace Falwell and Dobson)? How can you present the unchanging Gospel message in ways that
are interesting and appealing for these generations? And how do you accomplish these things without comprising theological commitments? The
difficulty of these questions is compounded because Evangelicals view
their message to be counter-cultural. While they believe that they offer
something people desperately need, it is not something people necessarily
want. Or, to borrow another Evangelical idiom, being a follower of Jesus
may be a better life, but it is not an easier life. Bill is particularly attuned
to these problems as a member of a declining Mainline denomination, as
the pastor of a congregation that is predominantly middle-aged and older,
and as the pastor of a congregation located in a city full of young families and only a few miles from a large university flooded with twenty and
thirty-something students and faculty. Bill's most recent inspiration for
addressing these problems has come from the "Emerging Church" movement (Gibbs and Bolger 2005; Kimball 2003).

In the late 1990s a group of young pastors and church workers—affiliated only loosely through social networks, seminaries, paradenominational institutions, and outreach conferences—began talking about the status of Christianity in American society and how the historical Evangelical approach to church life needs to change if it is to remain relevant. The Emerging Church "conversation" (read: movement) has coalesced around three areas of change. First, American Evangelicalism is a "modern" institution trying to witness to a "postmodern" culture. Core assumptions of modernity—namely, the commitment that humans are able to access universal propositions of truth—need to be recast if they are to be appealing (or, even sensible) to generations that prioritize doubt, the instability of language and meaning, and epistemological uncertainty. The result is the adoption of a "missiological" orientation. Witnessing to non-Christian America is equated with doing foreign missions, where the missionized do not necessarily know what Christianity is or assume a need for it.

Second, the seeker-sensitive model of congregational life—typified by Willow Creek Community Church—that catered to Baby Boomers and was so successful in the 1980s and 90s is becoming an outmoded formula. Younger generations increasingly want nothing to do with megachurches, PowerPoint sermons, and congregational life modeled on business corporate life. In its place, they want more intimate faith communities and worship activities that are more spiritually rigorous.

Third, in turn, there is a revival of interest in worship activities associated with Eastern Orthodox, "ancient," and "mystical" Christianities. This includes everything from the use of candles and incense to icon worship, *lectio divina*, high-church liturgy, prayer labyrinths, and the removal of the oratorical sermon from the center of worship life. While the interest in postmodern epistemology has impacted the theological and hermeneutic practices of Emerging Evangelicals, the "post-seeker" attitude and the turn to alternative worship has rearranged their ecclesiological decision making. All the while, these changes have retained a great interest in how to be a better Christian witness (cf. Bielo forthcoming; Flores 2005; Harrold 2006; Packard 2008).

Since the late 1990s the influence of the Emerging Church on American Evangelicalism has steadily widened. We have seen a veritable explosion of books, articles, blogs, podcasts, YouTube posts, and conferences opposing, advocating, and debating all things Emerging. We have seen the appearance of self-consciously Emerging communities across the United States. And we have seen established congregations—mainline and Evangelical alike—try to incorporate Emerging ideas into their local culture. Bill's efforts with IUMC are indicative of this latter case. When Bill arrived in 2002, the church was reeling from a series of interim pastors and a controversial female pastor who left in 2000, almost forcing the church to permanently close its doors. One of the first changes Bill instituted at IUMC was the addition of a second, "contemporary" worship service on Sunday mornings to try and attract a younger demographic. This experienced only mild success, and in the summer of 2005 it was brought to a temporary end. Bill then organized a "launch group" comprised of church members interested in reorganizing the contemporary service and creating a new "culture of outreach" that would fundamentally alter the congregational ethos toward witnessing. In late October 2006, following the hire of a new female assistant pastor—a recent graduate from a local seminary and trained to lead "multisensory" worship gatherings—"Oasis" was launched. IUMC describes this reimagined worship community as

> A new community of people seeking closer connection with God through interactive, authentic worship and living.
>
> Oasis is for people from all walks of life seeking, questioning, and finding God. (In other words everyone is welcome!! If you believe, if you don't believe, if you are wondering whether or not God cares about you or exists at all.)

Bill and others hope that Oasis will cater to the Emerging population of Christians and potential converts not being attracted by "traditional" worship, but who are assumed to be in abundance and waiting to be reached. The imagining and establishment of Oasis is a direct product of Bill's exposure and commitment to the Emerging Church. As of May 2008, Oasis averages roughly fifty attendants each Sunday. It is complete with candles by the hundreds replacing fluorescent lighting, a mix of music styles, burning incense, moveable prayer labyrinths, interactive art, and a spoken sermon that is frequently replaced with a multimedia presentation followed by a dialogue among those in attendance.

Bill's facilitation of the Tuesday Men and his leading role in guiding their backstage witnessing was also imbued with his interest in the Emerging Church. In this final example, the group had just finished reading Acts 2:42–47, which describes the fellowship of the 1st-century Christian Church. The study guide asked the group to comment on the nature of this relationship:

Jerry: This is gonna seem kind of strange. I was kind of comparing this to a business. You know, this is the start-up phase. And when you're in the start-up phase, you're really focused because you're trying to keep this thing going. And so, you got everybody going in the same direction. But then, as you get a more mature business, you know, people start looking at different directions. And the focus just changes.

Bill: That's a really good analogy. I like that a lot, because I think it's really true. In fact, it's funny that you should say that because I've been thinking about that a whole lot lately, just in regards to the church as a whole. And I've been even thinking in some radical ways, wondering whether a church ought to exist longer than about ten or fifteen years. . . . I think some places are beginning to discover that. Some of the stuff I've been reading on the Emerging Church really talks about new congregations, it's a different model, it's kind of the model we're looking at, where new congregations spring up almost as new churches inside the boundary of an existing church. And there's this new congregation and as another need arises there's, start another one. And just different ways of looking at things and different ways of reaching people. I think you're absolutely right. I think it's very, very easy once you get past the start-up phase, once things start going well, to lose that focus.

Bill's radical rethinking of congregational life and, by extension, of how best to "reach the lost," is structured by his interpretation of the Emerging Church. Underlying this particular reading from Acts 2 and the remainder of the group's study is a steady emphasis on what works and what does not in the effort to be a better Christian witness. Thus, from the backstage of the Tuesday Men's Bible study to the frontstage of Oasis, we see an American Evangelical pastor and his congregation taking seriously the wider discourse of being relevant.

* 6 *

Negotiating Self and Other

Meet Sandy. She spent most of her adult life raising two children and leading sales seminars for a management company. When she retired she was able to focus on a lifelong passion—teaching. Every year she makes multiple visits to parochial schools affiliated with nearby Lutheran churches to give lectures on Christian history and theology. And every Thursday from 10 a.m. to noon, she serves as the facilitator for a women's Bible study group at her own Lutheran church. Sandy values this responsibility, diligently preparing for each week's lesson, rarely devoting less than four hours to the task. While she enjoys this leadership role a great deal, she is often anxious about satisfying the women's expectations. Many of my conversations with her concerned the pros and cons of study texts, potential study resources, and different facilitation styles. She was always very interested to hear what other groups were studying and how other leaders led. Despite this anxiety and her tendency for self-deprecation, the women thought very highly of her pedagogical talents and the energy she invested week after week. They appreciated her attempt to involve everyone in the discussion and her use of multiple biblical commentaries for explicating study texts.

The LCMS Women belong to the same Missouri Synod Lutheran congregation as the LCMS Men (chapter 2). They met in the church library, and their usual attendance of ten to fifteen fit snugly around the large rectangular table in the middle of the small room. Shelves filled with books, videos, and Bibles sat a few feet behind our heads, giving the room a cozy and scholarly feel. The youngest member of the group was in her early fifties, though most were in their mid-sixties or early seventies. Nearly all of the women, including Sandy, are lifelong members of the Lutheran Church-Missouri Synod. The few exceptions to this joined the denomination in their early adult years.

During my initial visits in the late fall of 2004 they had just begun a new study: *To Live Is Christ: The Life and Ministry of Paul* (1997), an "in-depth women's Bible study" by Beth Moore, a popular Evangelical author and speaker. The study methodically moves through Paul's ministry in the book of Acts, incorporating relevant texts from the Pauline Epistles as readers follow the apostle's journey from city to city. The texts are supplemented with numerous intertextual references from both the Old and the New Testament. Along with the abundance of scriptural texts, much of the book consists of Beth Moore's questions and observations—ranging from personal anecdotes to biblical exegesis and original language commentary. Following Sandy's lead, the group focused primarily on Moore's open-ended questions that ask readers to apply biblical texts to their personal and congregational lives and then reflect on the consequences of those applications. The study is designed to last ten weeks. In between each meeting, individuals are to complete five days of private reading and reflection. When gathered together, groups are encouraged to watch a video in which Moore sermonizes on the week's lesson. However, Sandy worried that assigning "homework" might discourage some from attending. Instead, they adopted a different method of working through one day of reading and questions at each group meeting, turning the ten-week study into a fifty-plus-week study. After several months of this, Sandy suggested that they start moving at a faster pace, now worried that people were getting "bored." Everyone objected, assuring Sandy that they enjoyed "taking it slow" and "reading things thoroughly."

Along with Sandy's systematic leadership style, the group was characterized by a collection of distinctive personalities. Joyce's contributions were anticipated for being insightful, articulate, straightforward, and providing "the standard Lutheran answer." On the few occasions when Sandy could not attend, she relied on Joyce to facilitate. Lynn was equally reliable but for a much different reason. With a mix of stridency and humor, her right-wing political leanings added a shade of controversy and national relevance to the discussions. Barbara had an unmistakable presence, marked by her constant and infectious laugh. She was often late and rarely arrived without a mildly adventurous explanation of her delay. Once settled, though, she had a proclivity for incisive questions, just when discussions seemed spent.

These women are much more than study partners. They are close friends. Many were charter members who helped plant the church in the late 1980s. They travel together and spend time socially. Their husbands golf and work on projects with each other. Perhaps most frequently, they baby sit grandchildren together. This familiarity and closeness was transparent in their study discussions. Participants transitioned seamlessly among the intimate, supportive, scholarly, jovial, and controversial. The LCMS Women offer a case study for how Evangelicals self-consciously articulate conceptions of identity in group life.

Self and Other in Evangelical Identity

It is somewhat of a fiction to devote only this last empirical chapter to the question of Evangelical identity. Each of the preceding chapters, at least in part, has pursued how Bible study provides a vital locale for Evangelicals to perform notions of their religious self through dialogue and collective reading. In their attention to Bible interpretation, cultivating intimacy, participants' interests, and witnessing, groups are telling stories about what it means to "be Evangelical" in their own ways and in ways reliant on broader American religious discourses. In this chapter, though, I take a more focused approach and analyze how categories of religious identity are explicitly treated as an object of self-conscious reflection.

Articulations of identity in group Bible study are most commonly organized by the antinomy of self-other: the opposition of well-formed ideas about collective belonging with abstract and concrete descriptions of out-group representatives. David Hess (1993) classes this way of imagining identity as "dialogical," where "identity is constituted not by essential characteristics but instead by a set of relationships to the Other, or whatever is *not* the Self" (43, emphasis in the original; cf. Roberts 1998: 54–55). In this juxtaposition, social actors seek to identify how aspects of the self—regarding beliefs, actions, logics, and all other manner of expressions—are distinct and somehow favorable or superior to its antagonists. Depictions of cultural groups occupying the same sociohistorical space are presented, and a decisive separation is asserted between the others being eschewed and the self being claimed. In short, a great deal of energy is devoted to explaining who you are not in an effort to state who you are.

By framing notions of identity as a problem of self-other, Evangelicals are utilizing a logic that is visible cross-culturally and is perhaps a fundamentally human process. Many would argue that this relational dichotomy is a necessary foundation for intersubjectivity and the formation of individual consciousness. The intellectual tradition of symbolic interactionism, for example, suggests that all communicative action requires a knowing, reflexive self and an interlocutor recognized as other (Mead 1934). These two subject positions are the basis for evaluating the nature of an interaction, discerning intentions,[1] and constructing shared meanings. Among the more famously argued ethnographic cases is Keith Basso's work among the Western Apache Native Americans of eastern Arizona (1979). Basso explains how the generalized categories of "Whiteman" and "Indian" are made public through impromptu joking encounters in which Apaches mock the cultural incompetence of Whites. "[Joking] performances are little morality plays in which Western Apaches affirm their conceptions of what is 'right' and proper by dramatizing their conceptions of what is 'wrong' and inappropriate" (76). Basso's work clearly shows how conceptions of self among the Western Apache are communicated largely through their portrayals of this moral and cultural other. Similarly, Fredric Roberts (1998) asks among American Catholic liturgists, "How does the liturgical Self implicitly or explicitly represent the Other?" (55). In the Bible study context we can ask not only how the other is represented, but also which others are selected and how they are placed in relation to the self being articulated by the LCMS Women through their reading of Beth Moore and the Bible. As we will see, the process of selecting, representing, and evaluating others is informed by a series of cultural models and discourses evident in the history of Evangelicalism.

Among American Evangelicals, selves and others take shape around questions of theology, institutional history, religious practice, cultural affiliations (for example, national politics), and relationships with non-Evangelicals. In many ways, the history of Evangelicalism in America— indeed, the history of Christianity in the West—is a history of selves and others. Catholics are Catholics because they are not Orthodox. Protestants are Protestants because they are not Catholics. Wesleyans are Wesleyans because they are not Calvinists. Evangelicals are Evangelicals because they are not mainline Protestants, fundamentalists or charismatics. Charismatics are Charismatics because they are not Pentecostals. And perhaps most recent, progressive Evangelicals are progressive because they are not conservative Evangelicals. The many and varied expressions of Christianity in the United States encourage this play of identity, providing numerous everyday opportunities for empirical contrast and separation (cf. Bielo 2004). Within this economy of religious distinctions we can ask: how does the process of organizing identity by self-other relations unfold within particular traditions (for example, Missouri Synod Lutherans) and in particular social institutions (for example, group Bible study), and through particular forms of social practice (for example, collective reading)?

Lutherans and Evangelicals

American Lutheranism is dominated by three denominations: the Evangelical Lutheran Church in America (ELCA); the Lutheran Church-Missouri Synod (LCMS); and the Wisconsin Evangelical Lutheran Synod (WELS). These three Lutheran branches share a common lineage, establishing distinct denominational identities in 1988, 1847, and 1850, respectively (Noll 1992). They include more than 17,000 congregations and 8 million total adherents (Jones et al. 2002). The ELCA is the largest (more than 5 million), followed by the LCMS (more than 2 million) and the noticeably smaller WELS (more than 400,000) (Jones et al. 2002).

My inclusion of the LCMS as an "Evangelical" denomination is not a categorical move shared by all scholars of Christianity. More often, sociologists group the LCMS as a fundamentalist denomination (e.g., Mullin and Richey, eds. 1994). As a matter of self-identification, LCMS theologians (as Pastor Dave informed me during our first meeting together in August 2004) emphasize their uniqueness and prefer to describe their church as "confessional," signifying their acceptance of the doctrinal confessions set forth in the *Book of Concord*. The reasons for distinguishing Lutheranism from Evangelicalism are many. Various theological doctrines, in particular those involving the sacraments of communion and baptism, are commonly cited in support of this separation. However, the LCMS tradition is consistent with the wider Evangelical movement when it comes to other doctrines, such as an insistence on absolute biblical authority, a Triune God, the virgin birth of Christ, and a personal relationship with God. In addition to theology, my description of the LCMS as Evangelical is also justified on sociological grounds. LCMS congregations, including that of the LCMS Men and Women, participate in many of the same paradenominational organizations as other Evangelicals, watch the same religious television, listen to the same religious radio, read the same religious books, and use the same church programs (for example, *Forty Days of Purpose*).

As a case of religious identity organized by self-other relations, the LCMS is an exemplary choice. Lutheranism emerged during the 16th-century European Reformation primarily because of objections to the practiced theologies of the Roman Catholic Church. In the post-Reformation period, Lutherans set themselves apart from their competitors in the evolving religious economy (for example, Anglicans, Anabaptists,

Calvinists, Armenians) on doctrinal and liturgical grounds. The *Book of Concord*, the articles of faith that outline the whole of Lutheran theology, includes responses to the "erroneous articles" of "Anabaptists, Schwenkfeldians, New Arians, and Anti-Trinitarians." In the U.S. context, Lutheran immigrants in the mid-19th and early 20th centuries remained "a largely self-contained" religious entity for theological, ethnic, and linguistic reasons (Noll 1992: 216). These cultural enclaves are recognizable in 21st-century America by the strong concentration of all three Lutheran denominations in the Upper Midwest and Great Lakes regions (Jones et al. 2002), reflecting a history of migration, persecution, and settlement. Thus, from its 16th-century beginnings to its current manifestations, "being Lutheran" has largely been formed relationally in opposition to the Christianities (including other Lutheranisms) operating within the same sociohistorical setting.

Negotiating Self and Other in Group Bible Study

Based on my observations and analyses of eighteen group meetings, I cannot overstate the attention paid to the theme of denominational identity by the LCMS Women. The marking of textual materials alone was remarkable. The denominational affiliations of Bible commentators, authors, speakers, hymn writers, and Bible translators were constantly inquired about, if not immediately identified (usually by Sandy). The words and lives of Lutheran theologians—from Martin Luther to Dietrich Bonheoffer to Erwin Lutzer—were repeatedly recontextualized to help explain Moore's commentary and biblical texts. Self-deprecating jokes about this preoccupation concluded intense discussions, indexing a keen awareness of how much they talked about "being Lutheran." In addition to these very numerous but rather brief signifiers, the group exhibited a tireless concern with delineating the boundaries of their Lutheran self when reading scripture and *To Live Is Christ*. Below, I use five interactions to illustrate the varied ways that self-other distinctions appeared among the LCMS Women. These examples highlight both the continuities and the tensions that surround this play of religious identity.

Example One: January 13, 2005

The group had just finished reading Beth Moore's explication of Paul and Barnabas's trip from Derbe to Antioch (Acts 14:21–28):

Before we penetrate the heart of our lesson today, note the obedience of Paul and Barnabas to the great commission (see Mat. 28:19–20). Acts 14:21 tells us they ministered to the people in Derbe in two vital ways. They preached, which means "to evangelize," and they taught or *matheteuo*, which means "to instruct with the purpose of making a disciple." Paul and Barnabas were careful not to neglect evangelism or discipleship. Both are vital, life-giving elements in any New Testament church. (1997:64–65)

Sandy stopped and opened the topic for discussion:

Sandy: One commentator I read suggested that Matthew 28 had the sense of not just teaching, but also discipling. Setting up churches, discipling, setting up an order in the church, a way of continuing.

Lynn: See, I don't think that order is here today either. I think a lot of churches, new churches that are popping up, I don't think they're orderly. You know, they're fun, but I don't think there's order.

Sandy: Do people get baptized? Evangelized?

Joyce: Adults do.

Sandy: Taught in a relatively stabilized fashion?

Lynn: But taught, [[sighs]] I mean you would oft, oft, oft times never hear a word of law in months. It's much more Gospel and feel good and how to be good people.

Lola: Yeah. And sometimes I don't think they, I mean we, call it structure. Just to learn what our church stands for when you're first going. I think some churches, people just join and they don't really know what the basic beliefs are in that denomination.

Lynn: Well, the word of Gospel is not nearly so sweet unless you realize the, the law and the sin, and then you realize the sweetness of Gospel.

Sandy: It's interesting that the kinds of churches you might be talking about have very, kind of fairly strict lifestyles, or covenants. If you want to join that Assembly [of God] church across town, you'll covenant with them not to do certain things.

Lynn: Yeah. I'm thinking of the much more casual churches.

Sandy: Like the Vineyard churches?

Lynn: Yeah. Mhmm. And we have one, in fact, I went to a travelogue and I looked down and there was a bulletin. So, I was, during the intermission I was looking at the bulletin for this [local church]. And you know, it was a lot of nice. And grace is important, oh my. But that word of law should still be there. And I think that's why they're so casual these days, because there isn't the balance with the law.

Sandy: Remember when members of Zion came over, we had the green hymnal, that's the ELCA hymnal. . . . The order of service was such that the confession of sins is separate from the service. And you can have it or not. A number of times our pastors, they didn't choose to have a confession of sins.

Lola: Well, I have a friend who will not say the confession of sins because she says she is not a poor, miserable sinner. She said, [[defiant tone]] "I'm not."

Lynn begins the self-other work by equating "new churches" with a troubling lack of "order." Lola adds that these churches are also missing the element of "structure" that is so vital for Lutherans. Lynn continues this critique, adding "casual" to the running list of objections. Sandy adds a final problem regarding the absence of the "confession of sins" from other churches' liturgies.

This exchange includes four themes that populated the group's identity discourse: First, distinct Christian others are identified. In this case, three separate others are named. The first two occupy the same category of "new churches" and are represented here by the Vineyard Fellowship and a local Assembly of God church. The former is a neocharismatic denomination with a small but thriving community in the local area. The latter is the largest Pentecostal denomination in the United States, and the church to which Sandy refers boasts the largest membership of any church in the city. The third other is closer kin, the ELCA, the largest Lutheran denomination in the United States.

Second, distinct features of the LCMS Women's version of the Lutheran self are articulated. This interaction places three specific notions of identity at stake: the needed doctrinal balance of teaching both law (humanity's fallen nature, the reality of sin in the world today, and the necessity of spiritual redemption) and Gospel (forgiveness of sins through Jesus' sacrifice on the cross), as well as the institutional practice of mandatory theological training for all members, most visible as youth catechism and adult conversion classes and the inclusion of the confession of sins in the weekly worship liturgy.

Third, there is transitivity between separate dimensions of the others under consideration. Here, the initial classification of "orderliness" and the later addition of "casualness" are cast as part of the same general problem.

These are not theological or liturgical synonyms and therefore indicate a moment of conceptual linking where participants unite their different objections to "new churches."

Fourth, the Lutheran self is presented as consistent with an example from the Bible, lending authority to the self and divesting it from others. In this first example, Matthew 28 and the practice of "discipline" are said to be evidenced in LCMS practice. This fourth theme is picked up in the next interaction.

Example Two: April 7, 2005

To help contextualize Paul's ministry in the city of Ephesus (Acts 18 and 19), Beth Moore suggests reading 1 Corinthians 16:19: *The churches in the province of Asia send you greetings. Aquila and Priscilla greet you warmly in the Lord, and so does the church that meets at their house*:

Sandy: So, what does that tell you is going on there? What are Aquila and Priscilla doing?

Marcy: They were hosting meetings.

Sandy: House church, just like home groups.

Marcy: They would probably have had communion at theirs, wouldn't they?

Sandy: Mhmm.

Marcy: Didn't they always sit down and break bread together?

Sandy: Almost never without. We don't do that here because of our rule about ordination and the way we treat the sacrament. It has to be blessed by an ordained pastor.

Marcy: Right.

Sandy: So, here we are, people of house churches, just like our home groups. And in fact, in the home group concept, because it started in an evangelical background, it's not as sacramental as we are. Home groups and say, the Assembly [of God] Church, I imagine that they have them. Or, Trinity [Church], they would have communion in the home groups, because they don't consider that you need to have that sacrament. It is a sacrament, but it's not as regulated.

Lynn: I don't think it is a sacrament. They call it "public communion." But they don't call it, like, we talk about "Word and Sacrament."

Sandy: Mhmm.

Lynn: They do have baptism, but they're adults. But I don't think they call it the sacrament of baptism.

Carole: I think the big thing with those churches, and I speak for the Assembly [of God] Church, is having people profess that they believe Christ is their Lord and Savior and that they are born-again or whatever. You have to profess this. I know with the motorcycle group that my daughter is involved with now. They get them to come to church and they take off their patches that say all these horrible things. But to be part of this group you have to do this. You have to believe that Christ died for your sins. This is what they are really wanting these people to do. Whether they just say they do and then they ride off into the sunset, I don't know.

Lynn: But it's "what I did." "I came to you." And we say, "We were called *by* the Holy Spirit." And I think that's the difference. It wasn't what I did to come. It was that "the Holy Spirit called me by the Gospel, enlightened me with His gifts, sanctified in" . . .

[[overlapping]]

Sandy: "In the one true faith."

Much like the first example, this discussion is grounded in an attempt to align Lutheran practice with biblical practice. While the conclusion is the same—the Lutheran self is a biblical self—the journey there is quite different. It begins oddly, with Sandy pointing out how Lutheran churches seem inconsistent with scripture while "Evangelical" churches seem to uphold the practice of serving communion in home groups. In her explanation, Sandy references the Assembly of God Church from the first example along with Trinity, a Willow-Creek modeled megachurch that has the second-largest membership in the city. The seemingly favorable position of these two others is quickly dismissed. Carole and Lynn emphasize, respectively, the tenuous and misplaced motivation of these "Evangelical" others. The closing, cooperative recital of Lutheran creed by Lynn and Sandy restores the Lutheran approach to its elevated position, reasserting the parallel between the Bible and their own denomination.

In these first two interactions, the separation between self and other is clear, as is the interpretation of that separation: Lutherans are biblical, others are not. Ultimately, it is the ideological principle of biblical authority that frames these articulations of religious identity. Yet, rather than simply assert that the Lutheran position coincides with that of scripture, the group constructs lengthy comparisons with different Protestant traditions. The women's references to the Vineyard, Assembly, and Trinity are most likely a result of these churches' success in the city's religious ecology and their affiliated denomination's success in the American religious economy compared to the national decline of LCMS membership. The implicit question is twofold: how different are we from growing churches? And how much of that difference is integral to Lutheran identity and how much is negotiable for the sake of increasing membership? Through this play of self and other, the women reflect on the traditions (for example, holy sacraments) and beliefs (for example, God's law of sin and judgment) they understand as truly vital to "being Lutheran."

Example Three: February 17, 2005

This interaction occurred at the very beginning of the meeting in response to Beth Moore's interpretation of the character Lydia from Acts 16:11–15. Moore argues that Lydia played a key role in spreading Christianity to Europe, indexing the influence of "Christian businesswomen" in the early church. After a few minutes of applauding the working mothers in their own congregation, Julie raises an objection:

Julie: You know, when I read this I was a little bit upset with Beth Moore because I thought she was giving Paul more credit than he deserved. Because Lydia was already attending church and it made it sound, to me, that she was saying, you know, he brought her to the Lord. I mean, he did baptize her and I'm sure he strengthened her, but she was already there.

Joyce: Was she studying Judaism? I mean, she was there at the gate where there was a group praying. It doesn't say what she was.

Sandy: *She worshipped God.*

Joyce: I wondered the same thing. *She worshipped God.* So, as a Jewish God? It doesn't say.

Sandy: *Worshipped God. The Lord opened her heart to respond to Paul's message.* And his message would, of course, have been about Jesus.

[five-second pause]

Joyce: Or, maybe his message was, "Repent and be baptized." Maybe she had heard of Jesus before. But the Bible doesn't tell us that.

Julie: You know, sometimes when I read her slant on things I'm not sure it's not just her slant. Kind of like you asked initially, "had we heard this before?" I don't know, it just made me feel a little uneasy when I read it.

Sandy: You don't have to swallow it hook, line, and sinker.

[[Group agrees]]

Julie: Well, that's kind of the way I was feeling about it. But I thought, "That didn't feel comfortable."

Sandy: Well, I think there are points of departure here. She's really not in our denominational context. And I think, frankly, she talks about writing in-depth Bible studies. You can get so in-depth that you find yourself kind of out on a limb in certain areas. Don't you think? A couple of times I have run into that with her, where she's worked herself so into a corner that this over here doesn't quite match what's over there. This is one of those cases where she rather assumes that out of maybe one paragraph in the Bible on Lydia, she assumed that Lydia opened up the Gospel to an entire continent.

Julie: I guess as a general, I don't like speculation. You know, I don't like speculation. If my husband asks me what I think about something I say, "I don't think anything about it. I don't have enough background information." You know, I just don't like speculation. That's the feeling I got with this particular lesson was, there's too much speculation in it.

Joyce: I had a pastor in the past that put too much of his own idea in. And it made me so nervous that I told him, "How can you say that? That is not in the Bible. How can you preach that from the pulpit?" He could always throw in his own little feeling on it.

Julie: Yeah, there's a place in the Bible where it says, *don't take away or add to.*

Joyce: Yeah.

Julie: And maybe that's where I get my thing about speculation from, I don't know.

Sandy: Your pastor got so far afield, in fact, he's not in the . . .

[[interrupted]]

Joyce: Right, he's not in the Lutheran Church anymore.

The identity work performed by the women here is based on three sets of associations. First, hermeneutic procedures deemed as "speculation" are opposed to proper forms of biblical exegesis. On three occasions, Joyce observes that Moore veers from what is stated explicitly in the Bible. Sandy successfully mixes metaphors to equate Moore's "speculation" with going "out on a limb" and backing herself "into a corner." And Julie overtly states her unease with such interpretive excess. Second, "speculation" is assigned as a characteristic of how others read scripture. Moore's Baptist affiliation and Joyce's now ex-Lutheran pastor are used to link "speculative" reading with being outside the Lutheran church. Third, these two associations create a conceptual space for inferring what typifies Lutheran scriptural exegesis. If speculation is inappropriate, and if others speculate, then the remaining Lutheran self is left to represent proper forms of interpretation. In establishing these three associations, the group tacitly invokes the discourse of literalism that pervades American Evangelicalism (chapter 2), and they argue for its legitimacy. In their casting of the difference, the problems of inferential speech belie the appropriate conduct of "Bible-believing," "literalist" Christians. As with the first two examples, this interaction demonstrates a clear separation between Lutherans and their others and a clear evaluation of that dissonance. The fourth example follows the thread of "speculation" but begins to illustrate how the LCMS Women's articulations of identity are not always so decisive and are likely sources of tension.

Example Four: March 31, 2005

In her exegesis of Acts 18, Moore poses an application question: "What about you? Has God ever used you at a time when you felt weak, with little to offer? If so, when? What happened?" After a brief silence, Julie begins:

Julie: I can. My sister-in-law, who is a Baptist, when my boys were being baptized, she attacked me like I was doing something evil. Baptists don't believe you should baptize children until they're of age to know what they mean.

Barbara: Well, what do Baptists believe then if something should happen to that child before they come of age?

Julie: They'll go to heaven because they're just children. They don't know any better.

Lynn: Well, that's kind of what we believe of the unbaptized infant. We believe they're going to heaven, but the Bible never says exactly.

Joyce: I think some of those faiths believe that God makes allowances for children, and He has other plans for certain situations.

Sandy: Well, He may. But that's not what He says. So, I don't know. What do you think?

Lynn: We also do not know what happens to an unborn baby that dies before it's baptized. We assume because God is loving and gracious that that baby's going to heaven. But scripture does not tell us for absolute fact.

Sandy: It's an enigma.

Joyce: Yes it is. One of those questions.

Beth: And that's one of the questions that nobody can answer.

Joyce: Well, now, David says *he will see his son in heaven*. His first son that died.

Sandy: Oh, you know what, I saw a picture of David's genealogy in my study Bible somewhere. And David's first wife had no child. [Name unclear] had Annon. Abigail had Kilea. Meacha had Absolom, Tamar. Hagath had Adonijah. Bathsheba's down at the bottom. She had Solomon, plus three other sons. And then, finally the last one, Abigail had Abishea, Joab, and Asahil.

Joyce: So, it doesn't say, Bathsheba's first son, doesn't give a name there.

Sandy: No. And it certainly wasn't David's first son. So, I don't know that we can take anything from that.

Here, the LCMS women wrestle with the subject of eternal salvation for unbaptized infants who die. They begin just as they did in the third example: Julie introduces the difference between Lutherans and Baptists. However, Lynn complicates the typical self-other narrative with her claim that "the Bible never says exactly" what the answer is for this particular question. To continue opposing Baptists and Lutherans means risking the implication that Lutherans "speculate" as much as Baptist others. Sandy and Beth evade the problem by relegating it to the class of "an enigma" and "one of those questions." Joyce attempts to restore the biblical ground for the Lutheran position (and thus restore the interrupted self-other depiction) by referring to the genealogy of David in the Old Testament. Sandy picks up on the attempt but to no avail. Recounting David's lineage provides no clear answers. This interaction, then, reveals some of the negotiation that is required in the group's identity discourse. They eventually have to back away from their usual derision of a defined other (Baptists) for the sake of salvaging what they consider to be a proper interpretive relationship with the Bible. In the end, this proves more important for maintaining their posture toward Lutheran identity than reiterating what they already know about their differences with Baptists (and what they are likely to state again as soon as the opportunity arises).

Example Five: May 19, 2005

The first four examples present the LCMS Women consistently elevating their Lutheran self over a variety of Christian others. Even in the previous case, in which some salvage work was required, the interaction comes and goes without any explicit challenge to the appropriateness of LCMS theology or practice. Yet, such a uniform and unanimous picture is incomplete. On several occasions, an ambivalence surrounding their sense of self was drawn into sharp focus and stern disagreements quickly followed. In this final example the group takes up the contentious issue of female ordination. They began by reading Acts 2:18, the Apostle Peter's re-contextualization of the Old Testament prophet Joel: *Even on my servants, both men and women, I will pour out my Spirit in those days, and they will prophesy*:

Barbara: So, Beth Moore asks us, "Upon whom did God say He would pour out His spirit in Acts 2:18?"

[three-second pause]

Julie: Well, women. . . .

[four-second pause]

Barbara: If that happened so long ago, why does the Lutheran Church-Missouri Synod not let women read or let women do anything? [[Laughs]]

Judy: They left that part out of their Bibles.

[[Laughs]]

Becky: Well, there is another verse, though, that says *the women should not be teaching over the men*. Personally I always thought there's plenty for women to do. We have so much we can do we don't have to lead men's Bible studies. But I think men and women are unique. God made us differently and I think that men think and process in different ways, most of them.

Barbara: That's right.

Sharon: So, you agree with the Missouri Synod, that women shouldn't be involved in, you agree with that? I mean, you really think that that's what God meant?

Judy: I went to a church the whole winter, a Presbyterian church, and the head pastor was a woman. And originally I thought, "Mmm. I'm not gonna like this." But once she started preaching and doing her sermon she was just preaching the Word, and it just came out of a female mouth and body. And it was the same. It had absolutely no different impact. And she was dynamic.

Sharon: Well, in the Lutheran, ELCA, they have women pastors.

[[Several women affirm]]

Sharon: And so I've been to church with that because some of my husband's family belongs to the ELCA. And I think they do a great job.

Becky: I'm not saying that I feel it's sacrilege or that it's black and white. But because of that one passage that I can remember, and there might be more, I do think God is a God of order and he did choose twelve disciples that were men.

Sharon: But that was what was acceptable at that time.

Becky: That's right. And God used women all the way through the Bible. I mean, there's Dorcas and all the other ones in Acts.

Marie: God used women a lot more than other men ever used women. He really did elevate them.

Sharon: Well, I just don't think that they should be held down. I think it's wrong not to allow women to participate in the service. I think they should participate in every way.

Marie: Well, now, Missouri-Synod passed that they participate in the service, though.

Sharon: Did they finally pass that?

Marie: Women can hold the office of president and vice-president.

Sharon: There's still a lot of them, though. It depends on what kind of pastor you have too. My daughter's church out in Wisconsin, it's like going to a different church. It is *so* backward. I mean, they don't let women do anything. I think the pastor is just very conservative. He just won't allow that.

Marie: Do you notice there's no joy there?

Sharon: Oh, there isn't any. And you know what, it isn't growing all that fast either. So, I see that as a real turn-off for a lot of folks.

Lola: I guess I kind of feel like Becky. I don't think it's wrong. But I feel uncomfortable in a church when a female is preaching. I guess it's because I've always been brought up that way.

Sharon: Well, we have a niece. She went to college and was an engineer and had a wonderful job. But she always felt that she had been called by God to preach. All her life she thought she wanted to be a pastor. And so, she went to the ELCA Church and she is a pastor in California. So, that might be one of the reasons I feel a little different about it. But I didn't mean to get you off on this.

Barbara: No. That's fine.

Becky: Well, that's always good to talk about, though. I mean, and I feel if someone feels called by the Spirit, I'm not gonna argue with what the Spirit is telling someone to do. I mean, there are women professors. There have been women missionaries for years. So, I think if God called someone, that's between them and God.

[[Several women agree]]

Barbara begins by opposing LCMS doctrine with what appears to be a straightforward biblical truth. Becky responds with a proof-text of her own from the New Testament epistle of 1 Timothy. Interestingly, she does not try to assert that this text somehow makes proper sense of the text from Acts, implicitly invoking the textual ideology of biblical continuity. Rather, she finds it sufficient to simply present the alternative that supports the LCMS position. This does not sit well with several other participants. Sharon directly challenges this and, along with Judy, presents two Protestant others (Presbyterians and ELCA Lutherans) who adhere more closely to this particular text from Acts concerning female ordination. Marie attempts some brief repair work, acknowledging that the LCMS does allow women in positions of church governance, but this is largely ineffective for bringing about any consensus. Instead, Sharon continues with her critique, ultimately using her daughter's "very conservative" LCMS congregation to illustrate how this particular doctrine has negative impacts for church growth.

Unlike the second example, in which the momentary elevation of an other is dismissed, the lagging Lutheran self is left to linger and the strict separation of self and other falls apart—if only temporarily.

This interaction is particularly revealing because it blends several powerful discourses in American Evangelical culture and recalls the very real possibility that Bible study can produce unresolved tensions. In and among the self-other work being accomplished, these women invoke discourses of theological doctrine, gender ideology, and church growth. Much like the LCMS Men (chapter 2), the group's reading of this biblical text occurs alongside deep convictions about the fundamental (read: divinely designed) differences between males and females. Evangelical women, too, have well-defined ideas about the nature of the sexes and how these translate to church life. Unlike the LCMS Men, though, there is a sharp divide within the group (namely Sharon and Becky) about what those differences are and where those boundaries lie.

Ultimately, this tension—as with all the disagreements I observed in this and other groups—was not severely divisive, and their discussion that morning eventually moved on amiably to the next reading. But while it may not have caused any permanent damage, this example does remind us that the ever-present potential for tension in Bible study can disrupt the progression of predictable narratives—in this case, positing a separation between selves and others.

Selves, Others, and Denominationalism

There is a certain curiosity in examining articulations of identity among a group of individuals that claim a drastically similar sense of self. In this type of institutional context, there is no advertising of identity needed and no motive of conversion. Yet, identity is still performed in these encounters, still put on display for others to see. Here, a group of Lutheran women met once a week to read and discuss a biblical commentary on the life of Paul. But in doing so, they managed to grant a great deal of attention to explaining "who they are," despite the abundance of shared knowledge already present about the subject.

The identity discourse of these women is organized by the opposition of self and other. This "dialogical sense of Self" (Hess 1993: 43) is articulated through sets of contrasting relations between the boundaries of a well-defined Lutheran self and numerous, equally well-defined Christian others. These women's version of the Lutheran self is constituted by its separation from ELCA Lutherans, "new churches" of various stripes, and Baptists, among others. It is constituted through questions of liturgy, doctrine, theological education, and biblical hermeneutics. And this local discourse of self-other is articulated alongside a variety of larger Evangelical discourses, from the legitimacy invested in "literalism" to gendered ideologies of how men and women are "made" differently. For the most part, the LCMS Women come to the clear conclusion that the Lutheran self is appropriate, correct, and ultimately, biblical. However, this is not always the case, and it is not always achieved in a seamless fashion. In the fourth interaction, for example, they must retreat from their usual critique. And in other cases, like the final example, they turn the critique on themselves. Their identity discourse, then, seems to require a certain negotiation of both self and other. This negotiation occurs on several fronts, all of which reflect the current status of the LCMS denomination in the American religious economy and the features that have historically distanced it from other traditions. As evidenced by the LCMS Women, tensions arise around issues of inclusion and exclusion, necessary and unnecessary traditions, Bible interpretation, and the implementation of specific theological doctrines. As global, national, and local religious ecologies continue to shift, I suspect the concerns of individual groups like the LCMS Women will follow suit, mimicking the contexts they are embedded in.

The LCMS Women's play of self and other calls attention to one of the most widely accepted sociological theories of American Christianity:

denominationalism. As the argument goes, the history of Christianity in the United States is one founded and subsequently dominated by denominational traditions from Western Europe. To speak of early religious life in America is to speak of Congregationalist, Presbyterian, Baptist, Episcopalian, Quaker, Lutheran, Reformed, Methodist, and Roman Catholic church bodies (Finke and Starke 1992). In addition to a few Protestant denominations that began on American soil, these European traditions oriented conceptions of religious identity for at least the next 150 years. The historic denominations in America provide sets of doctrines to accept or negotiate, a means of self-identification, and a means of evaluating others' religious affiliation (Finke and Starke 1992; cf. Conkin 1997; Noll 1992).

As the argument continues, this era of denominationalism began to fade in the years following World War II, marked by the institutional development of ecumenical organizations, parachurch groups, and nondenominational seminaries (Wuthnow 1988). The rise of the postdenominational era in American Christianity was crystallized by the appearance and popularity of nondenominational megachurches. By the end of the 20th century, the majority of American Evangelical congregations seemed to gravitate toward other affiliations, such as being a "Willow Creek church" or a "Purpose Driven church," rather than being a Methodist, Presbyterian, and the like. Among other reasons, avoiding denominational ties meant avoiding the accumulated social, ethnic, economic, and theological baggage that accompanied each tradition. For mainline and Evangelical Protestants, the waning of these church structures reflected an institutional form whose currency had run out in the American religious economy (Wuthnow 1988).

The anthropologist Fredric Roberts (2005) critiques the strict postdenominational thesis among mainline Protestants. In a four-year ethnographic study that included eight mainline congregations from four denominations, all quite successful in their local religious ecology, he found that congregants placed a high level of belonging with their respective church tradition. In short, being Baptist and maintaining a Baptist identity was very important for these believers. In place of any empirical evidence to support the decline in denominational affiliation, he found instead a widespread fear and anxiety among church leaders that the importance of denominations was disappearing from American religious life.

The case of the LCMS Women in this chapter raises similar questions about the denominationalism thesis among American Evangelicals. As discussed earlier, Lutherans are not archetypical Evangelicals, and this extends to their sense of denominational identity. Much like the way in which the Prayer Circle illustrates the theme of intimacy, the LCMS Women represent a rather exaggerated case of how articulations of identity are grounded in denominational terms. And yet, placing identity in a self-other framework and appealing to denominational ties was a consistent observation among most of the remaining project groups. For the LCMS Women, being Lutheran was not just an issue to be considered, it was *the* issue, overwhelming any discussion of religious identity. A close look at group Bible study allows us to assert this challenge to a taken-for-granted idea in the study of American Christianity. In turn, this analysis demonstrates once again how valuable Bible study is as a site of dialogue for Evangelicals and as a site of observation for ethnographers interested in Evangelical culture.

Conclusion

Group Bible Study in
American Evangelicalism (Reprise)

Evangelicalism has helped shape the course of American history, and this influence shows no signs of disappearing. As I begin this final chapter, Sunday morning news plays in the background, questioning the role of each candidate's religious faith (Evangelical, Catholic, Mormon) in the 2008 U.S. presidential election. In late November 2007, Rick Warren and his "Purpose Driven" community hosted their annual "Global Summit on AIDS and the Church," garnering national and international media attention and praise. One year earlier, a far more negative media campaign reported on Ted Haggard—Colorado megachurch pastor and then president of the National Association of Evangelicals—and the news of his ongoing sexual relationship with a male prostitute. Haggard had just recently appeared in the widely popular and widely controversial documentary film *Jesus Camp* that was released in September 2006. In April 2006, the Gospel of Judas[1] was released to the public after years of restoration and translation. A few weeks later, the film version of *The Da Vinci Code*[2] debuted. Both reignited debates about the boundaries and authority of Christian scripture and the borderlines of heresy and spiritual exploration. National controversy swirled in the fall of 2005 around Intelligent Design theory after court cases in Pennsylvania and Kansas ruled whether or not it should be taught in public school science classrooms alongside Darwinian evolution. This brought attention to biblical themes of creation, as well as the broader issue of what (if any) value biblical education might contribute to elementary and secondary school curricula. In November 2004, George W. Bush was reelected to the U.S. presidency, indexing the political capital of Christian Right voters and the power of biblically infused rhetoric to communicate with this audience. Evangelical books steadily appear on religious and secular best-seller lists with sales exceeding tens of millions and birthing cottage industries of complementary products.

The sheer power and presence of Evangelicalism in America's public life and gate-keeping institutions has impelled scholars of all stripes to grapple with the contours of Evangelical culture. In particular, sociologists of American religion and anthropologists of Christianity have committed to look ethnographically at the public and private lives of Evangelicals. Taken together this research has covered an impressive range of social domains and discourses, including congregational life (e.g., Ammerman 1987; Eiesland 2000; Luhrmann 2004; Malley 2004; Miller 1997; Watt 2002), sermon performance (e.g., Harding 2000; Muse 2005; Witten 1993), conversion narratives (e.g., Stromberg 1993), power brokers (e.g., Lindsey 2007), faith-based activism (Elisha 2004, 2008), parochial education (e.g., Wagner 1990), parachurch organizations (e.g., Balmer 1989; Bartkowski 2004), fellowship groups (e.g., Griffith 1997), fiction reading (e.g., Frykholm 2004; Neal 2006), health regimens (e.g., Griffith 2004), economic practices (Bialecki 2008), and sexual ethos (e.g., DeRogatis 2005). In fact, it is difficult to locate an arena of Evangelical culture that has not at least been commented on, if not studied systematically. Through all of this research, scholars have returned to a series of fundamental questions: what organizes the Evangelical imagination? Where and how is this imagination structured? What are the channels of its circulation? And how do the details of this imagination interact dialectically with meaningful forms of social practice? In short, where can we look to see Evangelical culture "in action"?

Surprisingly, sociologists and anthropologists of American Evangelicalism have paid little attention to one of the most vital social institutions that serves as a site of cultural production for Evangelicals: group Bible study. In this book I have provided the first in-depth, comparative ethnographic analysis of Evangelical Bible study in an attempt to understand the link between this institution and the broader Evangelical imagination. We have considered five case studies from three denominations: the LCMS Men, the Prayer Circle, the Iconoclasts, the Tuesday Men, and the LCMS Women. These groups varied in their demographic compositions, the texts they read, and how they organized the group experience. I used these cases to illustrate five themes that characterize Bible study life: Bible reading, spiritual intimacy, participant interests, models of witnessing, and conceptions of religious identity. In each of these analyses we saw how the appearance of these issues in these particular groups spoke directly to broader themes in Evangelical culture, from hermeneutic presuppositions and procedures to fundamental assumptions about the nature of Christianity, nascent forms of Evangelicalism, and widely accepted sociological explanations of American religion. In addition, this analysis of Bible study life has observed how numerous other tensions and discourses that populate the Evangelical imagination (for example, postures toward church growth, nonscriptural texts, gender ideologies, Bible translations, prayer, and church history) are integrated into the practice of group reading and discussion.

All of this has been toward one end: to argue that group Bible study is a crucial institution in the cultural life of Evangelicals. In pursuit of this, I have stressed a select few theoretical and methodological principles that provide a foundation for this research. I return to three of these here in hopes of crystalizing what is so valuable about a comparative ethnography of group Bible study.

Why Bible Study?

Bible study as dialogical space

An initial premise of this research, and an assumption that has been borne out time and again, is the character of group Bible study as a social event. While small groups certainly do include elements of rote memorization, highly ritualized behavior, predictable and mundane interactions, and finely rehearsed performative acts, it is by nature none of these. Rather, Bible study is an event defined by open, reflexive, and critical dialogue about central models of belief, logic, and action. It is a social space where Evangelicals reflect on—sometimes skeptically, sometimes confidently—questions of text, theology, morality, history, identity, spirituality, and a seemingly endless string of practical applications. In this regard, Bible study rightly appears as a unique event for Evangelicals, a dialogical space that offers something quite different than worship services, accountability partners, board meetings, outreach activities, fundraisers, social outings, revivals, parachurch gatherings, and the like. This quality of Bible study emerges around the practice of collective reading, highlighting the social significance that imbues the relationships produced among readers and their texts.

Because of its dialogical character, Bible study occupies an important position between social theory and empirical observation. Among the central concerns of social and cultural analysis is the motivation to explain underlying logics of thought and action and to identify the material and ideological processes that actively shape those logics. Scholars, in turn, seek out social locations that provide a glimpse into the processes of becoming, remaining, and changing. This leads some to colonial archives, others to rites of passage, everyday performances, entertainment spectacles, and so on. But no matter what cultural scene one is interested in, his or her theorizing must reckon with the potential dissonance between the question the individual is asking and the event he or she is observing. Thus, Bible study is not only a unique event for Evangelicals, but it is also unique for ethnographers. In particular, Bible study serves as a site for the production of knowledge. As groups read and talk together they make explicit their relationships to various forms of cultural knowledge. In some cases this process is largely habitual and largely a matter of reproducing taken-for-granted aspects of the Evangelical imagination. Certainly we see this in the strict adherence to a defined textual ideology surrounding the Bible. American Evangelicals uphold a long history of understanding and reading their sacred text in particular ways, even if they differ in the interpretive conclusions they settle on. In other cases this process takes on a self-conscious character and what was tacit becomes (at least temporarily) an object of reflection. I am reminded here of the LCMS Women's self/ other discussions and the very intentional ways that they communicated their discourse of identity. In either case, Bible study allows for the playing out of both continuity and tension in Evangelical culture and for observing the local and (inter)national discourses that bind and disrupt. It is this unique capacity of Bible study—its status as a dialogical event of production and reproduction—that highlights its importance, which initially drew my attention and that should now keep our attention.

Bible study and text-action

Group Bible study is an event dominated by two forms of social practice: reading and communication. The reading that takes place, as well as the talk surrounding that reading, is not a passive affair. By this I mean that groups do not simply take up their various texts, consider them, and forget their impact until the next meeting or some random, future encounter with the same text. The analysis in the preceding chapters has made it very difficult to maintain such an evaluation of collective reading. Quite the opposite, in fact, the type of reading featured in this book speaks to a dynamic relationship between text and action. The interaction that takes place between Bible study participants and their texts is productive, informing the worldview of these readers and their ways of being and acting in the world. In short, what happens in Bible study does not stay in Bible study. It travels well beyond the confines of the group into the participants' lives as spouses, parents, employers, employees, consumers, activists, and citizens. Perhaps the most compelling example of this is the Tuesday Men. Here, we see a constant feedback loop between talk about witnessing in Bible study, acts of witnessing in the world, return to Bible study, return to the world, and so on. The comparative ethnography presented here keeps in focus the reality that the social lives of Evangelicals—so important to American life, from national politics to public education—is intimately coupled to their lives as readers and small group members.

This relationship between text and action in group Bible study also draws attention to the social life of scriptures. Sacred texts—like the Christian scriptures—are not only sources of spiritual revelation, they are also powerful incitements to action. In turn, Evangelicals take their Bibles with them in all that they do. Even when absent as a material artifact, scripture remains present as an embodied and remembered text structuring Evangelicals' engagement with the world. This mandate of the Evangelical imagination—that the Bible should not just be read but also followed—makes the sites of interaction between Evangelicals and scripture extremely valuable for understanding how the process of application works. The analyses I have provided contribute to this very important question of how scriptures circulate through the words, texts, and institutions of Evangelical culture. Moreover, my fieldwork raises some intriguing questions regarding the breadth of Evangelical reading. While books like Philip Yancey's *The Jesus I Never Knew* would never be mistaken for scripture by Evangelicals, they may very well be treated like scripture when it comes to the transitivity among reading, discussion, and action. For this reason, the framework of "textual economies" (chapter 4) is equally important in the anthropological study of Christianity as "textual ideologies" (chapter 2).

Bible study and ethnographic methodology

My approach to group Bible study was ethnographic in nature, which meant I spent extended time with actual groups while they actually performed this social event. In this way, the work presented here is part of a much larger project interested in the qualitative study of American Evangelicalism and American religion and culture more broadly. At least with respect to the ethnography of Evangelicalism, sociologists and anthropologists have relied most heavily (and in some cases, exclusively) on a combination of participant observation and structured interviews. These two methods are vital forms of ethnographic data collection, and both are tools I used throughout the course of my fieldwork. But they both have limitations and should not constitute the whole of our methodological imagination.[3] In particular, participant observation (which, in most cases, translates to the recording of hand-written field notes during and after moments of observation) is largely restricted to documenting behavior, given the limits of human memory and the ability to reproduce spoken dialogue. And structured interviews, while they are able to elicit reflexive commentary from social actors, are always bounded by the artificial situation and performative quality of the interview setting. This research, then, was partly an attempt to break with a sole reliance on this methodological pairing.

As I discussed in the introduction and chapter 1, my analysis of Bible study life is grounded in concerns with face-to-face social institutions and the interactions they produce. This required the ability to reproduce Bible study conversations, as well as the verbal and nonverbal cues that accompany talk. To do so, I tape-recorded Bible study meetings, allowing my field note work to concentrate on nonverbal actions, and I transcribed each recording for both the verbatim content of talk and the paralinguistic features of speech. This approach to documenting intersubjective events is certainly not original and is something that sociologists and anthropologists of language have been keen to for decades. If anything, this research is a pioneering attempt to construct a comparative ethnography of a single (but vital) Evangelical institution around the use of tape-recording and transcription, supplemented by the instruments of observation, interviews, text collection, and questionnaire distribution.

Beginning a Conversation

I do not offer this account of group Bible study—from its theoretical interests to its methodological and analytical strategies—as the final word on this subject. At the very least, what I hope to have done here is draw attention to a significant and largely unexamined religious phenomenon in the hope of encouraging other scholars to contribute their own accounts. In this spirit of beginning a conversation I devote the last few pages of this book to three issues about which I myself am left wondering.

Disruption and Discord

Throughout this book I have kept an eye on the tensions that populate Bible study life in addition to the continuities that define it. Alongside interactions that suggest an unfailing uniformity among and between groups, I have featured divergent textual interpretations, individual participants consistently out of step with the remaining group members, and broader American and Evangelical discourses that create interpretive dilemmas. This began with Peter in chapter 2 and continued through the LCMS Men's discussion of democracy, Linda's distance from the rest of the Iconoclasts, Bill and Eddie's struggle over "vulnerability," and the friction surrounding the gendering of religious responsibilities in chapter 6. This evidence of tension is telling within the study of American Evangelicalism, as it indexes the heterogeneity among these religionists and the ability of this cultural category to persist in the face of such diversity. Indeed, there is a certain dexterity to the Evangelical sense of self because it is not continually in danger of collapsing due to the lingering of competing hermeneutics, priorities, and ideological commitments.

Still, if there is one consistent bias in my project sample, and selection of case studies, it is the appearance of stability in Bible study life. Disagreements—whether they were short-lived or recurring—were inevitable but never posed a debilitating threat to the otherwise collaborative, positive atmosphere in each of the Bible study groups. All maintained a good relationship among the members, resulting in group dynamics that were familiar, amiable, and committed to cooperation. This norm of congeniality does reflect a foundational goal of Bible study—to have a constructive spiritual experience together as a group. I observed a variety of terms used to capture this sentiment, such as "being fed" and "growing in relationship with God." But the term I encountered most frequently was "edification." Facilitators and participants alike spoke of joining and attending groups because they wanted to be "edified." They came to support each other, learn from each other, and share in a mutual maturation of faith. This expectation removes certain dynamics from the purview of desirable interaction. Things such as ongoing tensions and hostile debates were avoided at all cost, keeping discussions from being overly contentious and protecting the norm of edification. But what happens when "being edified" is not so easy to come by? What happens when serious conflicts among participants do not disappear? I encountered only one case in the nineteen groups I worked among where this was visible: the UMC Women.

This group of seven women attended the third United Methodist congregation in the project sample (see chapter 1 and Downtown UMC). They met every Tuesday afternoon for two hours. They took turns playing the role of facilitator and selected texts of study only by unanimous agreement. The UMC Women were the only group in the sample that was not predominantly Evangelical. Of the seven regular members, only two were theologically conservative. Pat was a lifelong United Methodist and adhered closely to a progressive political ethos. Wanda, on the other hand, grew up as a United Methodist but spent most of her adult years in the neocharismatic Vineyard Fellowship. She returned to this particular United Methodist congregation several years ago because she missed the traditional hymns and community outreach she associated with the Methodist tradition. Wanda enjoyed being part of the group, but she was consistently and vehemently at odds with the theological positions held by others: resisting masculine references to God, dismissing the doctrine of original sin, and freely doubting the absolute authority of scripture, to name a few.

A month into my fieldwork, the tension between Wanda and the other members had escalated. Each week their confrontations lasted longer and became increasingly heated. When it came time choose a new study text, Wanda advocated for Bart Ehrman's *The Lost Christianities* (2003), a scholarly study of the Gnostic scriptures. She was sensitive to her role as the lone conservative and thought this a good compromise. Wanda was confident that the book's historical and textual evidence would convince the other members of the Gnostic scriptures' lack of authenticity, thereby forcing them to reconsider the nature of the orthodox canon (all this despite Ehrman himself being an avowed agnostic). The other women were interested in a (very) different text: *How to Know God* (2001) by Deepak Chopra, a well-known New Age author. While Chopra does make reference to the Christian scriptures, his spiritual imagination draws on a variety of other sources, including Eastern and Native American faith traditions. Despite Wanda's strong opposition, the other women chose *How to Know God* for their next study. The week they announced this was the last week Wanda attended. Between this meeting and the next, Wanda sent a lengthy email to the group. It informed them, among other things, of her decision to leave, her disgust with the Chopra decision, and her concern for their eternal salvation.

The discord of the UMC Women undoubtedly stemmed from theological (as opposed to relational) problems. The result was an increasingly argumentative series of disagreements, one individual eventually leaving the group and, soon after, the congregation. However, this is only one of many potential scenarios of what might occur in the wake of disruption to the norm of edification. Ultimately, we must ask how this type of group life—one where controversy rather than congeniality is typical—might impact the theorizing I have outlined in this book. What happens to Bible study as a dialogical space when the assumption of edification disappears?

Facilitators and Their Styles

The questions pursued in this book—about the cultural significance of Bible study for Evangelicals—are in many ways contingent on intersubjective questions about how the event of Bible study itself works. We have taken this issue up primarily in regards to the organizational qualities of group formats. The Prayer Circle was perhaps the most compelling example of how this interacts with foundational expectations about what Bible study is all about. An equally important set of questions ensues from the role of the facilitator in group life. The five facilitators who appeared at length here—Dave, Darren, Charlie, Bill, and Sandy—employed distinct leadership styles and had formative impacts on their respective groups. During my fieldwork I observed fifteen different facilitators, and the other ten individuals played a similar role in their group settings. Below I identify four elements of facilitator style that might be considered for a more thorough analysis of how the role of the facilitator actually structures group life.

AUTHORITY

How influential are the facilitator's words compared to the other group members'? This question of authoritativeness is crucial for understanding how the individual who leads shapes the life of a group. Individuals like Darren and Bill were particularly authoritative in their group contexts. Neither of these men was overbearing or forceful and yet other participants yielded to both. Whereas individuals like Charlie and Sandy were clearly the sole facilitators, their presence was not received as bearing any greater authority than anyone else's. This raises a necessary methodological question about how a trait like "authority" is best measured. In my analyses, I returned to several observations: the position of the facilitator in the church vis-à-vis other participants, length of facilitator's contributions, frequency and intensity of disagreements with the facilitator, and reactions to facilitators correcting other's contributions. These were effective but could be complemented by a sorting methodology in which group members are asked to rank each participant in terms of their perceived authority.[4] This could help match emic views of authority with the analyst's own empirical measures.

METHOD

How do facilitators approach the planning of group meetings? The leaders I encountered practiced a wide range of styles when it came to preparing for and organizing weekly meetings. Sandy, for example, always devoted at least four hours to preparation, where others spent only a few minutes. Similarly, a variety of formats were practiced, from the precisely ordered to ordered chaos. And in cases like the Prayer Circle and the LCMS Men, the defined structure of group meetings contained important lessons for what the group prioritized and what they expected from the experience of meeting together. Still, other revealing questions remain to be asked: where do facilitators find their models for organizing meetings? Do facilitators have well-formed ideas about why one format is beneficial over another? And how do they respond to objections or complaints regarding their chosen style?

CONVERSATION MANAGEMENT

How do facilitators guide Bible study discussions? As I have emphasized throughout this book, the conversations that comprise weekly meetings are the definitive feature of group life. And more than any other subject position, facilitators are charged with managing how these conversations unfold. Among the facilitators I observed there were numerous styles available for accomplishing this and numerous discursive strategies involved in doing so. In particular, the following questions were useful in thinking about what type of management style facilitators favored: did leaders pose open- or close-ended questions? Closed questioning usually resulted in a greater number of topics covered, shorter discussions, fewer members contributing, and the constant pursuit of "correct" answers. Were disagreements encouraged or muted? Encouraging disagreements seemed to reflect an ideology that such debate was not disruptive for group life, assuming that amiable argument was useful for eliciting meaningful ideas. Did facilitators lecture? Generally, leaders tried to avoid lengthy exhortations, thinking that members do not come to group to be preached to but to discuss in a collegial environment. However, all facilitators had the ability to talk extensively and all transitioned into this mode on occasion. Such lecturing in Bible study life could be a revealing phenomenon, signifying moments of insight into groups' ongoing dialogue around specific topics.

How and why do facilitators choose texts for study? Much of what happens in Bible study life is connected to the text being read and discussed. Facilitators are not always solely in charge of selecting the study text, but they usually direct how the selection process unfolds. Books of the Bible, nonscriptural books, videos, online and print periodical articles, and audiotapes were all used as the basis for discussion, and they were chosen for a variety of reasons. Sometimes the facilitator had read the text before, enjoyed it, and thought it appropriate for the group. Texts were also selected based on national popularity, by recommendation from other groups and individuals, and familiarity with an author's previous work. Facilitators also used a variety of methods for choosing texts of study, from simply making the selection themselves to more democratic approaches in which all participants were asked to present a possibility or to vote on possibilities given by the facilitator. Apart from the process and motivation of text selection, though, other questions linger about how texts come to appear in group life. One in particular intrigued me throughout my fieldwork, though I never devoted explicit attention to it: under what circumstances do facilitators choose texts that challenge rather than support established beliefs and group expectations?

The only hint of this came from the LCMS Men (chapter 2). Just prior to their second book study, Dave shared with me the three texts he planned to choose from. The first was St. Augustine's *The Confessions*, the famous spiritual autobiography dating to the 5th century. He loved the idea of using a book with such antiquity but decided against the classic work because he thought the language was overly arcane and would distract most members. His second choice was Stephen Arterburn's *Every Man's Battle: Winning the War on Sexual Temptations One Victory at a Time* (2000). The book addresses sexual "sins," such as addiction to pornography, and it promised to introduce topics and levels of intimacy foreign to the group's inclinations toward textual analysis and heady debate. Dave constantly sought ways to push the men outside their "comfort zone," but when I asked why he decided against this book he replied only, "I don't think they're quite ready for that yet." The text Dave ultimately chose was Os Guinness's *The Call: Finding and Fulfilling the Central Purpose of Your Life* (1998). Written by a well-known Evangelical author, the book is not terribly different from others the group has read. As several participants told me during the study, it shares the theme of giving life a "biblical purpose" with Rick Warren's mega-popular *The Purpose Driven Life* (2002) but conveys it in a more "intellectual" style. Despite Dave's final choice to use a more predictable text of study, the possibility of a more challenging book has great potential in thinking about Bible study as a site of knowledge production. This line of inquiry could prove quite helpful for identifying occasions in which Evangelicals self-consciously resist the received categories of their faith and tradition and in which facilitators purposefully attempt to alter the established ethos and norms of the group's experience.

These four areas—authority, method, conversation management, and text selection–certainly do not cover the entirety of facilitators' styles, but they do provide some concrete points of entry into a comparative analysis. More than any other subject position in Bible study life, the role of the facilitator has extensive and discernible impacts on what happens in groups from week to week. In turn, a continued ethnography of Bible study life should be concerned with developing more systematic ways of thinking about how facilitators conceptualize and perform their responsibilities.

Dialogical Spaces

Beginning with the opening narrative of this book, I have emphasized the uniqueness of Bible study in the lives of Evangelicals. At the risk of inconsistency, I would like to conclude by posing two questions that shift attentions away from this claim.

(1) Given the rise of Internet culture and computer mediated communication, are there online spaces that resemble Bible study?
Via the blogosphere, chat rooms, online communities, and podcasts, Evangelicals are having more and more of their dialogue online. I would never forecast that these virtual contexts are slowly, and exhaustively, replacing the face-to-face encounter. However, their steady proliferation does present a scenario of discourse and knowledge production to be considered alongside group Bible study as performing similar cultural work (cf. Doostdar 2004). In both spaces, ongoing conversations are held, opinions and texts are exchanged, and norms for interaction are cultivated. Will Evangelicals come to rely on (if they have not already) these online,

intersubjective sites in the same way that they have group study? Should theorizing about the formation of discourses and dispositions—for example, regarding textual hermeneutics or religious subjectivities—among Evangelicals now be sketched as a dialectical exchange between the face-to-face and the virtual? I suspect the answer to this latter question is increasingly an affirmative one, which means that scholars will have to begin dividing their analytical attention more evenly.

(2) Given what I have argued about group Bible study, are there any lessons available for discourse communities in civil society?

I do believe the groups featured here have something to tell us about maintaining productive sites of dialogue in other social contexts. There is an oft-heard lament in American society (one I empathize with greatly) about the state of our public discourse. Can we not do better than the rapid exchange of sound bytes and the hostile conditions of radio and television interviews? Is there a way to create more meaningful interactions around our most pressing social concerns? Perhaps a positive response to this type of questioning can be located among the kind of group this book has explored. There is something to be said for devoting an extended amount of time every week explicitly to the act of dialogue. And there is something to be said for sustaining communities that prioritize open, reflexive, and critical conversation. Alongside other cases of collective reading, group Bible study contains valuable insights for interacting closely, continuously, and cooperatively with the written word. Still, a word of caution is necessary next to the suggestion that Bible study can be looked to as a model. As I described in numerous examples throughout this book, groups often engaged in intense, lengthy discussions around an issue or text, only to move on without any attempt at resolution (cf. Bielo 2008). Moreover, the interpretations settled on in the midst of Bible study are not always translated in full, and sometimes not even in the least, to lived experience. Despite their virtues, conversation and dialogue cannot stand as the final solution to cultural divisions and destructive social problems, seeming useful but disguising diagnoses. Thus, while I am more than willing to advocate for the lessons that Bible study can offer civil society as an intersubjective, knowledge-producing event, I am less willing to do so uncritically and without particular reservations.

In June 2004 I began a comparative ethnographic project on the Evangelical phenomenon of group Bible study. Now, some four years later, I am concluding this account. The experience of collecting, analyzing, writing, presenting, and rethinking Bible study data has prompted several certainties in my mind. Top among them is this: no other institution in Evangelical life is as crucial for sustaining and reflecting on the Evangelical imagination as is group Bible study. In this book I have attempted to demonstrate the various ways in which this statement is proven true. As sociologists and anthropologists of Christianity continue to raise questions about Evangelical culture, I hope this book will be both a constant resource and a constant reminder to incorporate Bible study (and other sites of open, critical, reflexive dialogue) into research agendas. My hope here is, again, only to begin a conversation, not end it.

Notes

INTRODUCTION

1. Outside the American context, Eva Keller (2005) has provided an insightful and thorough ethnography of how scripture figures in the cultural life of Seventh-Day Adventists in Madagascar. However, Keller's analytical attention does not attend to the details of talk and interaction in contexts of group Bible study.

2. As a denomination, the United Methodist Church in America is characterized by internal theological divisions at the regional, district, and congregational levels. Perhaps more than any other Protestant denomination in the United States, United Methodism includes a cross-section of progressive, moderate, Evangelical, and charismatic Christians (Kirby et al. 1998). Two of the three congregations included in this project were predominantly Evangelical, while the third was more typically United Methodist in terms of its internal heterogeneity. However, the United Methodist groups that appear in this book (chapters 4 and 5) overwhelmingly adhere to conservative Evangelical theology.

3. Wuthnow distinguishes "Sunday school" from "Bible study" in his research. However, given my own emphases on institutions, reading, and discourse, I see no need to draw a sharp distinction between these two forms of group study. In regard to Wuthnow's estimation of more than 30 million weekly Bible study participants, I suspect that this number has only increased since the time of his survey given the growing numbers of national church membership and the expanding Evangelical publishing industry. Unfortunately, I can only suspect because I do not have the national, quantitative data to empirically support this assertion.

CHAPTER 1

1. This sampling rationale produced at least one inherent bias in the resulting data. By focusing on congregations with extensive Bible study opportunities, I most likely missed smaller congregations and churches struggling with increasing their membership. In turn, groups that might have been preoccupied by severe congregational controversies were not part of my data.

2. In the initial sampling pool I included all Protestant congregations for comparative purposes, not just those from historically Evangelical denominations.

3. It is noteworthy here that Janet's objection was not to my presence in any women's Bible study, as I spent several months observing one that she facilitated on Wednesday mornings. The awkwardness, she thought, would stem from these particular groups of women.

4. All specific church names are pseudonyms. This particular church is not represented in any of the case studies in the chapters to follow.

5. This was the home church of the Iconoclasts, who appear in chapter 4.

6. This was the home church of the Tuesday Men, who appear in chapter 5.

7. This was the home church of the LCMS Men (chapter 2) and the LCMS Women (chapter 6).

8. This was the home church of the Prayer Circle, who appear in chapter 3.

9. This particular church is not represented in any of the case studies in the chapters to follow.

CHAPTER 2

1. My attention was drawn to this definition by Modan (2007).

2. All Bible references are from the New International Version (NIV) unless otherwise indicated.

3. GodMen is an Evangelical group for men founded in 2006 by conservative Christian comedian Brad Stine. The organization's website reports on its "About" page: "Welcome to GodMen, where you'll find power, honesty, courage and your tribe of brothers. We have committed to see what would happen if, for one day, our faith and its struggles would be discussed with absolute honesty, transparency and openness—not sugar coated or framed in church language but instead spoken in frankness and maturity. The GodMen event creates an environment familiar with and conducive to the way men are made comfortable and the unique way men interact. We are unique in that we provide audience-speaker dialogue and interaction in order to teach men how to shoulder each others' burdens, never to be alone again. Our ultimate desire is to encourage men to leave committed to daily acts of courage, guiding them into a new and fresh journey. Does this resonate with you and your search for meaning and truth? Then you are of our tribe—come walk with us and bring your unique life experience and perspective to our journey. We don't want you . . . we need you."

CHAPTER 3

1. The two individuals who withdrew from the group were a married couple. The wife was diagnosed with a terminal illness in late 2004 and they both, reluctantly, decided to limit their weekly commitments.

2. "For he chose us in him before the creation of the world to be holy and blameless in his sight. In love he predestined us to be adopted as his sons through Jesus Christ, in accordance with his pleasure and will."

3. "In a large house there are articles not only of gold and silver, but also of wood and clay; some are for noble purposes and some for ignoble. If a man cleanses himself from the latter, he will be an instrument for noble purposes, made holy, useful to the Master and prepared to do any good work."

CHAPTER 4

1. Long is able to make this claim because she sought a diverse sample of groups to observe. Much like my own analysis of Bible study, the ability to argue for what is particular and what is typical emerges from the availability of comparative data.

2. This United Methodist church was, until roughly ten years ago, a small "family" congregation that prided itself on the fact that "everybody knows everybody else." However, a rapid surge in residential development in the surrounding area created a boom in the church population. During my fieldwork, the congregation maintained an average Sunday worship attendance ranging from 750 to 850 people.

3. See Matthew 21:12–17.

4. This theological position is not reliant on a "literalist" (Crapanzano 2000) interpretation of the first chapter in Genesis. The notion of a fallen humanity is able to exist equally well in social contexts where the story of Adam and Eve is read as an actual, historical event, and in cases where it is read as an allegory depicting the spiritual status of humankind. The Iconoclasts were somewhat divided regarding this issue of Bible interpretation, with a slight majority inclined toward allegorical readings.

5. Focus on the Family is an international ministry organization based in Colorado and founded by Dr. James Dobson. Dobson is widely known within Evangelical circles, and in the field of American politics for his "pro-family" discourse and his outspoken views against homosexuality and abortion.

CHAPTER 5

1. The Acts of the Apostles appears after the four Gospels and before the Epistles in the New Testament canon. It has twenty-eight chapters and chronicles the beginning of the 1st-century Christian Church.

2. Matthew 28:19.

3. Eli Stanley Jones (1884–1973) was a Methodist theologian and missionary, best known for his work throughout the Indian subcontinent. Eddie, who initially recontextualizes the quote about witnessing, served as a missionary in India for several decades.

4. Forty Days of Community was the follow-up to Rick Warren's widely popular Forty Days of Purpose congregation-wide campaign. Structurally the two were similar, but the sequel shifted the emphasis from the individual to the corporate Christian life.

CHAPTER 6

1. The presumptive link between individual intention and meaning in Western language ideology has been well critiqued by linguistic anthropologists working in non-Western settings (e.g., Hill and Irvine, eds. 1992).

CONCLUSION

1. The Gospel of Judas is a Gnostic text dating to the 2nd century A.D. It was first discovered in 1983 and released to the public as an English translation in 2006. The text portrays Judas as a confidant of Jesus Christ who obeyed a direct command from Jesus to betray him, rather than the demon-haunted traitor that has dominated the orthodox Christian narrative.

2. *The Da Vinci Code* (2003) is a mystery novel written by fiction author Dan Brown. The book's plot centers on the claim that Mary Magdalene and Jesus were secretly married and had children together. Historically, this has been a marginal, if not heretical, belief in the orthodox Christian tradition.

3. Other data collection techniques that have been employed in the qualitative study of American Evangelicalism include the collection and review of textual materials, photography and other visual means of mapping religious space, and the use of questionnaires to complement in-depth interviews and/or observations.

4. I am indebted to Fredric Roberts for this suggestion (cf. Bernard 2006).

*   *   *

References

PRIMARY REFERENCES

———. 1978. *The Holy Bible: New International Version*. Grand Rapids, MI: Zondervan.

———. 2001. *The Extreme Word: New King James Version*. Nashville: Thomas Nelson Publishers.

Arterburn, Stephen et al. 2000. *Every Man's Battle: Winning the War on Sexual Temptations One Victory at a Time*. Colorado Springs: Waterbrook Press.

Brown, Dan. 2003. *The Da Vinci Code*. New York: Doubleday.

Chesterton, G. K. 1908 [1995]. *Orthodoxy*. Ft. Collins, CO: Ignatius Press.

Chopra, Deepak. 2001. *How to Know God: the Soul's Journey into the Mystery of Mysteries*. New York: Random House.

Cole, Neil. 1999. *Cultivating a Life for God*. St. Charles, IL: ChurchSmart Resources.

Ehrman, Bart D. 2003. *The Lost Christianities: the Battles for Scripture and the Faiths We Never Knew*. New York: Oxford University Press.

Gibbs, Eddie and Ryan K. Bolger. 2005. *Emerging Churches: Creating Christian Community in Postmodern Cultures*. Grand Rapids, MI: Baker Books.

Guinness, Os. 1998. *The Call: Finding and Fulfilling the Central Purpose of Your Life*. Nashville: Thomas Nelson.

Hybels, Bill and Mark Mittelberg. 1994. *Becoming a Contagious Christian*. Grand Rapids, MI: Zondervan.

Kimball, Dan. 2003. *The Emerging Church: Vintage Christianity for New Generations*. Grand Rapids, MI: Zondervan.

Moore, Beth. 1997. *To Live Is Christ: The Life and Ministry of Paul*. Nashville: LifeWay Christian Resources.

Ortberg, John. 2001. *If You Want to Walk on Water, You've Got to Get Out of the Boat*. Grand Rapids, MI: Zondervan.

Seay, Chris. 2002. *The Gospel According to Tony Soprano: An Unauthorized Look into the Soul of TV's Top Mob Boss and His Family*. New York: Penguin.

Vander Lann, Raynard. 1995. *That the World May Know*. Colorado Springs: Focus on the Family.

Warren, Rick. 2007. *The Purpose Driven Life*. Grand Rapids, MI: Zondervan.

Yancey, Philip. 1995. *The Jesus I Never Knew*. Grand Rapids, MI: Zondervan.

SECONDARY REFERENCES

Abu-Lughod, Lila. 1991. "Writing against Culture." In *Recapturing Anthropology: Working in the Present*, edited by Richard Fox, 137–62. Santa Fe: School of American Research Press.

Agar, Michael. [1996] 1980. *The Professional Stranger: An Informal Introduction to Ethnography*. San Diego: Academic Press.

Ammerman, Nancy T. 1987. *Bible Believers: Fundamentalists in the Modern World*. New Brunswick, NJ: Rutgers University Press.

———. 1997. *Congregation and Community*. New Brunswick, N.J.: Rutgers University Press.

Ando, Clifford. 2001. "Signs, Idols, and the Incarnation in Augustinian Metaphysics." *Representations*. 73: 24–53.

Arnold, Dean. 2006. "Why Are There So Few Christian Anthropologists? Reflections on the Tensions between Christianity and Anthropology." *Perspectives on Science and Christian Faith*. 58: 266–84.

Ault, James. 2004. *Spirit and Flesh: Life in a Fundamentalist Baptist Church*. New York: Alfred A. Knopff.

Ayres, Lewis. 2006. "Patristic and Medieval Theologies of Scripture: An Introduction." In *Christian Theologies of Scripture: A Comparative Introduction*, edited by Justin Holcomb, 11–20. New York: NYU Press.

Balmer, Randall. 1989. *Mine Eyes Have Seen the Glory: A Journey into the Evangelical Subculture of America*. New York: Oxford University Press.

Bahktin, Mikhail. 1934 [1981]. *The Dialogic Imagination: Four Essays*. Austin: University of Texas Press.

———. 1986. *Speech Genres and Other Late Essays*. Austin: University of Texas Press.

Baker, James. 1993. "The Presence of the Name: Reading Scripture in an Indonesian Village." In *The Ethnography of Reading*, edited by Jonathan Boyarin, 98–138. Berkeley: University of California Press.

Bartkowski, John. 1996. "Beyond Biblical Literalism and Inerrancy: Conservative Protestants and the Hermeneutic Interpretation of Scripture." *Sociology of Religion*. 57: 259–72.

———. 2001. *Remaking the Godly Marriage: Gender Negotiation in Evangelical Families*. New Brunswick, NJ: Rutgers University Press.

———. 2004. *The Promise Keepers: Servants, Soldiers and Godly Men*. New Brunswick, NJ: Rutgers University Press.

Basso, Keith. 1979. *Portraits of "The Whiteman": Linguistic Play and Cultural Symbols among the Western Apache*. Cambridge: Cambridge University Press.

Bateson, Gregory. 1972. *Steps to an Ecology of Mind*. New York: Ballantine Books.

Bauman, Richard. 2004. *A World of Others' Words: Cross-Cultural Perspectives on Intertextuality*. London: Blackwell Publishing.

Becker, Penny Edgell. 1999. *Congregations in Conflict: Cultural Models of Local Religious Life*. Cambridge: Cambridge University Press.

Bender, Courtney. 1994. "Praying for the Saints: Single Mennonite Charismatics and the Conundrum of Community." In *"I Come Away Stronger": How Small Groups Are Shaping American Religion*, edited by Robert Wuthnow, 225–50. Grand Rapids, MI: William B. Eerdmans.

Berger, Peter, and Thomas Luckmann. 1966. *The Social Construction of Reality: A Treatise in the Sociology of Knowledge*. New York: Doubleday.

Bernard, H. Russell. 2006. *Research Methods in Anthropology: Qualitative and Quantitative Approaches, 4th ed.* Walnut Creek, CA: AltaMira Press.

Bialecki, Jon. 2008. "Between Stewardship and Sacrifice: Agency and Economy in a Southern California Charismatic Church." *Journal of the Royal Anthropological Institute*. 14: 372–90.

Bielo, James S. 2004. "'Walking in the Spirit of Blood': Moral Identity among Born-Again Christians." *Ethnology*. 43: 271–89.

———. 2007a. "Recontextualizing the Bible in Small Group Discourse." *SALSA XIV:2006. Texas Linguistic Forum*. Vol. 50. Edited by Taryne Hallett, Simeon Floyd, Sae Oshima, and Aaron Shield, 1–9. Austin: Texas Linguistics Forum.

———. 2007b. "'The Mind of Christ': Financial Success, Born-Again Personhood, and the Anthropology of Christianity." *Ethnos*. 72: 315–38.

———. 2008. "On the Failure of 'Meaning': Bible Reading in the Anthropology of Christianity." *Culture and Religion*. 9: 1–21.

———. Forthcoming. "The 'Emerging Church' in America: Notes on the Interaction of Christianities." *Religion*.

Bielo, James S., ed. Forthcoming. *The Social Life of Scriptures: Cross-Cultural Perspectives on Biblicism*. New Brunswick, NJ: Rutgers University Press.

Boas, Franz. 1920. "The Methods of Ethnology." *American Anthropologist*. 22: 311–22.

Bowen, John. 1992. "Elaborating Scriptures: Cain and Abel in Gayo Society." *Man*. 27: 495–516.

———. 1993. *Muslims Through Discourse: Religion and Ritual in Gayo Society*. Princeton: Princeton University Press.

Bourdieu, Pierre. 1977. *Outline of a Theory of Practice*. Cambridge: Cambridge University Press.

Boyarin, Jonathan. 1989. "Voices Around the Text: The Ethnography of Reading at Misevta Tifereth Jerusalem." *Cultural Anthropology*. 4: 399–421.

———. 1993. Introduction. In *The Ethnography of Reading*, edited by Jonathan Boyarin, 1–9. Berkeley: University of California Press.

Boyarin, Jonathan, ed. 1993. *The Ethnography of Reading*. Berkeley: University of California Press.

Boylan, Anne M. 1988. *Sunday School: The Formation of an American Institution, 1790–1880.* New Haven: Yale University Press.

Boyle, Marjorie O'Rourke. 1977. *Erasmus on Language and Method in Theology.* Toronto: University of Toronto Press.

Bright, Pamela. 2006. "St. Augustine." In *Christian Theologies of Scripture: A Comparative Introduction,* edited by Justin Holcomb, 39–59. New York: NYU Press.

Brown, Candy Gunther. 2004. *The Word in the World: Evangelical Writing, Publishing and Reading in America, 1789–1880.* Chapel Hill: University of North Carolina Press.

Cannell, Fenella. 2006. "Introduction: The Anthropology of Christianity." In *The Anthropology of Christianity,* edited by Fenella Cannell, 1–50. Durham: Duke University Press.

Clifford, James. 1986. "Introduction: Partial Truths." In *Writing Culture: The Poetics and Politics of Ethnography,* edited by James Clifford and George E. Marcus, 1–26. Berkeley: University of California Press.

Clifford, James and George E. Marcus, eds. 1986. *Writing Culture: The Poetics and Politics of Ethnography.* Berkeley: University of California Press.

Coleman, Simon. 2006. "When Silence Isn't Golden: Charismatic Speech and the Limits of Literalism." In *The Limits of Meaning: Case Studies in the Anthropology of Christianity,* edited by Matthew Engelke and Matt Tomlinson, 39–62. New York: Berghahn Books.

Conkin, Paul K. 1997. *American Originals: Homemade Varieties of Christianity.* Chapel Hill: University of North Carolina Press.

Crapanzano, Vincent. 1980. *Tuhami: Portrait of a Moroccan.* Chicago: University of Chicago Press.

———. 2000. *Serving the Word: Literalism in America from the Pulpit to the Bench.* New York: New Press.

Csordas, Thomas. 1997. *Language, Charisma, and Creativity: The Ritual Life of a Religious Movement.* Berkeley: University of California Press.

Cummings, Brian. 2002. *The Literary Culture of the Reformation: Grammar and Grace.* Oxford: Oxford University Press.

Davie, Jody Shapiro. 1995. *Women in the Presence: Constructing Community and Seeking Spirituality in Mainline Protestantism.* Philadelphia: University of Pennsylvania Press.

DeRogatis, Amy. 2005. "What Would Jesus Do? Sexuality and Salvation in Protestant Evangelical Sex Manuals, 1950s to the Present." *Church History.* 74: 97–137.

Dewey, David. 2004. *A User's Guide to Bible Translations: Making the Most of Different Versions.* Downer's Grove, IL: InterVarsity Press.

Doostdar, Alireza. 2004. "The Vulgar Spirit of Blogging: On Language, Culture, and Power in Persian Weblogestan." *American Anthropologist.* 106: 651–62.

Eckert, Penelope and Sally McConnell-Ginet. 1992. "Communities of Practice: Where Language, Gender, and Power All Live." In *Locating Power: Proceedings of the Second Berkeley Women and Language Conference*, edited by Kira Hall et al, 89–99, Berkeley: Berkeley Women and Language Group.

Eiesland, Nancy L. 2000. *A Particular Place: Urban Restructuring and Religious Ecology in a Southern Exurb*. New Brunswick, NJ: Rutgers University Press.

Elisha, Omri. 2004. "Sins of Our Soccer Moms: Servant Evangelism and the Spiritual Injuries of Class." In *Local Actions: Cultural Activism, Power, and Public Life in America*, edited by Melissa Checker and Maggie Fishman, 136–58. New York: Columbia University Press.

———. 2008. "Moral Ambitions of Grace: The Paradox of Compassion and Accountability in Evangelical Faith-Based Activism." *Cultural Anthropology*. 23: 154–89.

Engelke, Matthew. 2007. *A Problem of Presence: Beyond Scripture in an African Church*. Berkeley: University of California Press.

Finke, Roger and Rodney Starke. 1992. *The Churching of America, 1776–1990: Winners and Losers in Our Religious Economy*. New Brunswick, NJ: Rutgers University Press.

Fish, Stanley. 1980. *Is There a Text in This Class? The Authority of Interpretive Communities*. Cambridge: Harvard University Press.

Flores, Aaron O. 2005. *An Exploration of the Emerging Church in the United States: The Missiological Intent and Potential Implications for the Future*. Unpublished Thesis (M.A.), Vanguard University. Department of Religion.

Frake, Charles O. 1964. "How to Ask for a Drink in Subanun." *American Anthropologist*. 66: 127–32.

Frei, Hans W. 1974. *The Eclipse of Biblical Narrative: A Study in Eighteenth and Nineteenth Century Hermeneutics*. New Haven: Yale University Press.

Frykholm, Amy. 2004. *Rapture Culture: Left Behind in Evangelical America*. Oxford: Oxford University Press.

Gilmont, Jean-Francois. 1999. "Protestant Reformations and Reading." In *A History of Reading in the West*, edited by Guglielmo Cavallo and Roger Chartier, 213–37. Amherst: University of Massachusetts Press.

Goffman, Erving. 1961. *Encounters*. New York: Bobbs-Merrill.

———. 1974. *Frame Analysis: An Essay on the Organization of Experience*. New York: Harper and Row.

Graham, Laura. 1995. *Performing Dreams: Discourses of Immortality among the Xavante of Central Brazil*. Austin: University of Texas Press.

Griffith, R. Marie. 1997. *God's Daughters: Evangelical Women and the Power of Submission*. Berkeley: University of California Press.

———. 2004. *Born Again Bodies: Flesh and Spirit in American Christianity*. Berkeley: University of California Press.

Hagen, Kenneth et al. 1985. *The Bible in the Churches: How Different Christians Interpret the Scriptures*. New York: Paulist Press.

Hanks, William F. 1987. "Discourse Genres in a Theory of Practice." *American Ethnologist* 14: 668–92.

Harding, Susan. 1987. "Convicted by the Holy Spirit: The Rhetoric of Fundamental Baptist Conversion." *American Ethnologist*. 14: 167–81.

———. 2000. *The Book of Jerry Falwell: Fundamentalist Language and Politics*. Princeton: Princeton University Press.

Harrold, Philip. 2006. "Deconversion in the Emerging Church." *International Journal for the Study of the Christian Church*. 6: 79–90.

Hatch, Nathan O. 1989. *The Democratization of American Christianity*. New Haven: Yale University Press.

Hatch, Nathan O. and Mark A. Noll, eds. 1982. *The Bible in America: Essays in Cultural History*. New York: Oxford University Press.

Hendershot, Heather. 2004. *Shaking the World for Jesus: Media and Conservative Evangelical Culture*. Chicago: University of Chicago Press.

Hess, David. 1993. *Science in the New Age: The Paranormal, Its Defenders and Debunkers, and American Culture*. Madison: University of Wisconsin Press.

Hill, Jane H. and Judith T. Irvine, eds. 1992. *Responsibility and Evidence in Oral Discourse*. Cambridge: Cambridge University Press.

Horton, Michael S. 2006. "Theologies of Scripture in the Reformation and Counter-Reformation: An Introduction." In *Christian Theologies of Scripture: A Comparative Introduction,* edited by Justin Holcomb, 83–93. New York: NYU Press.

Howell, Brian. 2007. "The Repugnant Cultural Other Speaks Back: Christian Identity as Ethnographic 'Standpoint.'" *Anthropological Theory*. 7: 371–91.

Hunter, James Davison. 1983. *American Evangelicalism: Conservative Religion and the Quandary of Modernity*. New Brunswick, NJ: Rutgers University Press.

Hymes, Dell. 1964. "Toward Ethnographies of Communication: The Analysis of Communicative Events." *American Anthropologist*. 66: 12–25.

Jeffrey, David Lyle. 1996. *People of the Book: Christian Identity and Literary Culture*. Grand Rapids, MI: William B. Eerdmans.

Johnstone, Barbara. 2000. *Qualitative Methods in Sociolinguistics*. New York: Oxford University Press.

Jones, Dale E. et al. 2002. *Religious Congregations and Membership in the United States 2000: An Enumeration by Region, State, and County Based on Data Reported for 149 Religious Bodies*. Nashville: Glenmary Research Center.

Keane, Webb. 2004. "Language and Religion." In *A Companion to Linguistic Anthropology*, edited by Alessandro Duranti, 431–48. London: Blackwell.

———. 2007. *Christian Moderns: Freedom and Fetish in the Mission Encounter*. Berkeley: University of California Press.

Keller, Eva. 2005. *The Road to Clarity: Seventh-Day Adventism in Madagascar.* New York: Palgrave Macmillan.

Kirby, James E., Russell E. Richey, and Kenneth E. Rowe. 1998. *The Methodists.* Westport, CT: Prager.

Kort, Wesley. 1996. *"Take, Read": Scripture, Textuality, and Cultural Practice.* University Park: Pennsylvania State University Press.

Kuper, Adam. 1999. *Culture: The Anthropologists' Account.* Cambridge: Harvard University Press.

Lambek, Michael. 1990. "Certain Knowledge, Contestable Authority: Power and Practice on the Islamic Periphery." *American Ethnologist.* 17: 23–40.

Levering, Miriam, ed. 1989. *Rethinking Scripture: Essays from a Comparative Perspective.* Albany: SUNY Press.

Lindsey, D. Michael. 2007. *Faith in the Halls of Power: How Evangelicals Joined the American Elite.* Oxford: Oxford University Press.

Long, Elizabeth. 1993. "Textual Interpretation as Collective Action." In *The Ethnography of Reading*, edited by Jonathan Boyarin, 180–211. Berkeley: University of California Press.

———. 2003. *Book Clubs: Women and the Uses of Reading in Everyday Life.* Chicago: University of Chicago Press.

Luhrmann, Tanya M. 2004. "Metakinesis: How God Becomes Intimate in Contemporary U.S. Christianity." *American Anthropologist* 106: 518–28.

Macquarrie, John. 1967. *God-Talk: And Examination of the Language and Logic of Theology.* New York: Harper and Row.

Malinowski, Bronislaw. 1922 [1984]. "Introduction: The Subject, Method and Scope of This Enquiry." In *Argonauts of the Western Pacific.* Long Grove, IL: Waveland Press.

Malley, Brian. 2004. *How the Bible Works: An Anthropological Study of Evangelical Biblicism.* Walnut Creek, CA: AltaMira Press.

Marcus, George E. and Michael M. J. Fischer. 1986. *Anthropology as Cultural Critique: An Experimental Moment in the Human Sciences.* Chicago: University of Chicago Press.

Mattox, Mickey L. 2006. "Martin Luther." In *Christian Theologies of Scripture: A Comparative Introduction*, edited by Justin Holcomb, 94–113. New York: NYU Press.

McGrath, Alister. 2002. *In the Beginning: The Story of the King James Bible and How It Changed a Nation, a Language, and a Culture.* New York: Anchor Books.

Mead, George Herbert. 1934. *Mind, Self, and Society: From the Standpoint of a Social Behaviorist.* Chicago: University of Chicago Press.

Meigs, Anna. 1995. "Ritual Language in Everyday Life: The Christian Right." *Journal of the American Academy of Religion.* 63: 85–103.

Metts, Wallis C. 1995. *Just a Little Talk with Jesus: An Analysis of Conversational Narrative Strategies Used by Evangelical College Students*. Unpublished Thesis (Ph.D.), Michigan State University. Department of Interdisciplinary Studies, College of Arts and Letters.

Miller, Donald. 1997. *Reinventing American Protestantism: Christianity in the New Millennium*. Berkeley: University of California Press.

Modan, Gabriella Gahlia. 2007. *Turf Wars: Discourse, Diversity, and the Politics of Place*. London: Blackwell.

Mullin, Robert Bruce and Russell E. Richey, eds. 1994. *Reimagining Denominationalism: Interpretive Essays*. New York: Oxford University Press.

Murphy, William P. 1990. "Creating the Appearance of Consensus in Mende Political Discourse." *American Anthropologist*. 92: 24–41.

Muse, Erika A. 2005. *The Evangelical Church in Boston's Chinatown: A Discourse of Language, Gender, and Identity*. New York: Routledge.

Narayan, Kirin. 1993. "How Native Is a 'Native' Anthropologist." *American Anthropologist*. 95: 671–86.

Neal, Lynn. 2006. *Romancing God: Evangelical Women and Inspirational Fiction*. Chapel Hill: University of North Carolina Press.

Noll, Mark. 1992. *A History of Christianity in the United States and Canada*. Grand Rapids, MI: William B. Eerdmans.

Nord, David Paul. 2004. *Faith in Reading: Religious Publishing and the Birth of Mass Media in America*. Oxford: Oxford University Press.

Ochs, Elinor. 1979. "Transcription as Theory." In *Developmental Pragmatics*, edited by Elinor Ochs and Bambi Schieffelin, 43–72. New York: Academic Press.

———. 1992. "Indexing Gender." In *Rethinking Context*, edited by Alessandro Duranti and Charles Goodwin, 335–58. Cambridge: Cambridge University Press.

Olson, Daniel V. A. 1994. "Making Disciples in a Liberal Protestant Church." In *"I Come Away Stronger": How Small Groups Are Shaping American Religion*, edited by Robert Wuthnow, 125–47. Grand Rapids, MI: William B. Eerdmans.

Packard, Josh. 2008. *Organizational Structure, Religious Belief, and Resistance: The Emerging Church*. Unpublished Thesis (Ph.D.), Vanderbilt University. Department of Sociology.

Pulis, John. 1999. "Citing [sighting] up: Words, Sounds, and Reading Scripture in Jamaica." In *Religion, Diaspora, and Cultural Identity: A Reader in the Anglophone Caribbean*, edited by John W. Pulis, 357–65. Amsterdam: Gordon and Breach.

Putnam, Robert D. 2000. *Bowling Alone: The Collapse and Revival of American Community*. New York: Simon and Schuster.

Radway, Janice. 1984. *Reading the Romance: Women, Patriarchy, and Popular Literature*. Chapel Hill: University of North Carolina Press.

Reed, Adam. 2004. "Expanding Henry: Fiction Reading and Its Artifacts in a British Literary Society." *American Ethnologist*. 31: 111–22.

Roberts, Fredric M. 1998. "Are Anthropological Crises Contagious? Reflexivity, Representation, Alienation, and Rites of Penance." In *Reconciling Embrace: Foundations for the Future of Sacramental Reconciliation*, edited by Robert J. Kennedy, 45–59. Chicago: Liturgy Training Publications.

———. 2005. *Be Not Afraid: Building Your Church on Faith and Knowledge.* Herndon, VA: Alban Institute Press.

Robbins, Joel. 2001. "'God Is Nothing But Talk': Modernity, Language, and Prayer in a Papua New Guinea Society." *American Anthropologist.* 103: 901–12.

———. 2004. "The Globalization of Pentecostal and Charismatic Christianity." *Annual Review of Anthropology.* 33: 117–43.

Roof, Wade Clark. 1999. *The Spiritual Marketplace.* Chicago: University of Chicago Press.

Rosaldo, Renato. 1989. *Culture and Truth: The Remaking of Social Analysis.* New York: Beacon Press.

Sherzer, Joel. 1987. "A Discourse-Centered Approach to the Study of Language and Culture." *American Anthropologist.* 89: 295–309.

Shoaps, Robin A. 2002. "'Pray Earnestly': The Textual Construction of Personal Involvement in Pentecostal Prayer and Song." *Journal of Linguistic Anthropology.* 12: 34–71.

Smith, William Cantwell. 1993. *What Is Scripture? A Comparative Approach.* Minneapolis: Fortress Press.

Street, Brian V. 1993. "Culture Is a Verb: Anthropological Aspects of Language and Cultural Process." In *Language and Culture*, edited by David Graddol, Linda Thompson, and Mike Byram, 23–43. Clevedon, Engl.: BAAL and Multilingual Matters.

Stock, Brian. 1996. *Augustine the Reader: Meditation, Self-Knowledge, and the Ethics of Interpretation.* Cambridge: Harvard University Press.

Stromberg, Peter. 1993. *Language and Self-Transformation: A Study of the Christian Conversion Narrative.* Cambridge: Cambridge University Press.

Tannen, Deborah. 1993. "What's in a Frame? Surface Evidence for Underlying Expectations." In *Framing in Discourse*, edited by Deborah Tannen, 14–56. New York: Oxford University Press.

Thompson, John. 1991. Editor's Introduction. In *Language and Symbolic Power*, authored by Pierre Bourdieu, 1–31. Cambridge: Harvard University Press.

Thuesen, Peter J. 1999. *In Discordance with the Scriptures: American Protestant Battles over Translating the Bible.* New York: Oxford University Press.

Titon, Jeff Todd. 1988. *Powerhouse for God: Speech, Chant and Song in an Appalachian Baptist Church.* Austin: University of Texas Press.

Turner, James. 2003. *Language, Religion, Knowledge: Past and Present.* South Bend, IN: University of Notre Dame Press.

Wagner, Melinda B. 1990. *God's Schools: Choice and Compromise in American Society.* New Brunswick, NJ: Rutgers University Press.

Ward, Graham. 1995. *Barth, Derrida, and the Language of Theology.* Cambridge: Cambridge University Press.

Warner, R. Stephen. 1988. *New Wine in Old Wineskins: Evangelicals and Liberals in a Small-Town Church.* Berkeley: University of California Press.

Watt, David Harrington. 2002. *Bible-Carrying Christians: Conservative Protestants and Social Power.* Oxford: Oxford University Press.

Wimbush, Vincent, ed. 2000. *African-Americans and the Bible: Sacred Texts and Social Textures.* New York: Continuum.

Witten, Marsha G. 1993. *All Is Forgiven: The Secular Message in American Protestantism.* Princeton: Princeton University Press.

Wolcott, Harry F. 1995. *The Art of Fieldwork.* Walnut Creek, CA: AltaMira Press.

Wuthnow, Robert. 1988. *The Restructuring of American Religion.* Princeton: Princeton University Press.

——. 1994a. *Sharing the Journey: Support Groups and America's New Quest for Community.* New York: Free Press.

Wuthnow, Robert, ed. 1994b. *"I Come Away Stronger": How Small Groups Are Shaping American Religion.* Grand Rapids, MI: William B. Eerdmans.

Zachman, Randall C. 2006. "John Calvin." In *Christian Theologies of Scripture: A Comparative Introduction,* edited by Justin Holcomb, 114–33. New York: NYU Press.

* * *

Index

*** * *

About the Author

JAMES S. BIELO is Visiting Assistant Professor in the Department of Anthropology at Miami University in Oxford, Ohio. He received his Ph.D. in anthropology from Michigan State University in 2007.